The Routledge Concise His Literature

This remarkably broad and informative book offers an introduction to and overview of World Literature. Tracing the term from its earliest roots and situating it within a number of relevant contexts from postcolonialism to postmodernism, Theo D'haen examines:

- the return of the term "world literature" and its changing meaning
- Goethe's concept of *Weltliteratur* and how this relates to current debates
- theories and theorists who have had an impact on world literature
- non-canonical and less-known literatures from around the globe
- the possibility and implications of a definition of world literature.

The Routledge Concise History of World Literature is the ideal guide to an increasingly popular and important term in literary studies. It is accessible and engaging and will be invaluable to students of world literature, comparative literature, translation and postcolonial studies, and anyone with an interest in these or related topics.

Theo D'haen is Professor of English and Comparative Literature at K.U. Leuven University, Belgium and has also worked in Holland, France and, America. He is Editor-in-Chief of the *European Review*, and President of FILLM (Fédération Internationale de Langues et Littératures Modernes) 2008–12.

Routledge Concise Histories of Literature series

The Routledge Concise Histories series offers students and academics alike an interesting and accessible route into the literature of a specific period, genre, place or topic. The books situate the literature within its broader historical, cultural and political context, introducing the key events, movements and theories necessary for a fuller understanding of the writing. They engage readers in the debates of the period, genre or region adding a more exciting and challenging element to the reading.

Accessible and engaging, offering suggestions for further reading, explanatory text boxes, bullet pointed chapter summaries and a glossary of key terms, the Routledge Concise Histories are the ideal starting point for the study of literature.

Available:

The Routledge Concise History of Southeast Asian Writing in English
By Rajeev S. Patke and Philip Holden

The Routledge Concise History of Nineteenth-Century Literature
By Josephine Guy and Ian Small

The Routledge Concise History of Science Fiction
By Mark Bould and Sherryl Vint

The Routledge Concise History of Canadian Literature
By Richard Lane

Forthcoming:

The Routledge Concise History of Twentieth-Century British Literature
By Ashley Dawson

The Routledge Concise History of World Literature

Theo D'haen

Routledge
Taylor & Francis Group

LONDON AND NEW YORK

First edition published 2012
by Routledge
2 Park Square, Milton Park, Abingdon, OX14 4RN

Simultaneously published in the USA and Canada
by Routledge
711 Third Avenue, New York, NY 10017

Routledge is an imprint of the Taylor & Francis Group, an informa business

British Library Cataloguing in Publication Data
A catalogue record for this book is available from the British Library

Library of Congress Cataloging in Publication Data
Haen, Theo d'.
    The Routledge concise history of world literature / Theo D'haen. – 1st ed.
    p. cm. – (Routledge concise histories of literature series)
    Includes bibliographical references and index.
    1. Literature–History and criticism. 2. Comparative literature. I. Title.
    PN523.H34 2011
    809–dc22

                                                              2011011107

ISBN 13: 978-0-415-49588-2 (hbk)
ISBN 13: 978-0-415-49589-9 (pbk)
ISBN 13: 978-0-203-80375-2 (ebk)

Typeset in Times New Roman
By Taylor & Francis Books

MIX
Paper from
responsible sources
FSC
www.fsc.org   FSC® C004839

Printed and bound in Great Britain by the MPG Books Group

Contents

Acknowledgements

It is a pleasure to thank some of the many people who, over the years, have offered me advice, suggestions, information, or simply the opportunity to bore them with my questions. What follows is a very incomplete list, and I immediately apologize to those whose names should have figured here but which, for one reason or another, but most probably through sheer forgetfulness on my part, do not. Thanks, then, to Carlos Álvar (Alcalá and Geneva), Hans Bertens (Utrecht), Jean Bessière (Sorbonne), Tomasz Bilczewski (Cracow), Helena Buescu (Lisbon), Paul Cornea (Bucharest), David Damrosch (Harvard), César Domínguez (Santiago de Compostela), Oana Fotache (Bucharest), Djelal Kadir (Pennsylvania State), Svend Erik Larsen (Aarhus), Sarah Lawall (Massachusetts at Amherst), Gunilla Lindberg-Wada (Stockholm), Saiyma Masood (International Islamic University at Islamabad), Liviu Papadima (Bucharest), Anders Pettersson (Umeå), Monika Schmitz-Emans (Bochum), Manfred Schmeling (Saarbrücken), Monica Spiridon (Bucharest), Mads Rosendahl Thomsen (Aarhus), Bo Utas (Uppsala). I apologize that, in the end, I have not used the information, nor taken up the advice, that some of those mentioned have given me. The reason for this is to be found in limitations of space, and because I did not want to present too disparate a "story" of world literature. The latter meant that, regardless of the fact that some of the material that was so kindly offered to me was interesting and useful, I had to discard it. In any case, any errors in the text that follows are exclusively my own.

Thanks also to my colleague Elke D'hoker at Leuven University who cheerfully filled in for my American literature course during my absence while writing this book, and to all other colleagues in the Literature Department of Leuven University.

Also thanks to the Belgian Fulbright Committee, and particularly its Director, Ms Margaret Nicholson, for granting me a one-semester senior research fellowship to Harvard.

In a former life I taught for many years at Leiden University, and I wish to thank all of my former colleagues there. Even though when I was working with them my attention was focused on postcolonialism and postmodernism rather than world literature, the many conversations I had with my then Leiden colleagues undoubtedly contributed to my general education as well as to my knowledge of literatures around the world.

Finally, thanks to all those who are dear to me for their patience and forbearance during the time it took me to write this book.

Introduction

The (re)turn of world literature

No other approach to literary studies has known as spectacular a success in the new millennium as that which goes by the name of "world literature." In fact, both the term and the study of what it covers have a long history. Until recently, though, these led a rather hidden existence. Most students of literature were aware, even if often only vaguely, that Goethe, somewhere rather early in the nineteenth century, had used the term *Weltliteratur*. Beyond the rather narrow circle of comparative literature scholars the concept had never really gained much currency until recently.

Even within comparative literature, for a long time the subject remained a minority concern at best, for much of its history restricted to a small elite of European academics, or European-born literary scholars exiled or self-exiled in the United States of America. Moreover, regardless of its "global" claim, world literature in its orthodox guise largely limited itself to the comparative study of some major, and sometimes some minor, European literatures. In the 1970s to early 1990s the subject seemed almost dead and buried. As of the turn of the twenty-first century, though, world literature has suddenly resurfaced. In fact, it is not only rapidly becoming the new paradigm for the study of literature in the USA, but also increasingly around the world – in Europe and in the fast-developing academic environments of, for instance, East and South Asia.

The return of interest in the subject was heralded in 1994 by the collective volume *Reading World Literature: Theory, History, Practice*, edited by Sarah Lawall. In 1999 there followed Pascale Casanova's *République mondiale des lettres*. Franco Moretti in 2000 published "Conjectures on World Literature" in the *New Left Review*. This article immediately drew heavy critical fire, and became the focus of much vigorous debate springing up in English on world literature. The various reactions to his article by Christopher Prendergast, Jonathan Arac, Emily Apter, and others provoked Moretti to "More Conjectures on World Literature," published in the *New Left Review* again in 2003. Prendergast in 2004 collected a number of articles, some of them, like his own leading off the volume, reactions to Casanova and Moretti, in *Debating World Literature*. Moretti continued the debate with *Graphs, Maps, Trees: Abstract Models for Literary Study* (2005), and "Evolution, World

Systems, *Weltliteratur*" (2006). In the meantime had appeared David Damrosch's 2003 *What is World Literature?* which quickly became the reference for most further discussions of the subject. In 2004 there appeared the English translation, *The World Republic of Letters*, of Casanova's 1999 French volume.

The 2004 American Comparative Literature Association report on the state of the discipline, prepared by Haun Saussy, with reactions by a number of leading American comparatists, among whom David Damrosch, Emily Apter, Djelal Kadir, and Françoise Lionnet, largely concentrated on the question of world literature. The expanded version, published in 2006 as *Comparative Literature in an Age of Globalization*, added further reactions from the likes of the eminent structuralist scholar Jonathan Culler and the postmodern specialist Linda Hutcheon. John Pizer in 2006 gave *The Idea of World Literature*. The same year also saw the publication of Emily Apter's *The Translation Zone: A New Comparative Literature*, which, even though its title makes no mention of it, is also heavily concerned with world literature. Mads Rosendahl Thomsen's *Mapping World Literature* appeared in 2008. Meanwhile, most leading journals in the field of comparative literature had also jumped on the world literature bandwagon. The British comparative literature journal *Critical Comparative Studies* published a whole issue on "Comparative Literature and World Literature" in 2006, with contributions by David Damrosch, Susan Bassnett, Jonathan Culler, Tomas Docherty, Djelal Kadir, and Linda Hutcheon. Many other journals carried important articles on world literature too, as did for instance *Comparative Literature Studies*. And the pace keeps accelerating. In 2009 Damrosch, who had quickly established himself as the most productive scholar in the field, published a small booklet on *How to Read World Literature*, for use in class, or by students. That very same year he followed up with an edited volume, *Teaching World Literature*. At the very moment of my writing the book you are now holding, a *Routledge Companion to World Literature* and a *Routledge Reader in World Literature* are in press. How did all this come about so suddenly, and where did it all start? What does it mean for how literature is read, taught, studied, and thought about worldwide?

Although the term "world literature," or more accurately *Weltliteratur,* may not have quite originated with Goethe, his use of it certainly made all the difference as from then on it spread like wildfire all over Europe. Unfortunately, though, Goethe never clearly defined what he meant by the term, and consequently it assumed various guises as the nineteenth and twentieth centuries wore on. Goethe probably simply meant the term to refer to the increased circulation of works of literature among European writers and intellectuals. Very rapidly, though, it also came to stand for the totality of all works of literature in the world, past and present. Hence, the nineteenth century saw the rise of comprehensive, at least so in intention, histories of world literature. In the beginning this was a German specialty, but the German example was widely followed almost everywhere, and this down to the present. Most of these works paid scant attention to developments outside of Europe. Some paid them no attention at all. Many of these histories gave their own national literature disproportionate space. Almost all concentrated, besides, on a few "major" European literatures. Chapter 1 traces the early history of *Weltliteratur*, discusses the various translations of the term in a number of European languages and literatures, and briefly preludes upon the discussion of its relationship with comparative literature to follow in another chapter.

Alternatively, over the nineteenth century there also arose the interpretation of world literature as the canon of the world's literary masterpieces. This canon was largely confined to European works. The aesthetic ideal largely determining the criteria for the selection of the canon was heavily indebted to humanism. Moreover, Goethe himself was heavily influenced by the classical tradition underlying humanism. All this has led to the charge that world literature is inherently Eurocentric. Chapter 2 examines this charge.

Almost concurrently with the spread of the term and idea of world literature there also emerged the beginnings of the discipline of comparative literature. In Chapter 1 I already briefly review how within comparative literature the issue of world literature led to a quest for terminological precision. In Chapter 3 I discuss how comparative literature, over the course of its history, has dealt with world literature. The first half of the chapter concentrates on the period up to, roughly, WWII and the continental European tradition, or on what is commonly labeled the "French" school of comparative literature. The second half focuses on the so-called "American" school rising to dominance after WWII.

A major difference between European and American ways of dealing with world literature lies in how research in, and the teaching of, world literature have been incorporated into university curricula. Until very recently in Europe interest in the subject has almost exclusively been the province of research. In contrast, in the USA it has, from very early on, informed course work on all levels of university education, and most particularly so undergraduate survey courses. The specifically American pedagogical investment in world literature is the subject of Chapter 4.

In Europe, the focus on research has led to systemic, rather than, as in the USA, pedagogical approaches to world literature. Chapter 5 discusses a number of these systemic approaches, briefly stopping at some Central and Eastern European theories from the middle of the twentieth century, and then quickly proceeding to more recent theories of French and Italian origin. The latter have significantly re-invigorated the debate on the subject. As such, they form the main interest of Chapter 5.

Already for Goethe, translation was an essential ingredient of world literature. Much neglected in most earlier study of literature, translation since the last quarter of the twentieth century has developed into a major field of study of its own. With the renewed interest in world literature translation studies has come to occupy a central position in literary studies. Chapter 6 traces the rise of translation studies in relation to the study of world literature.

Chapters 1 through 6 are mostly concerned with theories, methods, and approaches to world literature that have come to fruition in some of the major countries or linguistic communities of Europe and America – practically speaking France, Germany, and the United States – with only occasional pointers to developments elsewhere. In the final two chapters of this book the focus shifts to what is happening in some smaller, or in any event less hegemonic, in literary-theoretical terms, countries or regions in Europe, or to some larger areas beyond Europe and the United States. Chapter 7 concentrates on the relationship of postcolonial studies to world literature. In Chapter 8 we take a look at some exciting new initiatives taking place in Scandinavia, Portugal, Spain, and China.

Throughout it will become clear that world literature is not an arcane subject for ivory tower scholars. On the contrary, the debate over world literature as it has developed, and sometimes raged, over the last two centuries closely reverberates with the changes taking place in the world itself over that same period. What constitutes world literature, for whom, and when, and how one should describe it, study it, and teach it reflect changing constellations of power around the world: literary, intellectually, but also, and perhaps even foremost, economically, politically, and militarily. That is why world literature is such an interesting subject.

1 Naming world literature

Overview

In this first chapter we take a look at how "world literature" got its name, and at some of the fluctuations that name, and the idea or ideas it has stood for, have undergone over the past two centuries or so. Put at its simplest, we see the story of world literature coming full circle over these two centuries, with the more recent and most influential commentators adopting a position that is close to that of the man who first made the term popular. That man was the German writer Johann Wolfgang von Goethe (1749–1832). Until recently it has been commonplace to assert that he coined the term "*Weltliteratur.*" We now know that this is not correct. August Ludwig von Schlözer (1735–1809), a German historian who also wrote a world history, already used the term in print in his 1773 *Isländischen Literatur und Geschichte (Icelandic Literature and History*; Schamoni 2008, Gossens in press). Yet another German, the writer Christoph Martin Wieland (1733–1813), certainly used it early in the nineteenth century in a handwritten note to a translation of Horace's letters (Weitz 1987, Pizer 2006). However, none of these earlier uses has had the impact that Goethe's has had. Goethe first recorded the term in his diary on 15 January 1827. In his *Gespräche mit Goethe* (1836–48; *Conversations with Goethe*) Johann Peter Eckermann (1792–1854) notes Goethe on 31 January of the same year as saying that "national literature has not much meaning nowadays: the epoch of world literature is at hand, and each must work to hasten its coming" (Strich 1949: 349), and he would regularly return to *Weltliteratur* over the next 4 years, almost up to his death in 1832. In all, we have twenty-one rather brief passages from Goethe's own writings and his recorded conversation in which the term appears (Strich 1957: 369–72, 1949: 349–51). Ever since the publication of *Conversations with Goethe,* these passages have served as the inevitable point of departure for all further discussions on the topic. Yet nowhere in his voluminous writings does Goethe give a precise definition of *Weltliteratur*. In fact, Hendrik Birus (2000) details the notorious ambiguity or polysemy of Goethe's utterances on world literature. It is not surprising, then, that these utterances have given rise to ambiguities. These ambiguities, moreover, largely stem from Goethe's own historical situation. In what follows we enter into the twists and turns these ambiguities have led to with regard to "world literature."

Goethe's *Weltliteratur*

At the time of Goethe's taking an interest in *Weltliteratur* Europe had only relatively recently emerged from a period of violent warfare occasioned by the French Revolution and the Napoleonic Wars. Goethe had himself been actively involved in some of these events. Germany at the time was divided into numerous smaller, and a few larger, kingdoms, principalities, duchies, and the like. For the better part of his adult life, Goethe had been living in Weimar at the court of the Dukes of Saxe-Weimar. After the final defeat of Napoleon in 1815 Europe had entered into a period of pacification and political restoration. Goethe noted that under these circumstances an increase in the production and circulation of periodicals facilitated the exchange of ideas across Europe. In his own journal *Über Kunst und Altertum* (*On Art and Antiquity* Vol. 6, part 1), in an 1827 article on a French adaptation of his own play *Tasso*, he commented upon this as a sign of "the progress of the human race, of the wider prospects in world relationships between men," and it led him to the "conviction that a universal world literature is in process of formation in which we Germans are called to play an honourable part" (Strich 1949: 349). In an 1828 issue of *Über Kunst und Altertum* (*On Art and Antiquity*, Vol. 6, part 2), in an article on "Edinburgh Reviews," he elaborated: "these journals, as they gradually reach a wider public, will contribute most effectively to the universal world literature we hope for; we repeat however that there can be no question of the nations thinking alike, the aim is simply that they shall grow aware of one another, understand each other, and, even where they may not be able to love, may at least tolerate one another" (Strich 1949: 350). The "honourable part" Goethe saw reserved for the German language and its literature lay in German literature mediating between the world's literatures because of what he esteemed to be the German language's unique gift for translation. This, Goethe thought, would also enhance the prestige and standing of German literature in a Europe in which, contrary to the English and French cases, German literature did not enjoy the support of a strong nation state, and could not invoke a robust national identity. Through the use of the German language, then, and with German literature acting as a sort of arbiter for the dissemination of work in foreign languages throughout Europe, a transnational literature would come into being that would serve the cause of understanding and toleration among nations and peoples.

Weltliteratur, "letters" and literature

In an address to the Congress of Natural Scientists in Berlin, in 1828, Goethe further refined his earlier ideas. "In venturing to announce a European, in

Johann Wolfgang von Goethe (1749–1832) is generally accepted as having been the greatest German writer ever. He gained fame very early with a tragedy, *Götz von Berlichingen* (1773), and especially with his 1774 epistolary novel *The Sorrows of Young Werther* (*Die Leiden des jungen Werthers*) about an unhappy love affair that had all of Europe in tears. Other important works include the drama's *Faust* I and II (1808, 1832), the two-part novel of education *Wilhelm Meister's Apprenticeship* (*Wilhelm Meisters Lehrjahre*, 1795–96) and *Wilhelm Meister's Journeyman Years* (*Wilhelm Meisters Wanderjahre*, 1829), and the volume of poems *West-Eastern Divan* (*West-Östlicher Diwan*, 1819), inspired by the poetry of the fourteenth-century Persian poet Hafez or Hafiz. Next to the most important German, and many would say European or even world, writer of his age, Goethe was also a noted scientist. His novel *Elective Affinities* (*Die Wahlverwandtschaften*, 1809) looks at marriage, and the relationships between men and women, as analogous to chemical reactions. Goethe also was active as a geologist and botanist, and he elaborated a theory of colors that drew a lot of attention at the time.

fact a universal, world literature," he said, "we did not mean merely to say that the different nations should get to know each other and each other's productions; for in this sense it has long been in existence, is propagating itself, and is constantly being added to" (Strich 1949: 350). "No, indeed! The matter is rather this," he claimed, "that the living, striving men of letters should learn to know each other, and through their own inclination and similarity of tastes, find the motive for corporate action" (Strich 1949: 350). In the original German, Goethe uses "Literatoren," which is a rather neutral term. Goethe's translator's use of the term "men of letters" in this passage, though, accurately points to the double frame of reference Goethe seems to invoke here, and hence perhaps to his own final indecision as to what precisely he meant with *Weltliteratur*.

On the one hand, the term "men of letters" suggests that Goethe, while thinking of *Weltliteratur*, may have been harking back to the concept, predating the French Revolution, of the "Republic of Letters." This term refers to the communities of intellectuals, writers, and philosophers that during especially the seventeenth and eighteenth centuries kept in touch with one another, across Europe, by the exchange of, precisely, letters. What they corresponded about, more importantly, were "letters" in the sense of any writing about any kind of "knowledge," stretching from poetry to politics, from astronomy to astrology. The impact these writers had can best be gauged from the fact that it is their ideas, especially those of the so-called *lumières* or Enlightenment philosophers of the eighteenth century, that led to the French Revolution. In fact, they acted as a kind of independent "republic" next to, and often in disagreement with, the official state powers across Europe. In Goethe's day, periodicals had replaced letter writing as the main medium of intellectual exchange. The men writing and reading these journals in Goethe's view should assume the mantle of their earlier counterparts of the Republic of Letters, and strive for the same impact. *Weltliteratur* would then refer to an updated form of transnational communication among, in first instance, European, and in further instance "world," intellectuals, to use a term that in Goethe's days had not yet been coined.

Alternatively, the use of such a term as "men of letters" also hints at Goethe's unease with what he saw as unwelcome developments in his already increasingly "modern" and commercialized world, of which the enhanced circulation of journals and peridodicals was in itself a telling instance. In an 1829 essay on a German translation of Thomas Carlyle's *Life of Schiller*, and after having mentioned the inevitability of the coming of world literature, Goethe writes that "what suits the masses will spread and will, as we can already see now, give pleasure far and wide ... but what is really worth-while will not be so popular" (Strich 1949: 25). So, "the serious-minded will form a quiet, I might almost say an oppressed community," and find their main consolation, "in fact the greatest encouragement" in the fact that "Truth has its function and performs it ... if they discover this for themselves and can point it out to others, they will have a profound effect on their generation" (Strich 1949: 25; for a slightly different version of the same passage see Goethe, ed. John Gearey 1986: 227).

Weltliteratur here assumes the double guise of on the one hand signaling, positively, the intimate "commerce" or exchange of ideas between like-minded writers around Europe and on the other hand, negatively, that of the ever-faster and ever-increasing commercialization, including in the province of "letters," that Goethe saw taking place all around him. Later ages would rephrase this distinction as the opposition between *Literatur* and *Lektur*, or *Unterhaltungsliteratur* (Schneider 2004), that is to say between literature and popular literature. Goethe's aversion to the latter would eventually translate into the rejection of mass culture by, for instance, Theodor Adorno (1903–69) and most of the Frankfurt School, as well as their American followers, foremost Fredric Jameson.

The "commercial" reference of *Weltliteratur is* picked up by Karl Marx (1818–83) and Friedrich Engels (1820–95) in their *Communist Manifesto* (1848), where they posited that "in place of the old wants, satisfied by the productions of the country, we find new wants, requiring for their satisfaction the products of distant lands and climates. In place of the old local and national seclusion and self-sufficiency, we have intercourse in every direction, universal interdependence of nations. And as in material, so also in intellectual production. The intellectual creations of individual nations become common property. National one-sidedness and narrow-mindedness become increasingly impossible, and from the numerous national and local literatures, there arises a world literature" (Marx 2010:16). In essence, the opposition between these two concepts of "world literature" – the one referring to the circulation of what are in essence "high" cultural goods among an international elite of "connaisseurs," the other embracing all works of literature everywhere – keeps running through the subject's further history.

The use of the word "literature" in the final sentence of the previous paragraph points to a further ambiguity in Goethe's various pronouncements on world literature, namely that related to the uses of "letters" and "literature." Discussion of Goethe's *Weltliteratur* almost from the very beginning became caught up in a more general discussion about the concept of "literature" raging at the beginning of the nineteenth century (Hoesel-Uhlig 2004). In fact it is only at that moment that "literature" gained its present meaning, at least as used in Europe and by extension in the West, or in Western-inspired thinking on the issue. Until the end of the eighteenth century it was "letters" that covered all forms of written knowledge. At the end of the eighteenth century, largely as a result of the German philosopher Emmanuel Kant's intervention, "literature" comes to designate only that part of the overall mass of written material that is ruled by the aesthetic sense, or "taste," and not by any objectively verifiable claim to "truth." Implicitly, the question then shifts to what is "good" literature and what is not. Goethe's own unease with *Weltliteratur* in his 1829 essay on Carlyle's *The Life of Schiller* quoted above as possibly designating all "literature" regardless of "quality" reflects this shift. At the same time, the rise of literary historiography as a branch of the newly emerging "science" of history at the end of the eighteenth and the beginning of the nineteenth centuries redirected attention to "literature" as the archive of everything ever written that fits the category of literature newly defined. Consequently, after Goethe the interpretations put on *Weltliteratur* have mostly tended to vacillate between the aesthetic and the archival, between an exclusive canon of what is deemed aesthetically most valuable in, and as comprehensive a coverage as possible of, "all" literature. Only recently has there been a return to Goethe's original concept of *Weltliteratur* as a form of circulation – albeit, of course, with a difference.

World literature versus national literature

At first sight the greatest ambiguity of all is that Goethe pushed the idea of world literature in an age of intense nationalism. In Germany as in the rest of Europe, and later also in the Americas, during the nineteenth and twentieth centuries most effort would go into the writing of national literary histories. This was the logical cultural counterpart to the relentless process of political nation-building or consolidation going on across Europe. According to the tenets of Romanticism, each nation strove to ground its legitimacy in its own literary antecedents. Consequently, we see the first systematic histories of Europe's various national literatures appearing in the first part of the nineteenth century. This is not to say that there had been no earlier national literary histories. Italy, until beyond the middle of the nineteenth century, remained subdivided into a motley quilt of larger and smaller political entities, with no hope of political unification in sight. The unity of a political "patria" or "fatherland" thus lacking was looked for in literature, and particularly in what Claudio Guillén (1993: 27) calls a "common poetic patrimony." Guillén cites Giaconto Gimmá's *Idea della storia dell'Italia letterata* (1723; *The Idea of the History of Literary Italy*) and Marco Foscarini's *Storia della letteratura veneziana* (1752; *History of Venetian Literature*) as the earliest examples of such histories. In France a multivolume *Histoire littéraire de la France* (*Literary History of France*) started appearing in 1733. The latter, an encyclopedia rather than a proper "history," was inaugurated by the Benedictine monks of Saint Maur, continued by the Institut de France in 1814, and still later by a French academy, and continues until today. Invoking the authority of the *Histoire* of the Benedictines, next to that of, for instance, the French sixteenth-century writer and philosopher Michel de Montaigne, the early nineteenth-century author René de Chateaubriand, and others, Matthieu Richard Auguste Henrion (1805–62) published a one-volume *Histoire littéraire de la France au moyen âge* (*Literary History of France During the Middle Ages*) in 1827, with a second edition in 1837. In his foreword Henrion justifies his enterprise by saying that whereas French youth in the course of their studies are familiarized with Greek and Latin letters, they remain strangers to the various phases of "our country's civilisation" (1827: i; civilisation de notre pays). Similarly, he claims, whereas "the better kind of people" (les gens du monde) are well up on matters political, they "barely know anything about our literary history" (Henrion 1827: i; connaissent à peine notre histoire littéraire). The very first pages of Henrion's *Histoire* set the tone for much of what is typical of nineteenth-century national literary historiography. He immediately starts by claiming for French literature the succession to the giants of Greek and Latin literature. In a similar vein, albeit perhaps not always with the same *aplomb*, all national literary histories glorified their own literature. Henrion qualifies his work as an "*Essai*," "sufficiently brief not to lay claim to the attention for too long, yet sufficiently thorough to cover all essentials" (Henrion 1827: i; assez rapide pour ne pas détourner trop long-temps l'attention, assez détaillé pour qu'il renfermât les notions les plus essentielles).

The *Geschichte der poetischen Nationallitteratur der Deutschen* (1835–42, 5 vols; *History of the National Literature of the Germans*) by Georg Gottfried Gervinus (1805–71) is a totally different affair in its comprehensiveness as well as thoroughness. Not for nothing does Michael S. Batts choose the date of appearance of the first volume of Gervinus's history (as of the fifth edition, by

Matthieu Richard Auguste Henrion (1805–62) was a French lawyer, royalist, supporter of Napoleon III, and a Catholic Ultramontanist – which is to say a supporter of the authority of the Pope over that of the local or national clergy. He frequently contributed to Catholic periodicals, and wrote numerous works on religion in France.

Karl Bartsch, renamed *Geschichte der deutschen Dichtung*, 1871–74; *History of German Literature*) as the starting date for his own *A History of Histories of German Literature, 1835–1914* (1993). For Batts, Gervinus's *Geschichte* is "quite different from anything that had appeared before and [...] set a standard for the future" (Batts 1993: 1). In fact, Batts situates Gervinus's work as at the start of "Germanistik," that is to say the academic discipline of the study of German language and literature. Most other, at least Western, European countries followed suit in the course of the nineteenth century. In Holland, for instance, we have W.J.A. Jonckbloet's (1817–85) multivolume *Geschiedenis der Nederlandsche letterkunde* (1868–70; *History of Dutch Literature*). Although, as we briefly saw earlier, Goethe himself wanted to propagate world literature at least partially because he thought that German letters would be enhanced if they should succeed in playing a central role in the circulation of the world's literatures, and because in this way the relative inconsequence of the numerous but mostly small German entities in the political realm would be at least partially offset by the increased weight of German literature in the cultural realm, his aims in all this were cosmopolitan rather than narrowly nationalistic. In fact, for at least a number of commentators Goethe would have insisted upon his ideas on world literature in reaction to what he perceived as the narrowly patriotic concerns of his Romantic coevals. Perhaps it is more correct to say that he did so in a limited "window of opportunity," when Europe was still in recoil from the excesses of the Napoleonic period, and before the onset of the nationalist movements that would erupt across Europe as of about 1830, with the Greek rising of the early 1820s serving as ignitor.

Goethe so to speak bypasses the level of the nation because "Germany" in his day is not a unified country, and therefore in the eyes of Goethe German literature is at a disadvantage in comparison to English and French literature, both of which can count on the backing of a powerful national identity which they can and do give expression to. Understandably then, Goethe concentrates on the complementarity of the local and the universal, of the regional, expressive of the kind of identitarian realities operative in his own immediate context, with the universal, which in his case is primarily the European, level. In this he was partially undoubtedly also inspired by the early forms of Romanticism that emphasized the local or regional as the expressions of a genuine popular sense of "belonging," inspired by the rising nostalgia for a "home" in time and space brought about by accelerating modernity in the form of the twin forces of industrialization and increased mobility, or in other words precisely the increased "commerce" that Goethe saw as facilitating the advent of *Weltliteratur*. To use the terminology of Aleida Assmann (2010), Goethe lived in an age when Romanticism, in the figures of the brothers Schlegel and Grimm, building on the work of Herder, could still combine short-term individual and social memory alive in "folk-culture" with long-term cultural memory as embodied or enshrined in the works of artists and scholars built upon this folk-culture. After Goethe, national literary histories would start to serve as institutionalized forms of national memory.

Heine and world literature in nineteenth-century Germany

What are the various offshoots, then, to which Goethe's thoughts on world literature, and particularly the ambiguity imbued in them, gave rise? For John Pizer, in his *The Idea of World Literature: History and Pedagogical Practice* (2006), only one German writer active in Goethe's own lifetime practiced anything resembling Goethe's own original idea of world literature as signaling and at the same time promoting an intensified cultural exchange among nations. That writer, according to Pizer, is Heinrich Heine.

Heinrich Heine (1797–1856) was one of the most important German poets of the first half of the nineteenth century. He was born in Düsseldorf, then a small town, of Jewish parents. He later converted to Protestantism. Most of his adult life was spent in Paris, whence he moved permanently in 1831. Witty and ironical, Heine criticized not only fellow poets and writers, but also the German authorities, for which his work often fell victim to censorship. His move to Paris was inspired by a search for greater political and poetic freedom. Many of Heine's poems were put to music by famous composers such as Robert Schumann and Franz Schubert.

Heine, in a number of essays written during his Parisian years (1831–56), strove to make German culture better known to the French, and French culture to the Germans, and did so in both German and French. Heine herewith sought to update Mme De Staël's (1766–1817) views on Germany as presented in her famous *De l'Allemagne* of 1813, a work with which she had wanted to promote the understanding of German culture among the French, and that in many ways can be seen as having been the prelude of Goethe's *Weltliteratur*, but that had also propagated the German Romantic nationalism Goethe shied away from and Heine abhorred. At the time of Heine's writing, several other German essayists, such as Ludolf Wienbarg (1802–72) in an 1835 article (Wienbarg 1982), and Karl Gutzkow (1811–78) in an 1836 book, still defended *Weltliteratur*, and Goethe. Both Wienbarg and Gutzkow were members, with Heine, of what came to be known as the *Young Germany* movement. Even though he defended Goethe, with Gutzkow nevertheless there already emerges an emphasis on the national within world literature.

After Heine, if Goethe's *Weltliteratur* was invoked, it was either in the service of nationalism, or to reject it as a threat to national culture. The former we find with the already-mentioned Gervinus, who in his *Geschichte* praised Goethe for the important role the latter saw German language and literature play on the scene of world literature, but only in so far as it strengthened German nationalism and advanced German politics. A rejection

Mme de Staël or **Anne Louise Germaine de Staël-Holstein** was a Swiss writer and socialite who ran a famous literary salon in Paris, where she was born and spent her early life, and at her Castle in Coppet, a village on Lake Geneva. Mme de Staël's father held important positions under King Louis XVI, and she herself was involved in politics during the period of the French Revolution and its aftermath. She published various poems and novels, the most famous being *Delphine* (1802) and *Corinne or Italy* (*Corinne ou l'Italie*, 1807). She also published a number of essays of which the most important are *Sur la litérature considérée dans ses rapports avec les institutions sociales* (*On literature considered in its relations to social institutions*, 1800) and *On Germany* (*De l'Allemagne*, 1813), a philosophical and literary inquiry into German culture meant to further French understanding for its eastern neighbor.

of *Weltliteratur* as a threat to German national character we find in *Geschichte der Literatur der Gegenwart* (1840; *History of Contemporary Literature*) by Theodor Mundt (1808–61) (Pizer 2006: 63). Mundt was yet another member of *Young Germany*, the adherents of which, as nationalist fervor mounted in a Germany on the road to unification, finally achieved in 1871, increasingly turned against the cosmopolitanism of a Goethe and a Heine, in favor of a nationalist and patriotic stance. As Gossens puts it,

> Drawing upon the ideas of Herder, Schlegel and Hegel, Mundt, in a series of literary histories, elaborates a concept of world literature in which literature becomes representative of a nation's development. Thus, Mundt actively contributes to a literary historical approach that sees a world literary canon as consisting of the cumulation of national canons. This approach heavily marked the world literary histories written in the second half of the nineteenth century, and continues to be significant even for our contemporary views of the subject

> (Gossens in press: 8; Unter Rückgriff auf Herder, Schlegel und Hegel entwickelt Mundt in einer Reihe von Literaturgeschichten ein Konzept von Weltliteratur, bei dem die Literatur zum Repräsentanten nationaler Entwicklung wird. Mundt trägt damit wesentlich zu einer literaturgeschichtlichen Fundierung eines additiven, national orientierten Weltliteraturkanons bei, der die Weltliteraturgeschichten in den zweiten Hälfte des 19. Jahrhunderts, aber auch noch unser heutiges Weltliteraturverständnis nachhaltig prägt)

Philarète Chasles and world literature in nineteenth-century France

If in Germany, and in German, according to Pizer, only Heine can be taken to follow Goethe's lead in actively furthering *Weltliteratur* even without ever mentioning the term himself, in France the same can be said of Philarète Chasles (1798–1873). Chasles, because of his father's involvement with the Napoleonic regime, spent some of his youth in exile in England after the fall of Napoleon. Later, he would become a prolific literary critic and university lecturer in France, holding the prestigious Chair of Foreign Literatures at the Collège de France from 1841 to his death. Chasles did much to further the understanding of foreign literatures, and particularly English literature, in France. His "Goethean" spirit can plainly be seen from the opening lecture to a course on "Foreign Literature Compared" he gave at the Parisian Athénée in 1835. "The entire idea of this course," he tells his audience, "the unique purpose of the studies with which [they] wish to associate [them]selves" is to demonstrate "the distant influence of one mind upon others, the magnetism of one thought for another" (Chasles 1973: 20). The "admirable study he is involved in," he announces, is "the intimate history of the human race, it is the drama of literature, for the drama is no more than the relationships of men with men; it is the exchange of intellectual feelings among all the nations of Europe" (Chasles 1973; 21). As such, he traces how Italy borrows from the Classics, France and Spain from Italy, England and Germany from France, and all from each other, nor does he forget to mention the influence of Arab, Gothic, Byzantine, and Provençal antecedents. To each of the literatures mentioned, Chasles ascribes specific characteristics, evocative of what today we would perhaps call national characters, Italy being associated with the senses and the passions, Spain with lyrical genius, Germany with the mind. Mentioning Goethe, next to Luther, Leibniz, and Kant, Chasles praises Germany, "this eminently critical country," for its "vast literary understanding," and its "magnificent comprehension of all the intellectual phases of the world" (Chasles 1973: 25). Still, Chasles says, he is going to "concern [him]self primarily with France," because France is "the center, but the center of sensitivity; she directs civilization, less perhaps by opening up the route to the people who border her than by going forward herself with a giddy and contagious passion" (Chasles 1973: 21). "What Europe is to the rest of the / world," he claims, "France is to Europe; everything reverberates toward her, everything ends with her" (Chasles 1973: 21–22). France, Chasles maintains, is "always influenced by the foreign, always mistress of the influences she receives" (Chasles 1973: 22). Goethe had already been of the opinion that in the final analysis France stood to gain most from the dawn of *Weltliteratur*. In his own present, however, he had seen German literature as mediator for the world's literatures, a position that Chasles in his lecture, and in the remainder of his course, claims for France as "*Grand-Sympathique*" of the civilized world" past, present, and future (Chasles 1973: 22).

As the title of his lecture indicates, Chasles was implicitly inspired by the "comparative method" that in the nineteenth century came to dominate science, and that underpinned the findings of, for instance, the then new discipline of philology, but also of Charles Darwin later in the century. Although he himself never used the term, Chasles can therefore be considered one of the founding fathers of the discipline we now refer to as comparative literature. It is not a coincidence, then, that the opening lecture from his 1835 Athénée course from which I just quoted features as the first passage in Hans-Joachim Schulz and Philip H. Rhein's 1973 anthology *Comparative Literature: The Early Years*. In fact, the relationship between world literature and comparative literature has been an intimate yet tangled one from the start. I will come back to this in Chapter 3. For the time being, I will continue with the vicissitudes the term and concept of world literature underwent between Goethe's time and our present one.

Towards the end of his 1835 lecture Chasles derides the study of "literature" as concerned with phrasing, metaphors, and style, and instead of the study of "literary history" advocates that of "intellectual history" and the "history of human thought" (Chasles 1973: 33 and 35). Potentially, this opens the door to all kinds of writing being included, and indeed Chasles mentions "the Koran of Mohammed and the proclamations of Bonaparte; a madrigal of the Marquis de Pézay and the laws of Zoroaster" (Chasles 1973: 33). He proposes however not to "follow a systematic synthesis," but rather to take "a pleasure trip, a random walk, not a geometric march bound by rigid cadence" (Chasles 1973: 36). During this "walk" he will concentrate upon the "great writers," Cervantes, Rabelais, Shakespeare, and others such, all "great men" (Chasles 1973: 36), whom, to use the term the American writer and philosopher Ralph Walso Emerson in 1850 used for one of his books, he also saw as "representative men" for their times. Effectively speaking, then, this amounts to a canon, if not of "great works," then at least of "great writers." In the second half of the nineteenth century scholars and writers would more systematically work out what is only mooted with Chasles. By and large they abandoned the original Goethean concept of *Weltliteratur* as the transnational contemporary circulation of ideas among the authors and leading intellectuals of, in first instance, the nations of Europe. Instead, they interpreted world literature as meaning either the archive of all that had ever been written, even if often, in spite of Chasles's proposal, limited to *belles lettres* or "literature" in the more restrictive sense, or, more often, as the canon of "world masterpieces." Telling in this respect is *Great Writers: Cervantes, Scott, Milton, Virgil, Montaigne, Shakespeare*, a work published in 1907 by George Edward Woodberry (1855–1930), from 1891 to 1904 Professor of Comparative Literature at Columbia University in New York. Moreover, while Chasles in his insistence on France being the "center" (Chasles 1973: 21) could also find fault with French literature, blaming it for sometimes having made mistakes and even of having misled other European literatures into following its own wrong turns, and thus expresses "complete contempt for narrow-minded and blind patriotism," which he likens to the "love of an idiotic mother who suffocates her child in the diapers she wraps him in" (Chasles 1973: 23), later scholars often have no such scruples and, as the example of Mundt cited earlier shows, use world literature as a vehicle to implicitly promote their own national literature.

Histories of world literature

The center of world literary history writing throughout the nineteenth and early twentieth centuries, though, was undoubtedly Germany. Anders Pettersson calls Karl Rosenkranz's *Handbuch einer allgemeinen Geschichte der Poesie* (*Handbook of General History of Poetry*), published in 1832, the "first completed history of world literature" (Pettersson 2005: 57). For Gossens (in press: 11), the literary historians Hermann Hettner (1821–82), Johannes Scherr (1817–86), and Adolf Stern (1835–1907) were mainly responsible for popularizing and developing thinking on world literature in nineteenth-century Germany. Instead of insisting on the utopian dimension of a Goethean concept of world literature furthering the intellectual exchange of ideas across Europe, all three basically follow a cumulative approach, describing the literary production of discrete countries from a chronological point of view. In other words, with these literary historians world literature took a sharp turn towards standing for the entire literary production of the world, to be described by simply adding one to the other the national literatures of the various countries or cultures. In practice, coverage did not stretch to the entire globe, but usually remained focused on Europe, and even on a relatively limited part of Europe. In a series of works published from the mid-1850s through the early 1870s Hettner concentrates on the literatures of France, England and Germany during the Enlightenment. For Hettner these play the central role in the development of European and world literature during the period that interests him. Stern, in 1888, published the first literary history to actually carry the word "Weltliteratur" in its title: *Geschichte der Weltliteratur in übersichtlicher Darstellung* (*History of World Literature Clearly Explained*). Most interesting and influential, however, was Scherr, whose *Allgemeinen Geschichte der Literatur von den ältesten Zeiten bis auf die Gegenwart. Ein Handbuch für alle Gebildeten* (1851; *General History of Literature from Antiquity to the Present. A Manual for all Educated People*) aimed at a comprehensive while at the same time geographically representative overview of "the achievements in poetry and literary prose" (Gossens in press: 11; die Erzeugnisse der Poesie und schönen Prosa) of humanity, and this in a truly transnational approach, looking for structural and historical developments that transcended national and linguistic boundaries. Some years earlier, in 1848, Scherr had already published what in effect was an anthology of world literature with his *Bildersaal der Weltliteratur* (*Picture Gallery of World Literature*). Revised editions of this work appeared in 1869 and 1885.

Scherr's History, regularly updated by later scholars, went through eleven editions, with the last of these appearing in 1921. As of the edition of 1895 the work bore the title *Illustrierte Geschichte der Weltliteratur* (*Illustrated History of World Literature*). As Scherr, for obvious reasons, had to be selective in his presentation of the world's literature, he had to institute a canon, which he did on aesthetic grounds. Stern's work, unlike that of Scherr, did not go through repeated editions. Still, together these two provided the examples upon which most subsequent histories of world literature would model themselves, in Germany but also elsewhere. In Germany, according to Gossens, this took the form of a whole series of similar histories, mostly written by one single author and targeted for specific audiences. These audiences could be differentiated according to levels of difficulty and scholarship, that is to say they might be aimed at high school or university students. They might be meant for the use of the so-called "interested layman." But they might also select their canonical works according to the religious or philosophical orientation of the readership they aimed at. Thus, different histories might be used in Protestant and Catholic schools, for instance. Gossens insists that in most of these works "the foundational value of the ideas of transnationalism and cosmopolitanism needs qualification ... most often the aim is to foreground the special qualities of one's own nation" (Gossens in press: 13; die Denkfiguren von Transnationalität und Kosmopolitismus ... nur bedingt grundlegend sind ... meist geht es darum, die qualitativen Besonderheiten der eigenen Nation hervorzuheben).

Beyond Germany, the genre of world literature histories, because such we can now call it, as described by Gossens and modeled specifically upon Stern rather than Scherr, knew a great vogue especially in the Scandinavian countries, the Netherlands, and Britain, and also in the United States. J.C. Brandt Corstius (1963) and Anders Pettersson (2005) enumerate and briefly discuss many of these histories. Interesting to find is that terminology often differs from one country or language to another, and that "world literature" relatively rarely figures in the titles to these works. Earlier, we already saw that even in Germany *Weltliteratur* was only used late in the century in the title to such a work. In France, Chasles, while in effect writing what amounted to some sort of "world literature" history, preferred the word "comparaison" in his title. In Germany the term used most often in the titles to such works was "allgemein" (general), stressing the comprehensiveness and general reach of the work in question.

Corstius (1963) signals that many of these works, although the ambition overtly was to write a history of he world's literatures, in fact, and in line with what Gossens suggests above, ended up giving inordinate room to their native literatures, at the expense of "foreign" and especially non-European literatures. In order to forestall this possibility, authors sometimes opted to by-pass discussions of their native literature altogether. In this respect Corstius (1963) mentions Otto von Leixner's 1880–82 *Illustrierte Geschichte der fremden Literaturen* (Corstius refers to the 1899 2nd edition; *Illustrated History of Foreign Literatures*) as well as to Paul Wiegler's 1913 *Geschichte der fremdsprachigen Literaturen* (*History of Literatures in Foreign Languages*). In 1911 Von Leixner's work was translated and revised for a Dutch public as *Der Wereld Letterkunde voor Nederlanders bewerkt door P.A.M. Boele van Hensbroek* (*The World's Literature Revised for the Use of the Dutch by P.A.M. Boele van Hensbroek*). In his foreword, dated 1909, Van Hensbroek insists that he has very much changed Von Leixner's original, and justifies this from the extreme

German chauvinism he finds with that original, and therefore the need to remake it "in line with the endeavor to make a book about Holland" (in overeenstemming met het streven, een boek voor Nederland te maken; Van Hensbroek 1911: vi). In fact, Van Hensbroek is not less chauvinistic than von Leixner, of course. At the same time, the Dutch book does carry the term "world literature" in its title. Yet, it excludes Dutch literature itself, while including the literatures of Holland's colonies.

World literature and comparative literature

In France, Corstius (1963) mentions Frédéric Loliée's 1903 *Histoire des littératures comparées*, translated in 1906 as *A Short History of Comparative Literature from the Earliest Times to the Present Day*. In fact, the change from Loliée's "littératures comparées" to the English version's "comparative literature" is not a coincidence. Towards the end of the nineteenth century the term "comparative literature" had gained entrance in the English-speaking world first through a lecture course that Charles Chauncey Shackford gave at Cornell University in 1871, and in the inaugural lecture to which he expatiated upon the discipline, and then through a book with the title *Comparative Literature* by Hutcheson Macaulay Posnett in 1886. In France, Germany, Italy, and other continental European countries the discipline of "littérature comparée," "vergleichende" or "allgemeine und vergleichende Literaturwissenschaft," or "letteratura comparata" had been building throughout the second half of the nineteenth century (Pichois and Rousseau 1967). In England, Matthew Arnold (1822–88) translated the term, from the French, as "comparative literature" in 1848 (Pichois and Rousseau 1967: 19). From the very beginning, "world literature" almost inevitably became the province of this new discipline. This, however, was not Goethe's *Weltliteratur,* but rather that of Scherr and his contemporaries, and therefore in effect that of a representative canon. Moreover, as also indicated before, this canon largely was restricted to literatures in European languages, and even primarily in a few major European languages, foremost French, English and German, with Italian and Spanish as distant seconds, and then the occasional other, smaller, European literature, often depending upon the provenance or linguistic skill of the discipline's practitioner in question. I will come back to the relationship between world literature and comparative literature in a later chapter. For the time being I just want to point out that the systematization of the discourse on world literature occasioned by its assumption by comparative literature led to a distinction between various terms used to indicate some of the various offshoots to which Goethe's use of the term had given rise to begin with.

Shackford started off his 1871 lecture by positing that "literature is a vast subject, and what is called universal literature is not only vast, but too often vague" (Shackford 1973: 42). Later on he also uses the term "general literature," without it being entirely clear whether he simply sees this as synonymous with universal literature, or rather as equivalent to the French "littérature générale." When he speaks of "structural affinities" (Shackford 1973: 43) this rather seems to indicate the latter, with its pursuit of the common traits of different literatures in their historical evolution and relations, a suspicion that is confirmed by his subsequent discussion of specific genres arising in comparable circumstances in different countries, or as passing from one country to another. Pichois and Rousseau warn that French "littérature générale" should not be confounded with American "General Literature" which, they say, should rather be likened to French "philosophie de la littérature" or German "Literaturwissenschaft" (Pichois and Rousseau 1967: 94). For them, the only valid French translation for Goethe's *Weltliteratur* is "littérature universelle," which in English translation for them becomes "World Literature" (Pichois and Rousseau 1967: 102).

As we saw, for Shackford universal literature was the totality of literature, in fact, almost an oxymoron for "literature," regardless of language or location. Even if Claudio Guillén is not quite fair when in his *The Challenge of Comparative Literature* he says that for Pichois and Rousseau "littérature universelle" is reduced to the "*Who's Who* of the most illustrious authors" (Guillén 1993: 65), it is true that for them "world literature in essence aims to review and explain those masterpieces that are the patrimony of humankind" (Pichois and Rousseau 1967: 102; la littérature universelle ... se propose au fond de recenser et d'expliquer les chefs-d'ouvre qui forment le patrimoine de l'humanité). Richard Moulton, in his 1911 *World Literature and Its Place in General Culture*, gives yet a further twist to the discussion. Admitting that the term "world literature" may "legitimately be used in more than one sense," he stipulates that he himself is "throughout attaching to it a fixed and special significance" (Moulton 1921: 6). "Universal Literature" he takes to mean "the sum total of all literatures," whereas "world literature," as he uses the term, "is this Universal Literature seen in perspective from a given point of view, presumably the national standpoint of the observer" (Moulton 1921, 6), a scope he somewhat later enlarges to "the English-speaking peoples" (Moulton 1921, 9). Albert Guérard systematized all this, at least in English, in his 1940 *Preface to World Literature* as follows:

> Certain authorities choose to establish a four-fold division: Universal Literature, World Literature, Comparative Literature, General Literature. *Universal Literature*, in this scheme, stands for the fullest possible expansion of our field: it embraces all literatures, of all ages, in all languages, without insisting on their unity or their relations. *World Literature* is limited to those works which are enjoyed in common, ideally by all mankind, practically by our own group of culture, the European or Western. In both these cases, the word *Literature* applies to a body of literary works, not to their critical study. *Comparative Literature* and *General Literature*, on the contrary, are methods of approach. The first is concerned with the mutual influences between various national literatures;

the second with those problems that are present in the literature of every epoch and every country.

(Guérard 1940, 15)

Guérard's "comparative" and "general" Literature neatly correspond with the German *vergleichende* and *allgemeine Literaturwissenschaft*. Corstius (1963: 11) points out that already around 1920 the French comparatist Paul van Tieghem had called for a "littérature générale" in the sense meant by Guérard. In English, what Guérard calls general literature we would now probably sooner call theory of literature, as Guillén also argues (Guillén 1993: 66). Without reference to Guérard or any other predecessor in the matter, A. Owen Aldridge in 1986 largely reiterated Guérard's classification, with this difference that he defined world literature as comprising "the great works or classics of all times selected from all of the various national literatures," and Universal Literature as comprising, in a restricted and more practical sense, "all works that contain elements cosmopolitan enough to appeal to the average person in any literate culture" (Aldridge 1986: 56–57).

World literature, European literature

The almost exclusive concentration upon European or Western literature that Guérard signals can be seen as extending the national bias signaled by Moulton and his contemporaries to a wider cultural perspective, while still "usefully bracketing" literatures other than European or Euro-American. In 1901, in his inaugural lecture upon accepting the Chair of Comparative Literature at the University of Lyon, Fernand Baldensperger ironically commented: "European literature! – or, with the more ambitious term our neighbors use, world, or universal literature" (quoted in Corstius 1963: 7; la littérature européenne! – ou encore, selon la désignation plus ambitieuse qu'emploient nos voisins, la littérature mondiale, ou universelle). Although Baldensperger and Guérard were stating what was undoubtedly received practice in their days, Posnett, as well as a number of German scholars, had paid at least some attention to non-European literatures, albeit usually limited to (much) earlier periods, and often concentrating almost exclusively on works with a religious or mythological content. Still, the Dutch-language *Der wereld Letterkunde* referred to earlier opens with a 90-plus page section devoted to "Oostersche letteren" (Oriental literatures), chronicling Egyptian, Babylonian and Assyrian, Chinese, Japanese, Hebrew, Arab, Persian, and Indian literature, as well as that of the then Dutch colonial East Indies, that is to say present-day Indonesia, and this up to the nineteenth century, albeit of course in summary form. An even greater summary is the treatment that Walter Blair metes out to these same literatures in his 1940 *History of World Literature*. He devotes seventeen pages to what he calls "the beginnings of literature," and which in practice means discussing some early religious and philosophical texts, the most recent being the *Quran*, from non-Western sources. He then starts off his "proper" literary chapters with the Greeks, and thence continues with the "Western" tradition as world literature. Peter Ulf Møller mentions that Francis Bull's 1940 Danish *Verdens litteraturhistorie* (*World Literary History*) too "deals exclusively with European writers, in spite of its title" (Møller 1989: 20).

Pretty much the same thing applied to most other histories of world literature written in Western languages during most of the remainder of the twentieth century, according to Corstius who in his 1963 article briefly reviews the Argentinian Ezequiel Martínez Estrada's *Panorama de las literaturas* (1946; *Panorama of Literatures*), the Dutch F.W. van Heerikhuizen's *Gestalten der Tijden* (1951 and 1956; *Figures of the Ages*), the Swiss Robert Lavalette's *Literaturgeschichte der Welt* (1948, 1956; *Literary History of the World*), the latter's compatriot Eduard von Tunk's *Illustrierte Weltliteraturgeschichte* (1954–55; *Illustrated History of World Literature*), the German Erwin Laaths' *Geschichte der Weltliteratur* (1953; *History of World Literature*), and the Spanish Martín de Riquer and José María Valverde's *Historia de la literatura universal* (1957–59; *History of World Literature*; republished in 2010). Slightly better when it comes to including non-Western literatures are, still according to Corstius (1963), G. Prampolino's *Storia universale della letteratura* (seven volumes, 1948–53; *World History of Literature*), and the French three-volume Pléiade *Histoire des littératures* (1955–58; *History of Literature*) edited by Raymond Queneau. Typical for most of these histories continues to be that they pay a disproportionate amount of attention to their own national literature. Queneau, for example, devotes one of the three sizeable volumes of his history to (overwhelmingly) French literature and (some) other Francophone literatures.

Nor do things outside of the Euro-American ambit seem to have been much different.

The Indian scholar Krisha Chaitanya (pseudonym of K.K. Nair, b. 1918) wrote what is variously referred to as a nine-volume or a ten-volume *History of World Literature* (Bombay-Calcutta-Madras-New Delhi: Orient Longmans). I have only been able to consult the three volumes in the Harvard Library, published in 1964, 1965 and 1966, and which deal, respectively, with Ancient Mesopotamian and Ancient Egyptian, Ancient Greek, and Ancient Roman Literature. From what I have seen, these follow the traditional pattern of earlier twentieth-century such overviews, especially as written in the United States. In fact, Chaitanya explicitly refers to the example of the American John Drinkwater's *Outline of Literature* (1923). Drinkwater also served as an example for publications on world literature in China.

Rabindranath Tagore and Maxim Gorky on world literature

Closer to Goethe's original ideas on *Weltliteratur*, yet inflected by their particular conditions, were those of Rabindranath Tagore (1861–1941) and Maxim Gorky early in the twentieth century. On 9 February 1907 Rabindranath Tagore gave a lecture entitled "World Literature" to the Indian National Council of Education in which he explicitly stated that, "Comparative Literature is the English title you [those that invited him] have given to the subject I have been asked to discuss ... in Bengali I shall call it world literature" (Tagore 2001: 148). In their note to this piece the editors of *Rabindranath Tagore: Selected Writings on Literature and Language* say that in this "he was probably influenced by Goethe's term *Weltliteratur*" (Tagore 2001: 376). In his lecture, Tagore went to great lengths to claim literature as the expression of all of humanity. "If we realize that universal humanity expresses itself in literature," he said, "we shall be able to discern what is worth viewing in the latter" (Tagore 2001: 148). Drawing upon Indian mythology, and extensively metaphorizing, Tagore construes literature as a "second world around the material one," in which humankind extends itself "through the creation of feelings and ideas" (Tagore 2001: 150). "It is time," he finds, that "we pledged that our goal is to view universal humanity in universal literature by freeing ourselves from rustic uncatholicity; that we shall recognize totality in each particular author's work, and that in this totality we shall perceive the interrelations among all human efforts at expression" (Tagore 2001: 150).

In 1919 the Moscow-based Soviet publishing house "World Literature" inaugurated, in Russian translation, a series comprising more than 1500 book-length works dating from the French (1789) to the Russian (1917) Revolutions. The occasion led Maxim Gorky (pseudonym of Aleksey Maximovich Peshkov [1868–1936]) to write a celebratory essay. From his explicit mention that within the People's Commisariat for Culture a number of people have been appointed "to publish the works of the most important writers from England, America, Hungary, Germany, Italy, Spain, Portugal, the Scandinavian countries, France, etc." (Gorky 1969: 37; um die Bücher der bedeutendsten Schiftsteller Englands, Amerikas, Ungarns, Deutschlands, Italiens, Spaniens, Portugals, der skandinavischen Länder, Frankreichs usw. Herauszugeben), one might perhaps conclude that the publishing venture under consideration would, in essence, be Eurocentric. Gorky states, though, that a further aim is to acquaint the Russian people also with "the literary achievements of the East – the literature of India, China, Japan, and of the Arabs" (Gorky 1969: 38; dem literarischen Schaffen des Ostens – der Belletristik Indiens, Chinas, Japans und der Araber). What mattered most for Gorky, of course, was to recuperate the idea of world literature for the ideology of the newly created Soviet state in the interest of which he labored. This recuperation ran along two lines. First, he claimed, "We notice, and we believe, that it is the aim of that powerful flood of creative energy embodied in images and words to wash away forever all distinctions between races, nations and classes, to liberate all peoples from the heavy yoke of having to struggle with each other, and to link all their powers in the struggle against the mysterious forces of nature ... and then it appears that the art of the word and of the image is the religion of all mankind, a religion that comprises all that is written in the sacred books of ancient India, in the Zand-Awesta, in the New Testament, and in the Quran" (Gorky 1969: 37; Angesichts des machtvollen Stroms der in Gestalten und Worten verkörperten schöpferischen Energie spürt und glaubt man, dass es das Ziel dieses Stromes ist, für immer alle Unterschiede der Rassen, Nationen und Klassen hinwegzuspülen, die Menschen von dem schweren Joch des Kampfes gegeneinander zu befreien und danach alle ihre Kräfte auf den Kampf gegen die geheimnisvollen Naturgewalten zu lenken ... Und dann scheint es, als sei die Kunst des Wortes und des Bildes die Religion der ganzen Menschheit, eine Religion, die alles in sich aufnimmt, was in den Heiligen Schrift des alten Indiens, in Zand-Awesta, im Evangelium und im Koran geschrieben steht).

Maxim Gorky was the penname of **Aleksey Maximovich Peshkov** (1868–1936), a Russian writer. Born poor, and orphaned at a very early age, Gorky lived and traveled all over the Russian empire, sharing the lives of its lowest laborers. As a journalist he attacked the Tsarist regime, and he was arrested many times. His stories and sketches of the downtrodden in Russia made him famous, however, and he became a personal friend of Lenin. Gorky was a proponent of socialist realism, supported the Russian revolution, and became one of the literary figureheads of the early Soviet regime.

Next to this more general, vague and quasi-religious motivation (fitting at least one strain of Gorky's thought, aiming to recapture the power of religion for the purpose of a secular commonality of all people) there is, however, a more direct aim, especially in relation to a series of shorter paperbound editions aiming at the widest possible distribution among the masses: "The paperbound editions aim to acquaint the widest possible readership as extensively as possible with the living conditions of the peoples of Europe and America, to show them which ideas, wishes and habits they share, and in which they differ, and to prepare the Russian reader for the absorption of that knowledge of the world and its peoples that literature so richly and vividly mediates, and that greatly facilitates mutual understanding between people using different languages" (Gorky 1969: 39; Die broschierten Ausgaben haben das Ziel, breiteste Leserkreise so allseitig wie möglich mit den Lebensbedingungen der Völker Europas und Amerikas bekannt zu machen, ihnen die Gemeinsamkeit und die Unterschiede der Ideen, Wünsche und Gewohnheiten zu zeigen und den russischen Leser für die Aufnahme jener Kentnisse über Welt und Menschen vorzubereiten, die Belletristik so reichlich und lebendig vermittelt und die das gegenseitige Verständnis der verschiedensprachigen Völker sehr erleichtern). Obviously, the kind of world literature here referred to answers to Gorky's socialist-realist desiderata under the guise of a Goethian *Verständniss* (understanding) between Europe's, and later the world's, various peoples.

World literature beyond Europe

Gorky's name would later be given to a Moscow institute explicitly dedicated to the study and propagation of world literature along Soviet lines. It is under the auspices of the Gorky Institute of World Literature that the multivolume *Istorija vsemirnoj literatury v devjati tomach* (*History of World Literature in Nine Volumes*) started appearing from 1983 in Moscow. The project never reached its full nine volumes, as the Soviet Union imploded after the eighth volume had appeared, and the work was discontinued. Nevertheless, the ambition was to produce a history in which all literatures would be "at home." Møller quotes R.M. Samarin, one of the early leaders of the project, as explicitly contrasting the endeavor he and his colleagues are engaged in with customary Western comparative literature practice privileging Western literature. Instead, he proclaims, "The Soviet History of World Literature will tell the story of how in the course of the centuries there arose a house of the literature of mankind, unified and miraculously diversified, embodying the creative genius of all the peoples of the world" (Møller 1989: 21).

Especially in Scandinavia, where there is a long tradition of world histories of literature, some histories of world literature published over the past few decades have explicitly aimed at presenting a non-Eurocentric picture of the world's literatures. However, as Møller demonstrates by a simple tally of pages, neither the Danish twelve-volume *Verdens Litteraturhistorie* (*Literary History of the World*) of 1971–73, edited by Edvard Beyer, F.J. Billeskov Jansen, Hakon Stangerup, and P.H. Traustedt, nor the later joint Scandinavian, though in fact mostly Danish, seven-volume *Verdens Litteraturhistorie* (*Literary History of the World*) of 1985–94, edited by Hans Hertel, devote as much space to non-European literatures as does the Soviet History (Møller 1989: 27–28). The Soviet *History of World Literature*, then, remains a fairly early example of the rejection of Eurocentrism in literary history. Of course, after WWII the call for a wider and fairer representation of the world's literatures has sounded ever louder the closer we approach the present, also in "the West." One of the most vocal advocates of opening up the canon of world literature to include non-Western works was the French comparatist René Etiemble (1909–2002), who as of the 1960s in numerous works and essays ridiculed the narrowness of a Western canon of world literature and in often provocative terms called for the inclusion of Asian and African works, not just from the remote past but also contemporary ones. However, it would take some time before Etiemble's injunctions were taken up.

Eurocentrism would of course come fully under attack in postcolonialism. Inspired by the work of Edward Said (1978 and 1993), himself building upon the theories of, primarily, Michel Foucault, but later also Gilles Deleuze and Félix Guattari, postcolonialism, emerging in the 1980s and reaching its peak in the 1990s, endeavored to widen the geographical scope of world literature, while the advocates of multiculturalism, gaining ground around the same time as did postcolonialism, strove for a fairer representation of all kinds of minorities, also from, but of course not limited to, Western literatures. Concurrently, postmodernism sought to do away with all hierarchical distinctions altogether, and hence argued either the impossibility of a canon, including of world literature, or its individual and as it were coincidental nature.

Postmodernism, postcolonialism, and multiculturalism were primarily phenomena of a cultural nature that sought to recalibrate the canon of world literature each from its own perspective. Of course, this is not to claim that they were unrelated to political and social developments beyond the realm of literature – in fact, especially postcolonialism and multiculturalism definitely had a political agenda. Still, the primarily economics-driven advent of globalization in the 1990s led to a wholly new approach to world literature.

In *La République mondiale des lettres* (1999, *The World Republic of Letters* 2004) Pascale Casanova, extrapolating Bourdieu's theories on social and cultural "capital" to the world market of literature, saw France, and particularly Paris, as the crucible where, at least between the seventeenth and the middle of the twentieth century, world literature was "made" in an ongoing process of critical recognition, translation, reception, and canonization. Meanwhile, Franco Moretti, Italian but working in the United States, in "Conjectures on World Literature" (2000), "More Conjectures on World Literature" (2003) and *Graphs, Maps, Trees* (2005) picked up on earlier work of his in *Atlas of the European Novel 1800–1900* (1998), using a combination of metaphors borrowed from the sciences with the world systems approach pioneered since the 1970s by the economic historian Immanuel Wallerstein to study, both synchronically and diachronically, the origin and spread of literary forms, motifs, and styles throughout the world.

In the United States, the shock of 9/11 and the awareness this induced of how in the newly "global" world not just of the economy but also of politics, ethics, and religion, and of terrorism even, the US could no longer shield behind its "exceptionalism," gave rise to an increased awareness also of the need to better understand the world beyond the nation's borders and that nation's interconnectedness with the world. One way in which this need translated itself was in a sudden and sharp increase in interest in world literature as a conduit through which to get in touch with the world's cultures. A first requirement to make the world, or more of it than had hitherto been the case, accessible to the US, was a greater emphasis on translation from the world's many languages into (American) English, and on seeing American literature and culture in relation to this new world constellation, both synchronically and diachronically. These various needs, and the solutions proposed, were explored in a number of books published since 9/11, most of them building on earlier articles. Emily Apter argues the case for translation, primarily synchronically, in *The Translation Zone: A New Comparative Literature* (2006). In *What Is World Literature?* (2003) David Damrosch puts the case for translation as a necessary instrument for, and at the same time an agent in, what he takes world literature to be, viz. "all literary works that circulate beyond their culture of origin, either in translation or in their original language" and this at any given moment, that is to say both synchronically and diachronically (Damrosch 2003: 4). As Damrosch puts it: "A work only has an effective life as world literature whenever, and wherever, it is actively present within a literary system beyond that of its original culture" (Damrosch 2003: 4). In this definition there are clear echoes of the idea of the German writer and philosopher Walter Benjamin (1892–1940) that foreign translation constitutes a work's "afterlife" (Benjamin 2000). At the same time Damrosch also comes close again to the original Goethean idea of *Weltliteratur* as an active principle in the world, rather than a list or series of "great works" or as a sum of all literature in all the world.

Conclusion

- Though Goethe was not the first to use the term "world literature," his use of it has had the greatest impact.
- Whereas Goethe meant world literature to refer to the increased circulation of literary works among European writers and intellectuals in order to promote a better understanding of each other's cultures, after Goethe the term variously also came to stand for the totality of all the world's literature and for a selection of "the best" of the world's works of literature.
- Almost from the very beginning world literature had to enter into competition with the rising tide of national literature studies, and it was often recuperated by the latter to implicitly glorify some national literature or other.
- Though Goethe himself had a lively interest in non-European literatures, world literature for most of its history has meant the literatures of Europe, and even then often only that of some major European literatures.
- Since the very end of the twentieth century we notice a return to Goethe's original concept of world literature, now enlarged to the entire world.

2 Goethe's *Weltliteratur* and the humanist ideal

Overview

For most of its history – that is, the history of the term, the concept, and the practice – "world literature" has been an exclusively European, or Euro-American, concern. Only in the last decade or so has the discussion really broadened to voices from beyond Europe and the Americas. The instigator of the concept, if not of the term, Goethe himself, has been accused of Euro-centrism because of three passages that seem to specifically conflate world literature and European literature. Strich defends Goethe against these charges by arguing that the latter was speaking on behalf of all, and not just European, humanity. Still, the fact that Goethe in his views of humanity was strongly influenced by his adulation of ancient Greece and Rome as interpreted by the Renaissance humanists and their more recent eighteenth-century followers in the eyes of his detractors proves that his ideas on *Weltliteratur* were pre-determined by a European "classical" norm, and hence inevitably Euro-centric. None less than Edward Said, trailblazer of postcolonialism and severe critic of European exclusionism, though, rushed to Goethe's, and humanism's, defense. Said sees humanism, in its Renaissance form, as grounded in philological research, and hence in the critical reading of texts, and particularly those texts that underpin Europe's own foundations. Humanism for Said is therefore inherently self-questioning. Said sees the philological method embodied in exemplary form in the work of the German scholar Erich Auerbach. Emily Apter, though, will defend the case of another German philologist – i.e. Leo Spitzer – claiming that he, like Auerbach but even more pronouncedly, opened up the philological method to reach beyond Europe and its literature. A third German philologist, Ernst Robert Curtius, forms a useful contrast to Auerbach and Spitzer.

Humanität and humanism

In an address to the Congress of Natural Scientists in Berlin, in 1828, Goethe referred to "a European, in fact a universal, world literature." The second passage appeared in 1829 in *Kunst und Altertum*, Vol. 6, part 3, where Goethe revised what first he had called "World Literature" as "European, in other words, World Literature." The final passage dates from 12 August of the same year, when in a conversation of Goethe's with the German historical novelist Willibald Alexis (pseudonym of Georg Wilhelm Heinrich Haring, 1798 – 1871) "there appeared references to a common European or World Literature." Fritz Strich, one of the most perceptive and thorough commentators on Goethe and world literature, and from whose book on Goethe I copied the three instances quoted (Strich, 1949: 250–51; passages 12, 16 and 17 respectively), defends Goethe from any such charge of Eurocentrism. Writing in 1945, well before the invention of the very term "Eurocentrism," Strich in the first chapter of his *Goethe and World Literature* warns that "in present-day speech practically no distinction is made between world literature and European literature – and this is a serious error" (Strich, 1949: 16). For Goethe, according to Strich:

> [W]orld literature is, to start with, European literature. It is in process of realising itself in Europe. A European literature, that is a literature of exchange and intercourse between the literatures of Europe and between the peoples of Europe, is the first stage of a world literature which from these beginnings will spread in ever-widening circles to a system which in the end will embrace the world. World literature is a living, growing organism, which can develop from the germ of European literature, and in his *West–Eastern Divan*, which was to throw a bridge from East to West, Goethe himself began the task of incorporating in it the Asiatic world.
>
> (Strich, 1949: 16)

Notwithstanding Strich's spirited defense of Goethe, it has to be admitted that even if the latter may have ideally meant the term *Weltliteratur* to embrace the entire world, it is also true that Goethe's own ideas about what that world was like, and what the role of *Weltliteratur* in it would be, were colored by his own belonging to a particular time and place. For Strich, Goethe saw as the first, and highest, aim of world literature "to foster the / growth of a common humanity in its most perfect and universal form: to advance human civilisation" (Strich, 1949: 12–13). Or, in another formulation: "It is in the idea of universal humanity that one finds the true source of world literature" (Strich, 1949: 37). Inevitably, these ideals of "common humanity in its most perfect and universal form" and "universal humanity" reflected contemporary thinking on the subject – as, for instance, in the *Briefe zur Beförderung der Humanität* (1793–97; Letters on the promotion of humanity) of Johann Gottfried Herder (1744–1803), or the writings of Immanuel Kant (1724–1804), who defined it as "the idea of the union of civility and virtue in one's relations with other people" (Eisler, 1930; die Denkungsart der Vereinigung des Wohllebens mit der Tugend im Umgange,

Anthr. 1. T. § 88 (IV 218)). In 1808, Friedrich Immanuel Niethammer (1766–1848), in his *Der Streit des Philanthropinismus und des Humanismus in der Theorie des Erziehungs-Unterrichts unserer Zeit* (*The Battle between Philanthropism and Humanism in Contemporary Educational Theory*), coined the term "Humanismus" in German. Needless to say, these late eighteenth- and early nineteenth-century ways of conceiving "humanity" and "humanism" themselves drew from a long history, and particularly upon classical antiquity as mediated by Renaissance Humanism.

The Middle Ages, especially after the Carolingian restoration of something resembling the ancient Western Roman Empire, had largely inspired itself upon Roman antiquity and upon a relatively small selection of Latin classics. The fall of Constantinople to the Ottomans in 1453 caused a massive transfer of Greek knowledge in the form of manuscripts, but also of Byzantine scholars seeking refuge, especially to northern Italy, thus giving an enormous boost to the growing Renaissance movement there. The study of ancient Greek literature and philosophy renovated European learning and education and made the classical world into the example to be emulated. At the same time, the invention and spread of the printing press sped up the production and circulation of texts that until then had been available in very limited numbers, and often in the form of collections of quotations and extracts rather than as complete texts. This led to the rise of philology in the comparative study of Latin, Greek, Hebrew, and, not much later, oriental languages such as Sanskrit. Partially, these studies served the ends of religion, of the established Church, and of imperial powers such as Habsburg Spain, as in the magnificent polyglot bibles produced for the Spanish crown by the Antwerp printing house of Christoffel Plantin (1520–89). However, they also served the more secular ends of smoothing the way for the beginnings of critical and empirical scientific investigation, and for redirecting attention from God to His creation, and especially to man and manmade things, or "humanitas." Scholars and writers who followed the latter path generally referred to themselves as "humanists," with some of the most famous names being those of Desiderius Erasmus (1466–1536) and Thomas More (1478–1535).

By the middle of the eighteenth century, when Goethe was born, Enlightenment thinking had, at least in scientific and scholarly circles, further loosened the bonds between God and nature, including man. Deism enshrined God as a remote "first principle," without any direct or immediate effect upon the world in any of its outward guises. At the same time the Enlightenment also promoted concern for the individual and "common man." Together with a renewed interest in classical antiquity spurred by, for instance, the extensive writings on especially Greek art of the German art historian and archeologist Johann Joachim Winckelmann (1717–68), and also by the mid-century excavations at Herculaneum and Pompeï, this led to a renewed form of Humanism – in German often referred to as "Neuhumanismus." This *Neuhumanismus* fed immediately into both Romanticism and Neo-Classicism. As the Greeks were seen as the original fountainhead of

European culture and civilization, creating as it were ex nihilo the arts, philosophy, and the sciences, they were also seen as proof of the creative power of "primitive" man, and hence also of the "folk." For Herder this legitimized his search for the "roots" of a "nation" in a people's language as embodied in its folk poetry. Goethe was also interested in folk poetry, and he discussed various instances of it in his writings. He saw such poetry, and folk literature in general, as expressive of a common core of humanity dressed up in a specific language or a specific people's particularities. However, this is not what he called "world literature." Rather, he termed it "world poetry." It only became world literature if it partook in the intellectual exchange among the nations and peoples.

Of course, similar interests flourished around Europe – for instance, with the so-called Scottish Antiquaries and James McPherson's Ossian poems. It is Herder, though, and after him the Grimm and Schlegel brothers, who systematized all this into the theoretical foundations of Romanticism, and hence laid the foundations of the study and teaching of national literatures. At the same time, an emphasis upon a Greek and Latin curriculum in the most highly valued forms of education, particularly the *Gymnasium* in Germany and in most public schools in England, and a general adulation of the classical ideal of man underpinned the rise of neo-classicism which, instead of the spontaneity, originality, and novelty propagated by Romanticism, favored measure, balance, and imitation, particularly of the classics. It is the combination of the qualities valorized by neo-classicism that constituted "Humanität," if we are to follow Kant when he writes that, "one part of philology is constituted by the humanities, by which we understand knowledge of the classics, which promotes the union of knowledge and taste, files away a person's raw edges, and furthers that communicative ability and urbanity of which "humanität" consists" (Eisler, 1930; Einen Teil der Philologie machen die Humaniera aus, worunter man die Kenntnis der Alten versteht, welche die Vereinigung der Wissenschaft mit Geschmack befördert, die Rauhigkeit abschleift und die Kommunikabilität und Urbanität, worin Humanität besteht, befördert, *Log. Einl.* VI (IV 50)). The earlier quote from Kant, where he fills out his definition of humanism, clearly also refers to a classical ideal. Most Romantic writers, of course, enjoyed a "classical" education.

Goethe in Italy

With his *Werther* (1774) in particular, along with his other *Sturm und Drang* (Storm and Stress) works published during the 1770s such as *Prometheus* (1773) and *Götz von Berlichingen* (1773), Goethe helped pave the way for Romanticism throughout Europe. In some way or other these works are also anti-authoritarian, whether it is against prevailing morals and religion, as when Werther commits suicide for love, or when Prometheus defies the Gods, or Götz the emperor. After his move to Weimar at the invitation of the Duke of Saxe-Weimar, though, Goethe increasingly turned neo-classicist in art, although for much of his life he stayed non-conformist in morals and religion (see Boyle, passim). His reading of Winckelmann, and the latter's example, incited Goethe to undertake an extended stay in Italy in 1786–88. During the two years he spent traveling the length of the peninsula and Sicily he closely acquainted himself with classical architecture, both Roman and Greek. Goethe published his *Italienische Reise* (*Italian Journey*) only in 1816–17, yet it is clear that his Italian experience served as catalyst for his "conversion" from *Sturm und Drang* proponent to Neo-Classicist, and to figurehead of so-called Weimar Classicism. This is especially clear in how he writes about the legacy of classical architecture in the South of Europe, represented by Italy, when compared to the medieval Gothic products of Northern Europe, and particularly Germany, as in the following passage, dated 27 October 1786:

> I walked up to Spoleto and stood on the aqueduct, which also serves as a bridge from one hill to the other. The ten brickwork arches which span the valley have been quietly standing there through all the centuries, and the water still gushes in all quarters of Spoleto. This is the third work of antiquity which I have seen, and it embodies the same noble spirit. A sense of the civic good, which is the basis of their architecture, was second nature to the ancients. Hence the amphitheatre, the temple, the aqueduct. For the first time I understand why I always detested arbitrary constructions, the Winterkasten on the Weissenstein, for example, which is a pointless nothing, a monstrous piece of confectionery – and I have felt he same about a thousand other buildings. Such things are still-born, for anything that does not have a true *raison d'être* is lifeless and cannot be great or ever become so.
>
> (Goethe, 1970: 124–25)

Part of this legacy is its rediscovery, and imitation, in the Renaissance by artists/humanists such as Palladio. In Padua, Goethe buys a catalogue of the works of Palladio, and in Venice he goes in search of the buildings of the master. On 2 October 1786 he visits a monastery designed by Palladio. Although only part of the original design has been actually realized, Goethe still finds that:

> Jahrelang sollte man in Betrachtung so eines Werks zubringen. Mich dünkt, ich habe nichts Höheres, nichts Vollkommneres gesehen, und glaube, daß ich mich nicht irre. Denke man sich aber auch den trefflichen Künstler, mit dem innern Sinn fürs Große und Gefällige geboren, der erst mit unglaublicher Mühe sich an den Alten heranbildet, um sie alsdann durch sich wiederherzustellen.
>
> (Goethe 2007: 71–72)

Auden and Mayer translate this passage as: "I am convinced I am right when I say that I never saw anything more sublime, more perfect, in my life. One ought to spend years contemplating such a work" (Goethe 1970: 80). This much foreshortened version fails to catch the real import the view of this building has for Goethe, and particularly its autobiographical implications. A fuller translation would read:

> One ought to spend years contemplating such a work. I think I have never seen anything more elevated, more perfect, and I believe I am not mistaken in this. But also picture to yourself the accomplished artist, born with an innate sense of the great and the pleasing, who first with an incredible effort schools himself after the classics, and then proceeds to recreate them through his own art.
>
> (My translation)

For Goethe, Palladio's greatness results, first, from his study of and, second, his imitation/emulation of the classics – especially the Greeks. Not only does this process correspond to the classical rhetoric recipe of *translatio, imitatio, aemulatio* (translation, imitation, emulation), it also closely parallels Goethe's own ambitions with his Italian journey. In a passage dated the following day, 3 October 1786, Goethe generalizes upon his earlier remark: "Palladio was strongly imbued with the spirit of the Ancients, and felt acutely the petty narrow-mindedness of his times, like a great man who does not wish to conform to the world but to transform it in accordance with his own high ideals" (Goethe, 1970: 81). The same thing applies for Goethe and his likeminded contemporaries, for Michelangelo, Raphaël, and most Renaissance artists. Of course, Goethe saw all this in relation to his own position. The link he makes between Palla-dio's imitation of the Greeks and the pettiness of his times obviously anticipates Goethe's own later yearning for *Weltliteratur* as a remedy for the fragmenta-tion of his own times. The link with humanism in its classical and Renais-sance variations and that of Goethe and his times is made in remarks such as that dated 3 December 1786, when during his extended first stay in Rome, he exclaims "the entire history of the world is linked up with this city, and I reckon my second life, a very rebirth, from the day when I entered Rome" (Goethe, 1970: 148), where he actually uses the German equivalent, "*Wie-dergeburt*," for "Renaissance" for his own feelings when experiencing classical art first hand. Earlier, in an entry dated Foligno, 26 October 1786, Goethe had expressed the same idea in more general terms when, having gone to look at a small antique temple described by Palladio, he concludes with: "I cannot describe the sensations which this work aroused in me, but I know they are going to bear fruit for ever" (Goethe, 1970: 121). From passages such as these it is evident that Goethe looks upon his Italian journey, and the exposure to the classics it brings, as an essential element in his own *Bildung*. From passages such as that quoted earlier, on the occasion of his visit to Spoleto, it is equally clear that when he lauds these same classics for having always aimed with their buildings at "bürgerlichen Zwecken" – that is to say, humanly practical and not god-centered purposes – he is highlighting their "humanity."

Andrea Palladio (1508–80) was an Italian Renaissance architect active in and around Venice during the sixteenth century. Heavily influenced by Greek and Roman architecture, his buildings, and the precepts upon which he based them as laid down in his *The Four Books of Architecture (I Quattro Libri dell'Architettura,* 1570), richly illustrated with engravings, remained the models for both public and private buildings all across Europe for the next few centuries.

The rediscovery of the Roman and Greek antiquities in the eighteenth century, through the excavations at Pompeï, Herculaneaum, and Paestum, and through the writings of Winckelmann, especially the latter's *Gedanken über die Nachahmung der griechischen Werke in der Malerei und Bildhauerkunst* (1755, *Reflections on the Imitation of the Greeks in Painting and Sculpture*) and *Geschichte der Kunst des Altertums* (1764, *History of Ancient Art*), gave rise to Hellenism, an adulation and glorification of especially Greek antiquity in its more expansive phase and its prolonged afterglow under Rome. As Martin Bernal, in a critical-negative sense in *Black Athena* (1987), and others in a more positive sense have shown, eighteenth-century Hellenism also led to the Germanic and English-speaking peoples claiming for themselves the right of succession to the Greeks as the creators of a Europe *sui generis*. Small wonder then that the American nineteenth-century woman author and friend of Emerson's Margaret Fuller, in her "Translator's Preface" to *Conversations with Goethe in the Last Years of his Life, Translated from the German of Eckermann*, labels Goethe "of German writers the most English and most Greek" (Fuller 1839: xvii). It is certainly also not a coincidence that Goethe's fist clearly neo-classicist work is his verse drama *Iphigenie auf Tauris* (1786, Iphigenia in Tauris), a re-working of earlier prose versions (1779 and 1781), and emphasizing human understanding, or "Humanität," over the inhuman demands of the Gods.

From the very beginning, then, for Goethe *Weltliteratur* and Humanism were closely linked. *Weltliteratur* was to fulfill the role that his own trip to Italy, and his exposure there to the revitalizing influence of classical antiquity, had played for him: to elevate the humanist individual, and the elite company of like-minded humanists and men of letters which he had in mind when speaking of *Weltliteratur*, to a higher awareness of what humanity was about, a form of both personal and collective *Bildung* (education), so to speak. In essence, then, his thinking about *Weltliteratur* was rooted in his humanist universalism which itself drew upon the Renaissance and Enlightenment thinking of the universal as an extension of the classical. That such a reasoning is at the heart of an important, and perhaps the dominant, stream in European thinking ever since the Renaissance, going back precisely to the latter's renewed engagement and interpretation of Greek thought, has recently been argued by Rodolphe Gasché, in his *Europe, or the Infinite Task: A Study of a Philosophical Concept* (2009). Gasché situates the thought of, respectively, the Austrian–German philosophers Edmund Husserl, the German Martin Heidegger, the Czech Jan Patocka, and the French Jacques Derrida, and without specifically referencing Goethe, in a European tradition that sees it as Europe's destiny to divest itself of its Europeanism precisely by spreading the idea of universalism to the rest of the world, that is to say the universalism of humanism, with the latter implying an awareness of the value of the individual – which complies with the Renaissance and Enlightenment interpretation of the classical idea of the human, and which needed this genealogy to firmly legitimate itself. Just as Husserl, Heidegger, Patocka, and Derrida rephrase this idea for the twentieth century, beginning to end, so Goethe does the same with regard to his own times and, making use of the historical "window of opportunity" offered to him by the period between the end of the Napoleonic wars and the onset of the ardent nationalisms of the second third of the nineteenth century referred to earlier, reformulates this idea in terms of world literature. That is also why Goethe, in contrast to a number of later theoreticians of world literature, particularly in the nineteenth century but partially well into the twentieth century, is not interested in drawing up a canon of world masterpieces, but is interested in what world literature, as he conceives it to be, can contribute to the *Bildung* of humanity by fostering the circulation of what he sees as the right kind of ideas and forms. As his discussions of Serbian folk poetry and Chinese fiction demonstrate, what constitutes the right kind of ideas and forms for Goethe is determined by their proximity to what he sees as universal "humanity," and that in turn is determined by the yardstick of the classical ideal that he upholds for everything.

World literature and philology

In practice, the classical and universalist genealogy of the "human" underlying Goethe's conception of world literature for the longest time largely limited the latter's reach to European literature, or, by extension, Western man and Western literature. Both Moulton and Guérard, writing for an American public in 1911 and 1940 respectively, make no bones about this. In the first chapter I already mentioned that Moulton distinguished between what he called "universal" and "world" literature, with the former covering all literature written anywhere in the world, and the latter that part of the former that was significant from a certain perspective, which for him was that of the English-speaking peoples. Therefore, he starts from what he calls the literary pedigree of those English-speaking peoples and, predictably so at the time he is writing, finds it in the fusion of what the English writer, educator, and cultural critic Matthew Arnold in *Culture and Anarchy* (1869) had termed the Hebraic and the Hellenic elements brought about by the spread of Greek rule under Alexander the Great. From there on Moulton traces the developments leading to English literature through the various phases of European cultural history: classical antiquity, Christianity, the Middle Ages, and finally the age of nation states and national literatures. However, he sees the latter as integrally taking part in what he calls European civilization. World literature, for Moulton, then, is what he calls in the penultimate chapter of his book "The Autobiography of Civilization" – that is, European civilization.

Guérard, in his Foreword, invokes Humanism as the ideal horizon of world literature, and clarifies that by Humanism he means "not the grammarian's delight, nor the austere faith of an Irving Babbitt, but simply our belief in the essential unity of the human race" (Guérard 1940: xii). Nevertheless, in his first chapter he resorts to the same distinction between universal and world literature that we also saw Moulton as making, and for him too "world literature is limited to those works which are enjoyed in common, ideally by all mankind, practically by our own group of culture, the European or Western" (Guérard 1940: 15). Moulton and Guérard were both Europeans, but they worked within the US academic system, and their books served a primarily educational purpose within that system. I will return to this in Chapter 4.

For the more recent discussions on world literature, humanism, and Eurocentrism as they have played especially in the United States as of the turn of the millennium, and particularly so after the events of 9 September 2001, Moulton and Guérard do not play a major role. That role is reserved for a number of European, and more precisely German, philologists of the first half of the twentieth century. Undoubtedly, the fact that two of these, Leo Spitzer (1887–1960) and Erich Auerbach (1892–1957), spent the final years of their lives and careers in the United States, where they exerted a powerful influence on the study of comparative literature, is not without importance here. Neither is the fact that the writings of Auerbach particularly were taken up both early and late in his career by Edward Said (1935–2003), himself Professor of English and Comparative Literature at Columbia University in New York for most of his career, and a (many would say *the*) driving force in the emergence of postcolonial studies in the USA and the world with his ground-breaking *Orientalism* (1978). Said himself had American and Palestinian roots and was raised in the Middle East, mostly Egypt. All his life he remained a forceful spokesman for the rights of the Palestinians, and his interest in postcolonialism was undoubtedly fueled by his own family history of exile. This was a history which, originating from different yet related circumstances, was also shared by Erich Auerbach, a German Jew who, because of the Nazis' coming to power in Germany in 1933, had to seek refuge in Turkish exile in 1935, the year of Said's birth. In Istanbul, Auerbach became Professor of Romance Philology as successor to Leo Spitzer, another Jewish scholar, born in Austria but working in Germany, who had moved to Istanbul for the same reason already in 1933. In 1969 Said, together with his wife, Maire, translated Auerbach's 1952 essay "Philologie der Weltliteratur" as "Philology and World Literature." It is in this essay that Auerbach, in words that recall Goethe's most famous statement on world literature, proclaims that "our philological home is the earth: it can no longer be the nation" (Auerbach 1969: 17).

In 2003, the year of his death, Said provided an "Introduction" to a new edition of Auerbach's *Mimemis: Dargestellte Wirklichkeit in der abendländischen*

Edward Said (1935–2003) was born of US–Palestinian Protestant parents in Jerusalem, then still part of the British mandate territory of Palestine. With the war over the foundation of Israël in 1947–48 Said's family moved to Cairo, where he was educated in French and English secondary schools. At the age of sixteen he was sent to the USA, where he undertook his university studies, graduating with a PhD in English Literature from Harvard in 1964. For the rest of his life he taught at Columbia University. Said is considered the founding father of the literary-critical movement known as post-colonialism with his extremely influential book *Orientalism* (1978). He was also a gifted music critic, and a powerful voice for Palestinian independence, serving for many years on the Palestinian National Council.

Literatur, a work written during the latter's stay in Istanbul while WWII was raging, published in German in 1947, and in an English translation (by Willard Trask) as *Mimesis: the Representation of Reality in Western Literature* in the USA in 1953. That introduction was republished in 2004 as part of what in effect would be Said's last, and posthumous, book: *Humanism and Democratic Criticism*. *Humanism and Democratic Criticism* contains the revised versions of three lectures Said gave in January 2000 at Columbia University in an annual series of lectures on aspects of American culture. In his "Preface" to the book Said stipulates that in 2003 he expanded and revised his original lectures, adding a fourth lecture on Auerbach's "humanist masterpiece" *Mimesis* (Said 2003: xv) and that later on he added yet another lecture on "The Public Role of Writers and Intellectuals." All changes, he insists, were made because of the "terrible events of 9/11" (Said 2003: xvii). The destruction of the twin towers in New York led to a "changed political atmosphere" in the USA and beyond, he argues, which sets "America" against the world, and the "West" versus "Islam." Yet, and with what I can only see as a submerged reference to Goethe's ideas on world literature, he contends that "far more than they fight, cultures coexist and interact fruitfully with each other" (Said 2003: xvi). And then he continues: "It is to this idea of humanistic culture as coexistence and sharing that these pages are meant to contribute" (Said 2003: xvi). Said finds the example for such a humanistic culture in Auerbach and to a lesser extent in Spitzer. The example of the latter will be taken up fervently by Emily Apter in her *The Translation Zone: A New Comparative Literature* (2006).

Auerbach and Spitzer were both members of what Hans Ulrich Gumbrecht calls "the great Romance scholars" in *Vom Leben und Sterben der grossen Romanisten* (2002; *Life and Death of the Great Romance Scholars*), a book in which he takes a close look at the careers of five major German scholars who have marked the discipline of Romance philology in the first half of the twentieth century: Karl Vossler, Ernst Robert Curtius, Leo Spitzer, Erich Auerbach, and Karl Krauss. Next to Auerbach and Spitzer, Curtius (1886–1957) is also of interest for recent discussions on humanism and world literature. It should not surprise us that the relevant statements on these issues by Curtius, Spitzer and Auerbach date from during or after WWII. These scholars had experienced first hand the decline of "humanism" under Nazism, and they felt the need to re-affirm this ideal.

Even if WWII presented the stronger challenge to the humanist ideals of a European civilization, WWI had already shattered the (until then) rather complacent and essentially bourgeois idea of a great common European civilization regardless of national peculiarities. After all, the Europe of before 1914 still comprised a number of major multilingual and multiethnic empires, such as the Austro-Hungarian, the Russian, and the Ottoman empires. Germany, still divided into many smaller – and some larger – states in Goethe's time, had become a powerful empire under Prussia. Italy had been united by Garibaldi under the House of Savoy. Certainly, national pride ran high everywhere, but violent eruptions of nationalism had largely been "neutralized" ever since the numerous revolts of 1848, and the even earlier revolutions leading to the independence of Greece and Belgium. However, the Balkans seethed with ethnic resentment, and the outbreak of WWI (in 1914) following the assassination of the Austro-Hungarian crown prince in 1914 blew the lid off the system of military and political balances and alliances that, with the exception of the Franco–German war of 1870, had kept Europe largely peaceful since Napoleonic times.

Ernst Robert Curtius

Ernst Robert Curtius, in the preface to the English (American) translation of his *European Literature and the Latin Middle Ages*, starts out by saying that his own interest in literature, especially in Romance literatures, and even more specifically in first instance in French, and contemporary French at that, literature was spurred by WWI, and by his desire to make Germany's arch-enemy, France, more understandable to a German public.

In fact, Gumbrecht, in his discussion of Curtius, speculates that the latter switched from pursuing a career in law (he obtained a doctorate at law in 1913) to one in philology because of the horrors he encountered as a soldier in WWI. From the study of philology proper, Curtius soon also turned to the study of modern English literature, particularly T.S. Eliot and James Joyce.

Increasingly though, as he argues in the preface to *European Literature and the Latin Middle Ages*, he became interested in Virgil and Dante, and in "what the roads were that led from the one to the other?" The answer, he says, "could not but be found in the Latin continuity of the Middle Ages ... and that in turn was a portion of the European tradition, which has Homer at its beginning and at its end, as we see today, Goethe" (Curtius 1953: vii). It is this tradition that Curtius saw as uprooted by WWI and its aftermath, "especially in Germany," as he puts it, and that, in 1932, led him to write a polemical pamphlet called *Deutscher Geist in Gefahr* (*The German Spirit*

Endangered), in which he pleaded for a "new Humanism." With the rise to power of the Nazis in 1933 Curtius abandoned the study of contemporary literature and turned to the study of the Latin Middle Ages, resulting in the publication, in German, in 1948, of the book he is now chiefly remembered for. This book, he stresses, "is not the product of purely scholarly interests ... it grew out of a concern for the preservation of Western culture" (Curtius 1953: viii) and "it grew out of vital urges and under the pressure of a concrete historical situation" (Curtius 1953: x). "In order to convince," he says, "I had to use the scientific technique which is the foundation of all historical investigation: philology"; yet he also hopes that it is clear that "philology is not an end in itself ... what we are dealing with is literature – that is, the great intellectual and spiritual tradition of Western culture as given form in language" (Curtius 1953: x).

Several items deserve commenting on here. Said mentions Curtius only in passing in *Humanism and Democratic Criticism*, in the chapter on Auerbach. It is clear though that he writes from premises strikingly similar to those of Curtius: the pressure of a concrete historical situation, the concern with Humanism to counter the rising tide of barbarism, and the turn to philology. Whereas Curtius wants his Humanism to bolster a tradition limited to the West, and specifically to Europe, and perhaps even Western Europe, Said aims for his Humanism to open out to the world. The continuity Curtius seeks is that of a particular idea of Western culture. The continuity Said strives for is that of philology as a scientific-investigative method. In doing so, Said returns to the original use and impact of philology as applied by the earliest, Renaissance, humanists – that is, as a critical method with which to probe all received ideas and all false continuities. From this perspective, and without Said ever mentioning as much, we might see the Renaissance not as continuous with the Latin Middle Ages but rather as breaking with them precisely because it questions all medieval doxa. The details of why Said found this use of philology with Auerbach rather than with Curtius we will come to in a minute – suffice to note for now that Gumbrecht draws a comparable parallel when it comes to Curtius' and Auerbach's attitudes toward the Western tradition as expressed in their respective masterpieces, *European Literature and the Latin Middle Ages* and *Mimesis*. When referring to Curtius' rationale, as given in the preface and as discussed above, for writing his *European Literature and the Latin Middle Age*, Gumbrecht asks:

> As if in those days it would not have been possible to do a little better. I mean an analysis or approach that would have been more apt to recognize in National Socialism also the proof for the falling apart of the European cultural tradition, rather than preaching its untrammeled conservation. The latter was precisely the reaction of the emigrant Erich Auerbach, who until his very death never again succeeded in regaining faith in political expectations founded on cultural traditions.

(Ob damals nicht auch Besseres am Horizont des Möglichen stand. Ich meine ein Denken, welches geeignet gewesen ware, im Nationalsozialismus auch die Evidenz für das Scheitern der europäischen Kulturtradition zu erleben, statt deren unversehrte Bewahrung zu predigen. Das genau war die Reaktion des Emigranten Erich Auerbach, dem es bis zu seinem Tod nicht mehr gelang, die auf kulturelle Tradition gesetzten politische Hoffnungen zu erneuern ...)

(Gumbrecht 2002: 67–68)

Earlier I suggested that Said, in the very first paragraphs of his Preface to *Humanism and Democratic Criticism*, makes an oblique appeal to Goethe's ideas on world literature to plead the coexistence and fruitful interaction of cultures, and particularly to gainsay the supposed opposition between the West and, specifically, Islam, and beyond this "the rest." Implicitly, along with other recent critics who do so explicitly, he sees Goethe as being at the beginning of an opening up of European culture and literature toward the world. Curtius, as we saw earlier, sees Goethe as the endpoint of a homogeneous European tradition that Curtius himself seeks to restore. In "Fundamental Features of Goethe's World," published in 1949 and collected in *Essays on European Literature* (1973, 1950 in German as *Kritische Essays zur europäischen Literatur*), Curtius pictures Goethe as an advocate of "aristocratic individualism" who sought "connection only with the 'most excellent'" (Curtius, 1973: 76), an elitist not in the political sense of the term, but rather in that of a select band of like-minded spirits past and present. Goethe, for Curtius, is "the final self-concentration of the western mind in a great individual" (Curtius, 1973: 90). Therefore, he is:

something more and something other than a German poet ... he is solidary with the spiritual heritage of Europe. He stands in the line of Homer, Sophocles, Dante, Plato, Aristotle, Virgil, Dante, and Shakespeare. The consciousness of his place in this series is very much alive in him. His piety towards the "fathers," his alliance with the "dignified men" of old and with the chorus of spirits of the past, his conviction that there is a realm of the "Masters," with whom he feels he belongs – this most characteristic and remarkable trait of his form of mind acquires its deepest sense only now. This consciousness of solidarity through the millennia Shakespeare could not have had, Dante only within the Latin tradition. To Goethe it was given as a legitimation and corroboration of his mission. It is a sign, so to speak, from "the alphabet of the universal spirit."

(Curtius, 1973: 90–91)

Curtius concludes his essay with reminding us that Goethe on occasion described himself as an "epigone poet," and that in a letter to Creuzer in 1817 he wrote that epigone poets such as him "must revere the legacy of our ancestors" and "bow before these men whom the Holy Spirit has inspired and dare not ask, whence or whither." That attitude, Curtius says, "can today be the one that a 'small number' adopts towards Goethe" (Curtius, 1973: 91). Obviously, he counts himself among this "small number." But I think his epigonism went further than mere reverence; he wanted to restore the tradition of the Master and re-establish the continuity of European culture.

Erich Auerbach

It is against the Goethe drawn by Curtius that Auerbach turns in chapter 17 of *Mimesis*, "Miller the Musician." *Mimesis* was written under the pressure of the same war as Curtius' *European Literature and the Latin Middle Ages*, not in Bonn, but in Istanbul. For Auerbach too it is philology, or what he calls the "method of textual interpretation," (Auerbach, 1953: 556) that underpins his findings. Other than Curtius, though, Auerbach does not chronicle the continuity of an unchangeable Western humanist tradition but rather the relentless "humanization" of that tradition from the ancients, both Greek and Latin, as well as Judaic, through a progressive intermingling of styles high and low, to French realism in the nineteenth century, when there is no longer a distinction of styles and the only thing left to form the subject of literature is "man." This is Humanism in its most bare and simple form – not heroes, not gods, but also not buffoons, the ones to be gloried or glorified, the others to be mocked and humbled, take center stage, but "man" pure and simple, and even "common" man at that. Goethe, Auerbach argues, could have played a major role in this development, and through him Germany. However, Goethe failed to fulfill the promise of his early work in this regard. And it wasn't just Goethe who failed in this respect. Friedrich Schiller, with an analysis of a passage from whose *Luise Millerin* (1782–83) the chapter in question starts, failed to make good on the promise of nascent realism which this early work shows. The reason, Auerbach argues, is to be found in the political division of Germany at the end of the eighteenth century. The numerous petty potentates autocratically ruling often-tiny territories did everything in their power to stem the rising tide of social and political revolution and maintain what was in effect a petty-bourgeois status quo. The youthful Goethe, as we have argued earlier, in his *Sturm und Drang* period, like Schiller in *Luise Millerin*, seemed poised to storm these bastions of privilege and immutability. However, after his conversion to neo-Classicism and his move to Weimar it is precisely those qualities that Curtius most admires in Goethe: his aristocratic individualism, his elitism, his loyalty to tradition, that make him shy away from social and political changes tending toward the inclusion of larger parts of the population, rising social classes, and in short what we would call democracy. The inclusion and depiction of the common man, then, which the French and the English novel increasingly successfully achieved during the nineteenth century, did not happen until much later in German literature. With Goethe's immense influence on nineteenth-century

German literature, next to Germany's political situation, acting as a brake, that literature never fully acceded to realism until, Auerbach argues, Thomas Mann's *Buddenbrooks* in 1901.

Edward Said

It is clear that Said recognizes in what he calls Auerbach's "humanist masterpiece" (Said 2003: xv) much of what he advocated himself over the course of his own career as a critic. Most of the relevant points are highlighted in the chapters, or lectures, preceding that on *Mimesis* in *Humanism and Democratic Criticism*. Most of them come down to how humanism and philology work hand in hand to constitute not only a continuous regime of investigation and critique, but also of self-critique. Said starts from the premise that "the core of humanism is the secular notion that the historical world is made by men and women, and not by God, and that it can be understood rationally according to the principle formulated by Vico in *New Science*, that we can really know only what we make or, to put it differently, we can know things according to the way they were made" (Said 2003: 11). This implies what the American scholar Djelal Kadir, taking his cue from Said's plea for a "worldly" criticism in *The World, The Text, and the Critic* (1983), has called the "worlding" (Kadir 2004) of both the work and the critic in the sense of a vivid awareness of their historicity, and particularly of the critic's self-awareness of her own relationship to her object of study and her discipline. This sensitivity Said recognizes in how Auerbach, starting from a close textual analysis, and along philological lines, relates each of the works he discusses to its particular historical setting not primarily by its content but by its use of language and structure. He also recognizes it in how Auerbach, at the end of *Mimesis*, stresses that each form of understanding is also a form of self-understanding at a particular time and in a particular place. This is clear in Auerbach's discussion of Goethe mentioned earlier when Goethe's reluctance to further the introduction of realism in German literature, and his conservatism in politics, or at least his refusal to actively uphold the causes of democracy and political unification in Germany in the post-Napoleonic era, are seen as possible causes for, or in any case as not having contributed to preventing, the unhappy fate that ultimately befell Germany, and Europe, at the time of Auerbach's writing of *Mimesis*.

  In the conclusion to *Mimesis* Auerbach defends why he does not offer any totalizing view of the Western tradition (and one immediately thinks of Curtius's *European Literature and the Latin Middle Ages*) but rather works from almost random passages, and from works that Auerbach himself claimed were chosen equally at random, on the basis of his own ready knowledge and from what he had to hand in Istanbul during the war. Instead of "one order and interpretation," Auerbach says, he offers "many," so that what emerges is a "synthesized cosmic view or at least a challenge to the reader's will to interpretive synthesis" (Auerbach 1953: 549, also quoted in Said 2003: 117). This resembles nothing so much as that contrapuntal approach that Said himself had unfolded in *Culture and Imperialism* (1993), and to which he returns in *Humanism and Democratic Criticism* when he notes that the term "canon" not only refers to a "law" but also to a musical piece in which various voices pursue and join each other (Said 2003: 25). Such contrapuntal reading then allows precisely for that permanent critique and self-critique that for Said are at the heart of Humanism: "that it is possible to be critical of humanism in the name of humanism and that, schooled in its abuses by the experience of Eurocentrism and empire, one could fashion a different kind of humanism that was cosmopolitan and text-and-language-bound in ways that absorbed the great lessons of the past from, say, Erich Auerbach and Leo Spitzer and more recently Richard Poirier, and still remain attuned to the emergent voices and currents of the present, many of them exilic, extraterritorial, and unhoused, as well as uniquely American" (Said 2003: 10–11).

To apply these lessons, for Said, is also to world oneself as a humanist critic: "It means situating critique at the very heart of humanism, critique as a form of democratic freedom and as a continuous practice of questioning and of accumulating knowledge that is open to, rather than in denial of, the constituent historical realities of the post-Cold War world, its early colonial formation, and the frighteningly global reach of the last remaining super-power of today" (Said 2003: 47). Especially in America, he argues, where so many people from so many traditions always have come and continue to mingle, such a "worldly" disposition is not only necessary, it is already inherent to the very make-up of the country: "American humanism, by virtue of what is available to it in the normal course of its own context and histor-ical reality, is already in a state of civic coexistence, and, to the prevailing worldview disseminated by U.S. officialdom – especially in its dealings with the world outside America – humanism provides little short of stubborn, and secular, intellectual resistance" (Said 2003: 49). Resistance, of course, is the term Said used earlier in *Culture and Imperialism* to refer to anti- and what we would now call postcolonial literature. That literature, in turn, can be seen as accomplishing what Auerbach says – in a passage at the very end of *Mimesis* that to me seems clearly not only to echo Goethe's ideas on world literature but also to extend them from Europe to the entire world – in rela-tion to Virginia Woolf's *To the Lighthouse*. In the final chapter of his book Auerbach discusses how Woolf's novel, like so many other Modernist works, is anchored in what he calls "the random moment." "The more [this] is exploited," Auerbach argues, "the more the elementary things which our lives have in common come to light," or, in other words, the greater degree of reality is achieved.

In this unprejudiced and exploratory type of representation we cannot but see to what an extent – below the surface conflicts – the differences between men's ways of life and forms of thought have already lessened.

[...] There are no longer even exotic peoples. A century ago (in Mérimée for example), Corsicans and Spaniards were still exotic; today the term would be quite unsuitable for Pearl Buck's Chinese peasants. Beneath the conflicts, and also through them, an economic and cultural leveling process is taking place. It is still a long way to a common life of mankind on earth, but the goal begins to be visible.

(Auerbach, 1953: 552)

In our age of globalization, but also of a return to ethics in literary studies, the passage of Auerbach's just cited begins to sound very much like an anticipated ethics of world literature, one moreover that certainly Said could unreservedly subscribe to. Small wonder then that precisely in his chapter on Auerbach, Said revises the former's negative judgment on Goethe, calling the latter a progenitor of the former and particularly of the "extraordinary attention to the minute, local detail of other cultures and languages" that the tradition of hermeneutical philology as embodied by Auerbach practices (Said 2003: 95). In a passage that may well reverberate with his Prefatorial remarks about the "much exacerbated conflict between what have been called 'the West' and 'Islam'," Said reminds us that Goethe "in the decade after 1810 became fascinated with Islam generally and Persian poetry in particular," and that it was during this period that he composed his *West-Oestlicher Diwan*. "During the 1820s," Said continues, "those earlier thoughts carried him toward a conviction that national literatures had been superseded by what he called *Weltliteratur*, or world literature, a universalist conception of all the literatures of the world seen together as forming a majestic symphonic whole" (Said 2003: 95). This sentence reminds us that Said was not only an insightful literary critic and theoretician, but also an accomplished musician. Robert Young comments in this regard that, "Said's writings on music were the one arena where he necessarily moved away from his chosen model of German philology, particularly the tradition of Auerbach" (Young 2010: 365). "The irony of Said's deep sense of affiliation to this tradition," Young adds, "was that its other branch, Oriental philology, was the very one that he attacked in *Orientalism* ... this constitutes the central contrapuntal paradox of Said himself, that he at once affirmed and placed himself in a tradition whose work also included that which he most vigorously denied" (Young 2010: 365). Looking back at the end of his life on his most influential book, *Orientalism*, Said called what he had tried to do in that book "humanistic critique" (Said 2003). He explicitated that by what he called "humanism" he meant "first of all attempting to dissolve Blake's mind-forg'd manacles so as to be able to use one's mind historically and rationally for the purposes of reflective understanding ... moreover humanism is sustained by a sense of community with other interpreters and other societies and periods: strictly speaking therefore, there is no such thing as an isolated humanist" (Said 2003). Finally, let us also recall that Said, together with Daniel Bairenboim, was the founder, in 1999, of the West–Eastern Divan Orchestra, bringing together young musicians from around the Near- or Middle-East, and most particularly including both Israelis and Palestinians.

Leo Spitzer

Like Said's *Humanism and Democratic Criticism*, Emily Apter's *The Translation Zone: A New Comparative Literature* "was shaped by the traumatic experience of September 11, 2001" (Apter 2006: vii). Apter is more concerned with the issues of translation and comparative literature, and therefore I will return to her book in more detail in following chapters. Here, though, I will briefly discuss the first part of her book, entitled "Translating Humanism," which deals with how Humanism has been adapted, or "translated," in the work of Leo Spitzer, the third "grosser Romanist" (great Romance scholar) in Gumbrecht's term, specifically in relation to Auerbach and Said's reading of Auerbach. Discussing "Saidian Humanism" in the chapter of the same title, Emily Apter voices her perplexity when reading Said's 2003 introduction to Auerbach's *Mimesis* at "what seemed to be a noticeable *lack* of attention to Auerbach's Eurocentrism" (Apter 2006: 69). Later on she will say that on a second reading she realized that, "Said was taking up the challenge of using Auerbachian humanism to fashion new humanisms, not merely because of a sober conviction that great books, on the grounds of their intrinsic merit, should continue to have traction in a global, increasingly mediatized culture industry, but more because of his belief that humanism provides futural parameters for defining secular criticism in a world increasingly governed by a sense of identitarian ethnic destiny and competing sacred tongues" (Apter 2006: 72). With particular reference to world literature and humanism, however, she contends that Said would have done better to use Spitzer as his *Ansatzpunkt* (Auerbach's own term for what provides the philological critic with an "entry" into the text) than Auerbach. Indeed, she claims that what she calls Said's "Welt-humanism" in *Humanism and Democratic Criticism* "is indebted not so much to Auerbach as to Spitzer," and she cites Said commenting Spitzer's statement in his famous 1948 essay "Linguistics and Literary History" that "the Humanist believes in the power of the human mind of investigating the human mind" with "Spitzer does not say the European mind, or only the Western canon ... He talks about the human mind *tout court*" (Apter 2006: 70; Said 2003: 26). Beyond this statement, though, Apter also sees other grounds for foregrounding Spitzer rather than Auerbach as prefiguring Said's ideas on a humanism that transcends the European.

Apter rehearses how Said conducts a running debate with Auerbach from the very beginning of his career, with the translation (together with his wife Maire) of Auerbach's "Philology and World Literature" in 1969, over his use of him in *Orientalism* and *The World, The Text, and the Critic*, down to *Humanism and Democratic Criticism*. As I have done earlier, she also stresses the parallels between Said and Auerbach, and particularly how Said himself repeatedly returns to Auerbach's condition of exile in Istanbul from 1935 to

1947. In contrast, Spitzer spent only three years in Istanbul, between when he fled Cologne, where he was succeeded by Curtius, in 1933, and his further move to the United Sates in 1936. Yet, Apter shows, on the basis of interviews with former students of Spitzer's and Auerbach's at Istanbul, it was Spitzer that next to the dozen languages or so he already knew when he arrived in Istanbul quickly added Turkish to this array while Auerbach apparently never learned the language. It was also in Spitzer's seminars that languages other than European ones featured. In fact, she argues, "the seminar also acted as a laboratory for working through what a philological curriculum in literary studies should look like when applied to non-European languages and literatures" (Apter 2006: 55). For this reason, Apter credits Spitzer with "inventing" comparative literature in its modern guise during his stay in Istanbul. "In retrospect," she concludes, "Spitzer's invention of comparative literature in Istanbul transformed philology into something recognizable today as the psychic life of transnational humanism" (Apter 2006: 64).

Finally, what of the question about Humanism's alleged or necessary Eurocentrism? As we have seen, it all depends upon what one means with "Humanism." If one means by that term a certain idea of a European tradition rooted in the classics and passed on from especially the Renaissance, but more likely from the eighteenth century to the present, especially in established forms of education, in the guise of a canon of great works, yes, it is Eurocentric and universalist in the worst sense – i.e. as projecting an ideal of European man as normative for the world at large. If, however, one means by it the marriage between philology as a critical method and a concern for the human, Humanism becomes universalizing in Said's sense of critique and self-critique. The Humanism of the Renaissance rests upon the re-discovery of classical civilization as the realm of the human instead of the divine, as was the case in medieval times. This is symbolized by the rediscovery of the human body as the legitimate and proper subject for art, as Kenneth Clark has convincingly shown in his celebrated study *The Nude* (1953), and by the philological study of texts not as divine revelation but as man-made. However, the adulation of the classics this initially implied also made them into a measure for conservatives to return to again and again, thus making Humanism for this group a permanent state in the past from which the present could only be a falling off. This adulation was for students of literature, and particularly world literature, still reinforced by Goethe's own continuous return to the classics, particularly the Greeks. The emergence of Humanism thus became for these conservatives the moment of fusion of classic/modern into a moment of stability, with Dante as the fulcrum of this meeting. This then also became the measure for Curtius who wanted to see continuity in European culture and literature, and hence of "eternal" Greek and Goethean values. His position, mutatis mutandis, was shared by other conservatives such as T.S Eliot, a correspondent of Curtius'. The other camp stressed the evolving aspect of "humanity" in Humanism. This is what Said sees Auerbach doing, and what he himself put into practice. This necessarily also implies a return to philology in the original spirit of Humanism: as a critical instrument to analyze man-made texts and worlds; Humanism not as the stabilization of Europe's past greatness but as Europe de-Europeanizing itself via self-critique; and in terms of world literature a Europe, to use Dipesh Chakrabarty's apt term, "provincializing" itself by universalizing its critical method.

Conclusion

- Because of Goethe's humanistic infatuation with ancient Greek and Roman culture, a world literature taking its cue from him, and especially from his insistence on the validity of the Classical as normative for universal humanity, has often been deemed inevitably Eurocentric.
- Goethe's Humanism was confirmed and deepened by an extended trip to Italy he undertook while still a young man, during which he avidly went in search of Ancient monuments.
- Humanism, however, is more than Ancient monuments; the rise of Humanism in the Renaissance also marks the rise of philology as investigative method to draw out the meaning of all kind of texts.
- The postcolonial critic and theoretician Edward Said insists precisely on the value of humanistic philology as an instrument also for self-critically investigating the foundations of Humanism itself, and of that European civilization It undergirds.
- Edward Said and Emily Apter draw on the examples of the German philologists Erich Auerbach and Leo Spitzer to argue that a world literature modeled upon Goethe's example and using humanistic philology as its instrument is not necessarily Eurocentric but is rather open to the world.

3 World literature and comparative literature

Overview

The study and teaching of world literature have traditionally been seen as belonging to the province of the discipline of comparative literature. The Hungarian comparatist Arpád Berczik even calls comparative literature the "applied science of world literature" (Berczik 1972: 159; die angewandte Wissenschaft des Weltliteratur). In fact, the actual teaching of something called "world literature" has mainly been confined to the United States, and we will return to it in Chapter 4. As to the actual study of world literature, if in most writings on comparative literature there is the obligatory, but often also perfunctory, nod to the term, just as often the possibility of actually "doing" world literature has been dismissed out of hand. This is especially true of the so-called "French" school of comparative literature, which from the mid-nineteenth to the mid-twentieth century practically commanded the field, and which heavily insisted on the "comparative" element in the discipline's practice. Moreover, in Europe or in the European tradition comparative literature in practice was the domain of a cultured elite naturally schooled in a variety of languages, often because of the specific political or other conditions they found themselves in. It is certainly no coincidence that many of the nineteenth-century forerunners of comparative literature, and of its earlier practitioners in the twentieth century, were Swiss or worked in that country. Additionally, the cultured elite in Europe during the nineteenth and early twentieth century as a matter of course understood, spoke and wrote French, and was educated with Latin and Greek as self-evident parts of the high school curriculum, with Latin often being a prerequisite for admission to university. Finally, scholars working in languages and literatures until WWII were almost invariably philologists, who as a matter of course studied European rather than single national literatures. In the United States circumstances were completely different, and when after WWII the lead in comparative literature passed from Europe to the USA this also had immediate consequences for the study of world literature. The scope of the literatures that could be studied broadened significantly, no immediate filiation between various works studied need be demonstrated, and more general topics could be broached. For various reasons, though, from the 1970s through the 1980s comparative literature, and world literature with it, were eclipsed by a rapid succession of theoretical movements that flourished in national literature, and particularly English departments, rather than comparative literature departments, at least in the United States. The recent renewed interest in world literature, though, has returned comparative literature to the center of American academe again. However, this is a much-changed comparative literature from its earlier days. Interestingly, though, the recent upswing of interest in world literature as fueled by comparative literature goes hand in hand with a re-discovery, or in any case a re-reading and re-interpretation, of a number of pioneers in the field of comparative literature that are being re-appropriated for present-day concerns. In what follows I sketch the intricate, though until recently not necessarily very intimate, relationship between comparative literature, especially in its "French" and "American" guises, and world literature.

Intimations of comparative literature

The birth of comparative literature coincides with Goethe's observations on *Weltliteratur*. It also coincided, as we have seen in the first chapter, with the emergence of a clear consciousness of national literatures and with the writing of their histories. It is not that histories of literature spanning a wider reach than a single country or one single language had not been written before. Guillén (1993: 27) mentions several eighteenth-century such histories which, like the first national histories he also mentions, and which I cited in the first chapter, were all written in Italy: *Della storia e della ragione d'ogni poesia* (1739; *On the History and Reason of All Poetry*) by Francesco Saverio Quadrio (1695–1756), the *Discorso sulle vicende d'ogni letteratura* (1760; *Discourse on What Happened in All Literature*) of Carlo Denina (1731–1813), and especially the seven-volume *Dell'origine, dei progressi e dello stato attuale d'ogni letteratura* (1782–99; *On the Origin, Development and Contemporary Situation of All Literature*) by Juan Andrés (1740–1817), a Spanish Jesuit who worked most of his life in Italy. The eminent Swiss-American comparatist François Jost, in his *Introduction to Comparative Literature* (1974), adds an even earlier Italian example to Guillén's: *Storia della vulgar poesia* (1698; *A History of Poetry in the Vernacular*) by Giovanni Mario Crescimbeni (1663–1728). Jost also mentions a number of examples from England and France. John Dryden (1631–1700), Jost points out, wrote a number of essays on various genres, as well as on comparisons between poetry and painting, in which he addressed more than one literature. In 1785, John Andrews (1736–1809) published a *Comparative View of the French and English Nations in Their Manners, Politics, and Literature.* In 1727 Voltaire (1694–1778) had already written an *Essai sur la poésie épique (Essay on Epic Poetry)* and in 1762 Jean-Baptiste-René Robinet (1735–1820) offered his *Considérations sur l'état présent de la littérature en Europe (Considerations on the Present State of Literature in Europe).* Most of these, however, do not correspond to what as of the nineteenth century we would normally consider "histories," that is to say they do not offer a continuous and reasoned narrative relating to people, works, and events.

The transnational study of literature as practiced by comparative literature, Guillén (1993: 27) argues, could only come into being "when two events occur: one, when a large number of modern literatures – literatures that recognize themselves as such – come into existence; and two: when a unitary or absolute poetics ceases to be an accepted model." Indeed, the older transnational literary histories that Guillén mentions start from the assumption of an accepted neoclassical model of a unitary or absolute poetics stretching back from their own times to the Greek and Roman classics, and from a sense of community over such poetics shared in the Republic of Letters mentioned in the first chapter. We might speak here, with the American comparatist Alexander Beecroft (2008: 95), who takes his cue from an article by the Indologist Sheldon Pollock (1996) on the Sanskrit "Cosmopolis," of a cosmopolitan system in which, at variance with what Beecroft calls a "panchoric system," in which "a literary language allows literature to circulate among a set of political entities sharing a native language (but likely not a political regime)," "a cosmopolitan literary language creates a cross-cultural system, in which speakers of many languages share a common literary idiom ... this language may be the cultural expression of a world-empire, or a nostalgic reminiscence of a former empire, or it may constitute a cultural world-empire without political ramifications." Writers, readers, and all men (and women) of letters before the end of the eighteenth century shared in such a cosmopolitan system on the basis of first Latin, later complemented by French, as commonly shared languages, as well as on the basis of a common understanding of what "letters" stood for. One of the ironies of history is that the German philosopher Immanuel Kant (1724–1804), who in his *Perpetual Peace: A Philosophical Sketch* (1795) defended cosmopolitanism and is still valued as one of the most important philosophers on the issue, with his *Critique of Judgment*, as briefly argued in the first chapter, also paved the way for the conception of "literature" as the new name for what until then had been known as "belles-lettres" within the general category of "letters" as an autonomous domain ruled by taste (judgment) and not by "truth," like science, and hence also for the separation of the unitary realm of "letters," as shared around Europe, into distinct national "literatures."

Once the new national literatures came into their own, they also called forth, in an almost Hegelian dialectic, a new internationalism in the form of both Goethe's *Weltliteratur* and the early stirrings of comparative literature. Guillén cites Joseph Texte (1865–1900), one of the earliest official comparative literature scholars, when looking back in 1898 at the birth of the discipline, as concluding that Romantic criticism had been "in one sense, an agent of *concentration*, and in another, an agent of *expansion*" (Guillén 1993: 28). It had been an agent of concentration in furthering national literatures; an agent of expansion by furthering the transnational dimension of literature. We can already see the combination of this twofold process in *De la littérature considérée dans ses rapports avec les institutions sociales* (1799; *On Literature Considered in Relation to Social Insitutions*) and *De l'Allemagne* (1810; *On Germany*) by the Swiss Madame (Anne Louise Germaine) de Staël (1776–1817), and *Littérature du midi de l'Europe* (1813; *Literature from the South of Europe*) by the equally Swiss Jean-Charles Léonard Simonde de Sismondi (1773–1842). These works, as I have also argued with regard to Goethe on *Weltliteratur,* simultaneously look back at the Republic of Letters and forward to the new Romantic era of national literatures.

Mme de Staël was the center of a cosmopolitan circle at her salon in Paris and her estate in Coppet, Switzerland, with as regular members a.o. Sismondi, the Swiss-French Benjamin Constant (1767–1830), and the German writer and philologist August Wilhelm (von) Schlegel (1767–1845). The celebrated British-Scots poet Byron (1788–1824) was also, during certain periods, a frequent visitor. Together, along with like-minded writers and thinkers across Europe, they can be considered as part of what the French critic Paul van Tieghem (1871–1959) in one of the earliest systematic treatments of comparative literature as a discipline calls the fourth cosmopolitan age in European letters: "After the Christian and Chilvalresque cosmopolitanism of the middle ages, after the humanist cosmopolitanism of the Renaissance, after the classicist and philosophical cosmopolitanism of the Age of Enlightenment, there appears a Romantic and historical cosmopolitanism that, more than its predecessors, takes into account national differences, deigns to accept them and does its best to understand them" (Van Tieghem 1931: 27–28; Apres le cosmopolitisme chrétien et chevaleresque du moyen âge, apres le cosmopolitisme humaniste de la renaissance, apres le cosmopolitisme classique et philosophique de l'âge des lumières, paraît un cosmopolitisme romantique et historique qui tient compte, beaucoup plus que ses prédécesseurs, des différences nationales, qui se plaît à les accepter et s'efforce de les comprendre). It is in this context that Van Tieghem refers to Goethe and *Weltliteratur:* "That is why Goethe, in 1827, spoke to Eckermann about world literature (*Weltliteratur*) as the totality of all singular literatures, a totality that one should take into account so as not to fall victim to national prejudices" (Van Tieghem 1931: 27; C'est ainsi que Goethe, en 1827, parlait à Eckermann de la "littérature universelle" [*Weltliteratur*] comme de l'ensemble des littératures particulières, ensemble qu'il faut savoir considérer pour ne pas être dupe de préjugés nationaux).

The works of De Staël and Sismondi are often cited as forerunners to comparative literature proper, as is the *Geschichte der Poesie und Beredsamkeit seit dem Ende des 13. Jahrhunderts* (1801–19; a twelve-volume *History of Poetry and Eloquence since the End of the Thirteenth Century*), by the German philosopher and critic Friedrich Bouterwek (1766–1828). August Wilhelm Schlegel actually used the word "comparison" in his *Comparaison entre Phèdre de Racine et celle d'Euripide* (1807; *A Comparison between the Phèdre of Racine and that of Euripides*). Certainly, "comparison" was a buzzword at the turn of the nineteenth century, though initially in the sciences rather than in literature. It indicated a scientific method that had become very popular especially in anatomy and philology. In the former field its main proponent was the French naturalist Georges Cuvier (1769–1832) who in 1800 had published his *Leçons d'anatomie comparée* (*Lessons in Comparative Anatomy*) and which had met with great success across Europe. In philology, the name of the English jurist and orientalist William Jones (1746–94) stands out. With his work on Sanskrit, relating it to most of Europe's languages as well as to Persian, and positing a common ancestry for them all, Jones is usually seen as the founder of comparative linguistics.

Comparative literature: the early years

The birth of comparative literature as a discipline proper is to be situated in France. Jost (1974) mentions as the earliest instance of the documented use of "littérature comparée" a *Cours de littérature comparée*, comprising a series of textbooks published in 1816 by Jean-François-Michel Noël (1755–1841) and several collaborators. As Jost hastens to point out, though, Noël's collection merely consisted of an assemblage of texts, without any truly comparative framework. The true origins of the discipline are to be found with Abel-François Villemain (1790–1870), Philarète Chasles (1798–1873) and Jean-Jacques Ampère (1800–864). In the 1820s, Villemain, professor of Eloquence at the Sorbonne, presented a series of lectures that resulted in a number of volumes published in 1828, 1829 and 1830 under the titles *Tableau de la littérature au XVIIIe siecle* (*Survey of Eigtheenth-Century Literature*) and *Tableau de la littérature au Moyen Age en France, en Italie, en Espagne et en Angleterre* (*Survey of Medieval Literature in France, Italy, Spain and England*), addressed to the "amateurs de la littérature comparée" (Guillén 1993: 24; amateurs of comparative literature). Ampère, in 1830, delivered his inaugural lecture to the Marseilles Athénée discourses on the "comparative history of arts and of literature" (histoire comparative des arts et de la littérature). Two years later he was appointed by the University of the Sorbonne in Paris, where he again referred in his inaugural lecture there to "this comparative study, without which literary history is not complete" (cited in Pichois and Rousseau 1967: 16; cette étude comparative, sans laquelle l'histoire littéraire n'est pas complete). Finally, Philarète Chasles, whom I already dealt with in some detail in the first chapter, dedicated his inaugural lecture at the Parisian Athénée in 1835 to "la littérature étrangère comparée" (foreign literatures compared).

Jean-Jacques Ampère (1800–64) was a French writer, philologist and literary historian. After first having published on German and Scandinavian folk poetry, introducing his French public to these subjects, he turned to the history of French literature, which he taught at the Sorbonne and the Collège de France. He also developed an interest in Dante, visited the United States in 1851, and eventually became a member of the Académie Française.

The new discipline received its popular consecration in France when the celebrated critic Charles-Augustin Sainte-Beuve (1804–69) in two articles on Jean-Jacques Ampère, in 1840 and in 1868, talks of "l'histoire littéraire comparée" and "littérature comparée," respectively. Though the importance of Ampère for the early development of comparative literature has always been recognized, until recently his work had not drawn any particular attention from the point of view of world literature. Now, however, and along the lines of what we will also see happening further on with such figures as Hugo Melzl and Georg Brandes, Ampère is in the process of being reclaimed as an alternative starting point for the actual discipline of comparative literature – alternative, that is, to what toward the end of the nineteenth century hardened into the "orthodox" form of comparative literature practiced in France, and under French influence in most of the Western academic world. Françoise Lionnet (2011: 328), in her contribution *The Routledge Companion to World Literature* sees Ampère as "an early advocate of a global approach to French literature, and a believer in its fundamental heterogeneity."

In 1847 Charles Louandre (1812–82), with a reference to Chasles, proclaims in the *Revue des Deux Mondes* that "the comparative study of literature has put in circulation a myriad of new ideas" (cited in Pichois and Rousseau 1967:18; l'étude comparée des littératures a mis en circulation une foule d'idées nouvelles). If from the 1840s on, then, comparative literature has become an accepted enterprise, at least in France, this is not to say that this new way of looking at literature also was honored with official chairs at French universities. For sure, a number of courses in comparative literature were instituted, mostly under the tutelage of chairs in foreign literatures, but no independent chairs. The first such chairs were created in Italy and in Switzerland. The very first chair would seem to have been created in Naples, although accounts differ to its regard. According to Jost (1974: 12) a chair in comparative literature was created in Naples in 1861 for the Italian scholar and politician Francesco de Sanctis (1817–83) who, however, could only take up his professorship in 1871. For Pichois and Rousseau (1967: 19), De Sanctis already became Professor in Comparative Literature at Naples in 1863 upon the creation of a chair there. In Switzerland a chair in "littérature moderne comparée" was created in Geneva in 1865. France followed in 1890 with the appointment of Joseph Texte to a newly created chair in Comparative Literature at the University of Lyons.

Beyond France: Hugo Meltzl and Max Koch

In the second half of the nineteenth century comparative literature spread to the rest of Europe, and beyond. The Hungarian periodical *Tudománytár*, founded in 1834, regularly reported on various European literatures (Berczik 1972). However, not everything that appeared in its pages unhesitatingly was in support of a Goethean *Weltliteratur*. In 1836 the journal published an article by the German poet and critic Wolfgang Menzel (1798–1873), a staunch opponent of Goethe and Heinrich Heine. Menzel blamed Goethe for what he considered the sins of the early "Young Germany" movement: "world citizenship, Saint-Simonism (a form of utopian socialism named after the French writer and social critic Saint Simon [1760–1825], *TD*), anti-religious attitudes, immorality" (Berczik 1972: 161; Weltbürgertum, Saint-Simonismus, anti-religiöse Einstellung, Immoralität). In Berczik's words: "the ill-guided young writers propagated a world literature in the sense of Goethe's which, if one is not careful, supplants national literature, Menzel says ... [and] ... in the final part of his essay he reproaches the 'Young Germany' writers that they proclaim the Republic of Literature, the 'World Republic,' and that 'this is being prepared for by world literature'" (Berczik 1972: 161; Die irregeleiteten jungen Schriftsteller verkünden im Sinne Goethes die Weltliteratur, die – wenn man nicht gut aufpasst – das nationale Schrifttum verdrängen wird, – sagt Menzel ... [and] ... im Schlussteil seines Aufsatzes wirft er den Dichtern des "Jungen Deutschland" vor, dass sie die Republik der Literatur, die "Weltrepublik" proklamieren, und "diese wird durch die Weltliteratur vorbereitet").

> **Young Germany** (Junges Deutschland) was the name given to a German social and literary reform movement between 1830 and 1850. Inspired by liberal ideas of French origin the writers making up the movement opposed nationalist and Romantic excesses. By the German authorities, and by conservative commentators, they were seen as dangerous revolutionaries, and their works were banned or censored. Heinrich Heine, although he formally had nothing to do with them, was often counted among them because his ideas were close to theirs.

More importantly, the first ever comparative literature journal properly so named was founded in 1877 in present-day Cluj (officially Cluj-Napoca) in Romania, but which at the time went by the names of Klausenburg in German and Kolozsvár in Hungarian, and which was the capital of the then province of Transylvania in the Austro-Hungarian Empire. Edited by Hugo Meltzl (1846–1908; also known as Hugo von Meltzl and Hugo Meltzl de Lomnitz) and Samuel Brassai (1800–97) the journal first appeared under a multilingual title, which in all languages used basically said it to be a "journal of comparative literature." As of 1879 it changed its title to *Acta Comparationis Litterarum Universarum*, and it is under this title that it entered the history of comparative literature. Meltzl became the sole editor upon Brassai's retirement in 1883, and this until the journal's demise in 1888. Brassai belonged to the Hungarian-speaking population of Transylvania, Meltzl to the German-speaking minority long established there. In the countryside around Cluj Romanian was the dominant language. Brassai's and Meltzl's journal not only reflected the multilingualism of the region, it actively promoted polyglottism as a standard for comparative literature. In the first of three parts of a programmatic article on the "Present Tasks of Comparative Literature" published in the first three issues of the journal Meltzl declared that "a journal like ours, then, must be devoted at the same time to the art of translation and to the Goethean *Weltliteratur* (a term which German literary historians, particularly Gervinus, have thoroughly misunderstood)" (Meltzl 1973: 56). In the second part, fearing that his emphasis on translation in the first part of his statement had been misunderstood, he hastened to correct himself and to substitute the "principle of translation" with "*the principle of polyglottism.*" Still, he declared, it should be obvious that,

> These polyglot efforts have nothing in common with any kind of universal fraternization ... the ideals of Comparative Literature have nothing to do with foggy, "cosmopolitanizing" theories; the high aim (not to say tendencies) of a journal like ours would be gravely misunderstood or intentionally misrepresented if anybody expected us to infringe upon the national uniqueness of a people. ... It is, on the contrary, the *purely national of all nations* that Comparative Literature means to cultivate lovingly ... Our secret motto is: nationality as individuality of a people should be regarded as sacred and inviolable.
>
> (Meltzl 1973: 59–60)

This leads Meltzl to mount a defense for small literatures, for the "spiritual life of 'literatureless peoples'," and thence also for "folk literature," even to the point of comparing the extinction of a people's literature to that of the people itself. Surely, he continues, this should be impossible "in a time when certain animal species such as the mountain goat and the European bison are protected against extinction by elaborate and strict laws" (Meltzl 1973: 60). Returning to the issue of "world literature," he claims it to be generally misunderstood in his day, "for today every nation demands its own 'world literature' without quite knowing what is meant by it ... by now, every nation considers itself, for one good reason or another, superior to all nations, and this hypothesis, worked out into a complete theory of *suffisance*, is even the basis of much modern pedagogy which today practically everywhere strives to be 'national'" (Meltzl 1973: 60–61). In the first part of his essay he had already given as his opinion that, "as every unbiased man of letters knows, modern literary history, as generally practiced today, is nothing but an *ancilla historiae politicae*, or even an *ancilla nationis*" (Meltzl 1973: 56). Meltzl concludes the second part of his essay as follows:

> True "world literature," therefore, in our opinion, can only remain an unattainable ideal in the direction of which, nevertheless, all independent literatures, i.e. all nations, should strive. They should use, however, only those means which we have called the two most important comparative principles, translation and polyglottism, never acts of violence or barbaric

hypotheses which will be profitable for nobody but which unfortunately appear occasionally even in the great European journals.

(Meltzl 1973: 61)

The principle of polyglottism had implicitly already been flagged in the journal's first name appearing as it did on its title page in eleven languages. In the third part of his programmatic statement, on "Decaglottism," Meltzl proposes ten working languages for the journal: German, English, French, Icelandic, Italian, Spanish, Portuguese, Swedish, Dutch, and Hungarian, next to Latin – no Romanian. In practice, most articles were in German and Hungarian. In its later years the *Acta* increasingly concentrated on one of the aspects that Meltzl highlighted as the province of what he considered "world literature" – that is to say, the folkloric – offering examples from around the world in the original with adjacent translations.

It should also be said that the *Acta*, notwithstanding its ambitions, and probably at least partially due to its relatively inauspicious site of publication, never had more than a few score subscribers and readers. These formed also the core of the Societas Comparationis Litterarum Universarum, labeled by David Damrosch, in his entry on Meltzl in the *Routledge Companion to World Literature* (2011: 15), as "probably the world's first Comparative Literature Association." Damrosch (2011: 20), concludes that:

> It is only in recent years that comparatists have begun to recover the fully global perspective that Goethe anticipated and that Meltzl's journal truly began to embody. We can now return to the origins of comparative literature with new appreciation for the complexities of the pioneers' situations, nowhere better represented than in Meltzl's polyglot anti-cosmopolitanism. Little read in Meltzl's lifetime, the *Acta Comparationis Litterarum Universarum* makes fascinating reading today, and it can help us create a study of world literature that truly deserves the name.

Neohelicon, a Hungarian comparative literature journal founded in 1973 by the Hungarian Academy of Sciences with the particular purpose of supporting the publication of the International Comparative Literature Association's ongoing series of literary histories in European languages, took as its subtitle "Acta Comparationis Litterarum Universarum," thus laying explicit claim to Meltzl's legacy.

It is not only *Neohelicon* and the Hungarians though that claim Melzl's legacy. In fact, if I have dwelt upon Meltzl in such detail it is because he has become somewhat of an iconic figure for comparatists, especially in the United States, since the beginning of the twenty-first century. Damrosch in particular, but in his wake others such as Haun Saussy, have seized upon Meltzl to at least partially reground the genealogy of comparative literature in the direction of a globalized multilingual, or polyglottal, discipline. I will return to why this is so later in this chapter – suffice to say (at this point) that not everyone agrees with Damrosch's benign view of Meltzl, and even less with the twist given to it by Haun Saussy (Saussy 2006b) in his own contribution to the 2006 volume *Comparative Literature in an Age of Globalization* he compiled for the American Comparative Literature Association (Saussy 2006a).

Reasoning that "philological study that incorporates both German and Hungarian cannot plot its course on cognates or common ancestors, for Hungarian belongs to a separate language family entirely; the science will have to suspend its allegiance to genealogical reasoning and take its bearings from reports of contact or similarity," Saussy (2006: 8) singles out Meltzl's inclusion of Hungarian as one of the working languages of the *Acta* as "the first in a long series of gestures by which comparative literature questions the criteria for inclusion in the set of objects known as 'literature,' ... and also the decisive swerve of an established academic discourse (the comparative philological method) toward a Goethean horizon in which world literature, coming from all directions, is whatever the world takes to be literature" (Saussy 2006: 8). Saussy is overlooking three things here. To begin with, Meltzl himself at the outset of the first part of his 1877 programmatic statement feels it necessary to insist that his new journal is not to be taken as a philological enterprise. Second, even if comparative philology, as Meltzl himself underlines, is indeed an "established academic discipline" in 1877, comparative literature, as Meltzl insists upon even more strongly, definitely is not. And third, as David Marno highlights, Meltzl's "polyglot anti-cosmopolitanism," in Damrosch's characterization, is not, as Saussy implicitly takes it to mean because of its inclusion of Hungarian, "a sign of his refusal to be complicit with the general trend of nationalist-historicist sciences in the nineteenth century," (Marno 2008: 38). Rather, Marno argues, it is "a position that has very transparent political motives: a last position accessible to someone who wants to advocate the literature of a country that had lost its war for national independence just two decades earlier, a country that around this time, in the aftermath of the 1867 compromise between Austria and Hungary, was becoming more powerful than it had been in more than 300 years" (Marno 2008: 40–41).

The fact is that not only did Meltzl not include Romanian as one of the working languages of his journal, but also he excluded all other languages of all other minorities in the Austro-Hungarian Empire: Czech, Serbo-Croat, Slovene, Slovak, as well as the language of that Empire's powerful neighbor (and neighbor particularly to Hungary) to the East, that is to say Russia. Meltzl's position on polyglottism, then, has at least as much to do with consolidating the position of his own country's language and literature in the contemporary political conditions as with his propagation of a Goethean *Weltliteratur*. In fact, in the second part of his 1877 programmatic statement Meltzl, when soft-pedaling on the importance of translation as announced in the first part, specifically in relation to Goethean world literature, had said that "the means should not be mistaken for the end ... Goethe was still able to conceive of his 'Weltliteratur' as basically, or even exclusively? (German) translation which for him was an end in itself" (Meltzl 1973: 58). Meltzl here seems to be implying that Goethe could afford his cosmopolitanism because even if he was comparing the position of German literature unfavorably with that of English and especially French literature, he was still writing from the comfort of a major language, and hence from a position of power. Meltzl's situation, when it comes not to his own native language, which was German, but to his national language, which was Hungarian (he gained some notoriety for holding his inaugural lecture as Professor of *Germanistik*, and against Gervinus's interpretation of Goethe's *Weltliteratur*, in Hungarian [Marno 2008: 40]), was exactly the opposite. He needs to defend polyglottism as a defense against the encroachment of German, yet he also needs to raise Hungarian above the status of the other minority languages in the Austro-Hungarian Empire, particularly Romanian. He does so by including Hungarian into his list of ten European literatures that according to him had achieved "classicism" (Schulz and Rhein 1973: 230). As Schulz and Rhein note, Melzl never precisely defines what he means by the latter term. He does list the works with which he sees each of these literatures acceding to "classicism." For Hungarian literature this is with the nineteenth-century writers József Eötvös (1813–71) and Sándor Petöfi. (1823–49).The latter was, next to a noted poet, also a revolutionary, who died most probably (his body was never found) in a battle for Hungarian independence. In his journal Meltzl repeatedly came back to the poetry of Petöfi, commenting upon it, translating it. Here again we can see Meltzl's dual interests in comparative literature as a discipline, a calling even, and a means of furthering patriotic concerns. It should be said, though, that Meltzl did pay critical attention to literature in Romanian and in languages other than his journal's ten working languages.

If for Damrosch and Saussy Meltzl is the good guy, and his journal the beacon shining bright at the beginning of the institutionalization of the discipline of comparative literature, lighting the way for present-day and future comparatists and world literature scholars; the bad guy is Max Koch (1855–1931), first Professor at Marburg and later at Breslau (now Wroclaw in Poland). In 1886 he founded the *Zeitschrift für vergleichende Litteraturgeschichte*, published in Berlin. Koch's journal published on almost the same things as Meltzl's, but did so exclusively in German, and from a German point of view. In fact, in his programmatic statement to his new journal Koch emphasized that "German literature and the advancement of its historical understanding will form the starting point and the center of gravity for the endeavors of the *Zeitschrift für vergleichende Litteraturgeschichte*" (Koch 1973: 77). Damrosch (2006: 110) remarks that, "Koch's journal must have seemed to Meltzl to represent not merely a personal affront but also a real step backward in scholarly terms." Meltzl's journal was almost immediately overshadowed by its more powerful rival, and in 1888 it ceased publication. Notwithstanding Damrosch's rather negative judgment on Koch and his journal, one has to admit that Koch was probably simply more in tune with the way comparative literature in Europe was developing than Meltzl. Koch too drew upon the legacy of Goethe and his *Weltliteratur*, but unlike Meltzl, who rejected Goethe's penchant for world literature in German translation in favor of polyglottism, he welcomed it, in his opening statement to his journal approvingly quoting Goethe's review of Carlyle's *German Romance* in *Über Kunst und Altertu*m VI, 2 that:

> True general tolerance will be achieved most surely when we leave untouched the special qualities of individuals and individual peoples but at the same time hold on to the conviction that the truly meritorious belongs to all mankind. For a long time now, the Germans have contributed to such a mediation and mutual acceptance. Those who know and study the German language find themselves in that marketplace where all nations offer their wares; by acting as interpreters, they enrich themselves.
>
> (Koch 1973: 75)

In the spirit of Goethe, then, Koch saw the use of German as the working language of his journal as actually promoting understanding among scholars of various nations because of its mediatory role. Indeed, while admiring Meltzl's principle of polyglottism, Damrosch admits that the actual number of articles published in languages other than German and Hungarian in Meltzl's journal, and especially in lesser known languages such as Icelandic, and even Latin, was very small. We may even wonder whether such polyglottism may not have hampered the journal's accessibility rather than enhancing it. In any case, Koch's approach, with its turn to literary history – "but all consideration of world literature is, after all, comparative literary history" (Koch 1973: 76) – was certainly closer to that of the French "school" (Guillén 1993: 47, prefers to call it the "hour") of comparative literature then becoming dominant in Europe and even beyond, rooted in positivism, and turning away from for instance folklore. Meltzl had increasingly turned to folklore in the later issues of the *Acta*. Koch noticed that the interest in Germany in such studies had been waning for some time while in other European countries journals specializing in folklore had been founded. Still, he invited contributions on the subject to his *Zeitschrift*, perhaps in an effort to undercut Meltzl here too, as Damrosch (2006: 110) suggests he also did in other ways. Nevertheless, Damrosch too seems forced to admit that Koch was more alert to the times when he states that "more broadly, the great-power perspective became dominant in Comparative Literature for a full century thereafter" (Damrosch 2006: 110). Moreover, as Schulz and Rhein (1973: 66) put it in their introduction to their reprint of Koch's opening statement to his journal, which kept appearing until 1910: "At a time when there was no other organ to propagate the aims and possibilities of the young discipline, Koch's two periodicals (next to the *Zeitschrift* he also edited nine volumes of *Studien zur vergleichenden Literaturgeschichte*, 1901–9) fostered, kept alive and shaped comparative literature and bestowed upon it the academic respectability that it needed."

Comparative literature: the French school

In his opening statement to the *Zeitschrift für vergleichende Litter-aturgeschichte* Koch quoted Moritz Carrière (1817–95), professor at the University of Munich, where he mainly lectured on aesthetics, on comparative literature as a "science" (Koch 1877 quoted in Schulz and Rhein 1973: 76, Carrière 1884). Certainly, this was in tune with the trend of the times, especially so in France which, although it was very late in recognizing the discipline with the institutionalization of dedicated university chairs, nevertheless during the second half of the nineteenth and the first half of the twentieth century continued as the undisputed center of comparative literature. As Guillén (1993: 35) stresses, summarizing René Wellek's survey of the history of comparative literature in the latter's *Discriminations* (1970), under the influence of the positivism of the French critic and literary historian Hippolyte Taine (1828–93), who based himself on the philosophy of August Comte (1798–1857), one of the founders of the discipline of sociology and one of the earliest philosophers of science, two principles, or perhaps preoccupations, predominated in the approach to comparative literature imposing itself in France as of the 1850s: *factualism* and *scientism*. Scientism meant that phenomena in literature had to be explainable from ascertainable causes. This is where Taine's famous triad "race, milieu, moment" appears, explaining, or reducing, everything human to the interplay between national character ("race" in the nineteenth century basically meant "nation" or "ethnicity," see for instance Robert Young 1995), the social environment, and historical time. In practice, this gave a strong boost to the study of national literatures as "naturally" emanating from, and giving voice to, a particular people's "national character" springing from precisely such interplay. The advent of Darwinian evolutionism would only strengthen this methodological tendency. Especially Ferdinand Brunetière (1849–1906), Professor of French Language and Literature at the École Normale in Paris, took a Darwinian approach to literature, as demonstrated in his *L'évolution de la poésie lyrique en France* (1894; *The Development of Lyrical Poetry in France*). As Guillén (1993: 36) puts it, "The literature of a country thus became a biological variety, a subspecies of universal literature; and the task of the comparatist was to be the elucidation of the cross-fertilizations and other grafts that link these subspecies and give rise to their mutations, hybridization, and growth ... the integrity of the individual components of literature was not in doubt, owing to a firm belief in the uniqueness of the character of each people." Under these conditions factualism then meant that such "elucidations" would have to happen on the basis of observable and demonstrable facts. In practice, this meant "comparing" works, authors, etc. from at least two different European literatures.

Brunetière and Fernand Baldensperger (1871–1958), together with Joseph Texte, who died very young in 1900, were the "face" of French comparatism around the turn of the twentieth century. In his opening address to the section on "histoire comparée des littératures" (comparative history of literatures) of a Historical Congress held in Paris in 1900, Brunetière readily admitted that "European literature is only a branch, or better yet a province, and maybe even a narrow province, in the almost infinite field of *Comparative Literature*" (Brunetière 1973: 159). At the same time, he also firmly pleaded sticking to European literature guided by "only one principle, which I hope you will understand as evident, and it is that the studies of comparative literature are related only to that which is comparable" and that "by a reasonable extension it follows that the productions of a great literature do not concern us except as we have seen the resultant consequences of this contact" (Brunetière 1973: 168). French comparative literature, then, mainly concentrated on so-called "influence studies." Indicatively, Texte, who was a pupil of Brunetière's and followed the guidelines for the study of literature laid down by the latter in his *L'évolution de la poésie lyrique*, started off his career with a book on *J.J. Rousseau et les origines du cosmopolitisme littéraire* (1895; *Jean-Jacques Rousseau and the Origins of Literary Cosmopolitanism*). Baldensperger did the same with *Goethe en France* (1904; *Goethe in France*). The same Baldensperger, who first had taught at Nancy and Lyon, in 1910 became professor at the Sorbonne, and together with Paul Hazard (1878–1944), himself likewise professor at the Sorbonne as of 1919 and from 1925 on Professor of Comparative Literature at the prestigious *Collège de France*, founded the *Revue de littérature comparée* (1921–).

Baldensperger held a visiting professorship at Columbia University (1917–19). In 1935 he became Professor and Chair of Comparative Literature at Harvard University, from which he moved to the University of California-Los Angeles in 1940 until his retirement in 1945. Hazard held a visiting professorship at Columbia University from 1932 to 1940. Thus, the influence of the French school of comparative literature stretched to the United States in the guise of its most prestigious universities – universities moreover that had been among the first to create chairs of comparative literature, Harvard in 1891 and Columbia in 1899. The handbooks on comparative literature that appeared in France in the first half of the twentieth century basically raised the ideas of Baldensperger and his followers to dogma. As late as 1951 Jean-Marie Carré, Baldensperger's successor at the Sorbonne, in his preface to his former pupil Marius-François Guyard's *La littérature comparée* (*Comparative Literature*), insisted that "comparative literature is not literary comparison," but that it is "a branch of literary history," and that it is "the study of international intellectual relations, of the actual connections that existed ... between the works, the inspirations, or even the lives of writers belonging to various literatures" (Carré 2009: 159). In a note, Carré repeats that, "the first general exposition (of the concept of comparative literature) was provided by our teacher Fernand Baldensperger in 1921" (that is to say in the first issue of the *Revue de littérature comparée*). He also refers to Paul van Tieghem's *La littérature comparée* (*Comparative Literature*) of 1931, which had been reprinted in 1946 (Carré 2009: 160), and which insists that "a clear and distinct idea of comparative literature supposes first of all a clear and distinct idea of literary history, of which it is a branch" (Van Tieghem 1931: 23, as quoted in English in Jost 1974: 25). And so it was, Guillén (1993: 37) somewhat ruefully notes, "that the idea of *Weltliteratur* was left far behind, its outlines blurred" in the French version of comparative literature dominant until WWII.

The changing of the guard: comparative literature after 1945

In his 1951 preface to Guyard's *La littérature comparée* Carré insisted that "comparative literature is not general literature," adding in a note that the latter is "a subject taught in the United States" (Carré 2009: 159–60). Perhaps Carré was thinking of the fact that already in 1901 Richard Moulton had been appointed professor of literary theory and interpretation and head of the department of general literature at the University of Chicago and that this same Moulton in 1911 had published *World Literature and Its Place in General Culture*. More likely, though, if we keep in mind that already Paul van Tieghem had defined "general literature" as being concerned with large syntheses, Carré was thinking of the trend, rapidly gaining ground in the USA after WWII, of teaching large "world literature" courses. In fact, ever since the middle of the nineteenth century the Anglophone world had been elaborating a comparative literature of its own, more geared towards Carré's "general literature" than towards the meticulous study of "rapports de fait" (factual relationships) as had become increasingly the habit, and indeed the prescription, in the French tradition. As already mentioned in Chapter 1, what Schulz and Rhein (1973: 41) call "the first known formal presentation concerning the discipline of comparative literature in the United States" was an address on "Comparative Literature" given by Charles Chauncey Shackford at Cornell University in 1871. Shackford is interested in the laws that govern "universal literature," and thinks that "the literary productions of all ages and peoples can be classed, can be brought into comparison and contrast, can be taken out of their isolation as belonging to one nation, or one separate era, and be brought under divisions as the embodiment of the same aesthetic principles, the universal laws of mental, social, and moral development: the same in India and in England; in Hellas, with its laughing sea, and Germany, with its sombre forests" (Shackford 1973: 42). "Literature," he declares, "can be studied not in the isolated works of different ages, but as the production of the same great laws, and the embodiment of the same universal principles in all times" (Shackford 1973: 46).

Hutcheson Macaulay Posnett

Ideas similar to Shackford's were taken up in a more systematic, some would say a more mechanical, way in England by Hutcheson Macaulay Posnett in his 1886 *Comparative Literature*, a book in which he claimed to have been the first to have elaborated "the method and principles" of the discipline (Posnett 1973: 186). As the title of the 1901 article – "The Science of Comparative

Literature" – in which he uttered these claims illustrates, Posnett was a staunch believer in "science," and therefore it should not come as a surprise that for him "the fundamental principles of Comparative Literature, as [he] formulated and illustrated them fifteen years [earlier, in *Comparative Literature*], are social evolution, individual evolution, and the influence of the environment on the social and individual life of man ... a scientific 'law' is only a brief summary of a vast number of observed and recorded facts" (Posnett 1973: 188–89). In *Comparative Literature*, when discussing "The Comparative Method and Literature," Posnett proclaimed that "the central point of these studies is the relation of the individual to the group. ... we therefore adopt ... the gradual expansion of social life, from clan to city, from city to nation, from both of these to cosmopolitan humanity, as the proper order of studies in comparative literature" (Posnett 2009: 59). "That cosmopolitan and world-wide spirit which is the servant of no one social group but the sympathetic friend of all," Posnett specified in 1901 with a reference to Goethe, "I studied in *Comparative Literature* under the name of 'world-literature,' and I illustrated its various characteristics by Hebrew, Greek, Latin, Indian, and Chinese examples" (Posnett 1973: 191). If Posnett can be accused, then, of having followed a narrowly positivist and social Darwinist road when elaborating his "principles and methods" of comparative literature, he certainly cannot be accused of limiting himself to Europe, even though he also seems to have thought that "the making of [the British] empire's literature ... going on before [his contemporary compatriot's] eyes" was a significant contribution to his "cosmopolitan spirit" (Posnett 1973: 191). Sounding a distinctly Goethean note, Posnett optimistically concluded that "now, when the science of Comparative Literature is a dream that has come true," it is a "study that is as certain to enlighten and expand the friendship of nations as to increase the knowledge and sympathies of individual men" (Posnett 1973: 206).

Posnett devoted a sizeable part of his book – pages 235–336 – to what he calls "world-literature." This is not the *Weltliteratur* of Goethe, though. In fact, when Posnett mentions Goethe in regard to world literature it is to insist that the latter, though what Posnett calls "the admirer of world-literature" (Posnett 1886: 42), still thought that "national literature is an outcome of national life, a spiritual bond of national unity, such as no amount of eclectic study or cosmopolitan science can supply" (Posnett 1886: 341). Nowhere does Posnett actually discuss Goethe's idea of *Weltliteratur*. Instead, his world literature is the third stage in a historically successive series composed of "clan literature," the literature of "the city commonwealth," "world-literature," and "national literature." World-literature to Posnett is literature produced in cultures held together by what he calls "religious" or "political" cosmopolitanism. Examples of the former are the Hebrew and Islamic cultures. Examples of the latter are the Greek, or perhaps better Hellenic, and Roman, or perhaps better Latin, cultures. "Between the world-religions of Israel and Islam and the world-cultures of Alexandria and Rome there are, no doubt, very wide differences," he admits, "yet, though the former reach universality through social bonds of creed and the latter reach universality through the unsocial idea of personal culture, the outcome of both is to rise above old restrictions of place and time, and to render possible a literature which, whether based on Moses or Homer, may best be termed a 'world-literature'" (Posnett 1886: 236). For Posnett, then, the determining characteristic of such a world-literature is its "severance of literature from defined social groups" or "the universalising of literature" (Posnett 1886: 236). Next to this "universal idea of humanity," further characteristics of Posnett's world-literature are "the critical study of language as the medium of sacred books or models of literary art" and "the rise of new aesthetic appreciations of physical nature and its relations to man" (Posnett 1886: 238). Next to the literatures already mentioned Posnett also sees Indian and Chinese literature as qualifying as world-literatures.

Though, as Schulz and Rhein (1973: 185) note, Posnett's *Comparative Literature* was initially greeted with some enthusiasm, especially in the United States, it quickly came to be seen as overly mechanical and dated in its methodology because of what was perceived as its over-reliance on social Darwinism. Of late, though, as has happened with other early advocates of comparative literature, Posnett has been recast as a convenient forefather of more recent trends in the discipline. In 2004 Simon During, after having given a brief description of Posnett's methodology, concluded that: "Posnett conceived of comparative literature as a social science which, along with the world-literature canon it addresses, forms a basis for the politics of cosmopolitan democratic individualism … it does so not just because literature uniquely articulates those structures through which individuals recognize themselves as connected to and formed by an increasingly wide range of distant social formations, but because the comparative method enables recognition of social and cultural differences and, hence, encourages the dissemination of relativism as well as entry into a single world system" (During 2004: 314). Here, During is obviously reclaiming Posnett for the more sociologically and systemically oriented form of comparative literature he also sees Pascale Casanova and Franco Moretti as advocating in their publications. I will return to the latter in Chapter 5. Beyond this, and even though there is no sign of his ever having read Posnett, some proposals put forward recently by Alexander Beecroft (2008), and to which I will also return in Chapter 5, show remarkable resemblances to Posnett's differentiation of literatures according to different forms of social organization.

Comparative literature in the United States: the early years

In his editorial to the newly founded (and short-lived) *Journal of Comparative Literature* (1903), George Woodberry (1855–1930), who briefly occupied the chair of comparative literature at Columbia University before retiring early and devoting the rest of his life to traveling, lecturing and writing, summarized the province of comparative literature as the study of sources, of themes, of forms, of environments, and of artistic parallels. In all these areas, he argued, a lot of work had already been done, especially under the influence of "German methods," but these concerned mostly the "externals of literature" (Woodberry 1973: 212). The question now became what was to be done with all this accumulated material? For Woodberry, the ultimate goal had to be the search for "the laws of the human soul" (Woodberry 1973: 213). He put forward that "to disclose the necessary forms, the vital moods of the beautiful soul is the far goal of our effort, – to help in this, in the bringing of those spiritual destinies in which human destiny is accomplished" (Woodberry 1973: 213–14). "With such thoughts in mind," Woodberry continued, "It may perhaps seem to some of us that the subject of international influences is not the main road of our travel." Instead, he advocated studying "the isolated phenomena of national literatures," feeling that "the approaching exploitation of the old literatures of the Orient" might be a fruitful field of investigation. In all this Woodberry is obviously holding a modest plea for the study of general literature, for the study of affinities, correspondences, parallels, and all those things that French orthodoxy disapproved of.

In 1894, Charles Mills Gayley (1858–1932), professor of English at the University of California, Berkeley, proposed the creation of a Society of Comparative Literature; in 1903 he published an article in *The Atlantic Monthly* in support of Woodberry's newly founded *Journal of Comparative Literature*. Gayley specifically interpreted Woodberry's editorial as "non-acceptance of a theory of evolution such as Brunetière's," and as a confirmation that "the study of international relations and influences is but one of the objects of Comparative Literature" (Gayley 1973: 101–2). In fact, Gayley saw anthropology as "the cradle of literary science" (Gayley 1973: 96) and finally called comparative literature "literary philology" (Gayley 1973: 103). All this did not prevent Baldensperger and other prominent European scholars from contributing to Woodberry's journal. Still, Carré's 1951 statement clearly shows the rift between the French and what since 1958 it has become customary to call the "American" schools of comparative literature.

The crisis of comparative literature

The years from Woodberry's premature resignation from Columbia to WWII were lean years for comparative literature in the United States. The subject had been rejuvenated somewhat by the arrival in the USA of a number of European scholars, mostly Jewish exiles from Nazi Germany, in the late 1930s and the 1940s. Prominent among these were Leo Spitzer, who arrived in the US in 1936, and Erich Auerbach, who came in 1948. But there was also René Wellek (1909–95), born in Vienna of Czech parents (Czechia being a part of the Austro-Hungarian Empire at the time of Wellek's birth), educated in Prague, and as of 1939 active in the United States, where in 1946 he founded the department of comparative literature at Yale University. Comparative literature in the US set much greater stock on interpretation, or hermeneutics, and on emphasizing the humanitarian dimension of literature than did the French school. The rift between the long-dominant French school of comparative literature and what since has come to be known as the "American" school (Guillén again insists on using "hour" instead of "school") plainly erupted on the occasion of the Second World Congress of the then recently formed International Comparative Literature Association in Chapel Hill, NC in 1958.

In a speech to the ICLA Congress at Chapel Hill Wellek condemned the

René Wellek (1903–95) was born in Vienna, Austria, of Czech parents. Fluent in German and Czech, he was educated at Prague's Charles University, where he moved in the circles of the Prague School structuralists. In 1935 he took up a teaching post at University College London, and on the eve of WWII moved to the US, eventually becoming Professor of Comparative Literature at Yale. In the 1940s, together with Austin Warren, Wellek published *Theory of Literature*, which for the next forty years was the most influential handbook for the study of literature in the United States. The book is widely seen as supporting New Criticism, while also showing the influence of European forms of structuralism. Wellek also wrote an eight-volume *History of Modern Criticism: 1750–1950*.

French school for its "obsolete methodology" which had laid on comparative literature "the dead hand of nineteenth-century factualism, scientism, and historical relativism," and instead advocated a more generous attitude towards what could be done under the label "comparative literature." Clearly echoing his own and Austin Warren's celebrated introductory handbook to the study of literature *Theory of Literature* (1949), Wellek argued for the study of the literary work of art's "literariness" (Wellek 2009: 169) and for a "holistic" conception that sees the work of art as a "diversified totality, as a structure of signs which, however, imply meanings and values" (Wellek 2009: 170). Once we do that, he contends, "man, universal man, man anywhere and at any time, in all his variety, emerges and literary scholarship ceases to be an antiquarian pastime, a calculus of national credits and debts and even a mapping of networks of relationships ... literary scholarship becomes an act of the imagination, like art itself, and thus a preserver and creator of the highest values of mankind" (Wellek 2009: 171).

Wellek soon received support from H.H. Remak, Professor of Comparative Literature at Indiana University, who, in the article with which he opened Newton P. Stallknecht and Horst Frenz's 1961 programmatic collection *Comparative Literature: Method and Perspective*, posited that comparative literature would best serve its purpose "by not only relating several literatures to each other but by relating literature to other fields of human knowledge and activity, especially artistic and ideological fields; that is, by extending the investigation of literature both geographically and generically" (Remak 1961:

10). For Remak comparative literature and world literature dealt with largely the same issues, but comparative literature did so in a more restricted form as to space and time. "Much of what he have been doing [in comparative literature]," he said, "is, in effect, comparative world literature" (Remak 1961: 12), the difference being that the former "is not bound to the same extent by criteria of quality and/or intensity" (Remak 1961: 13). Nor, did he add, did world literature necessarily involve the aspect of comparison, unlike comparative literature. Finally, he referred to the distinction made by van Tieghem with regard to "general literature" as dealing with large syntheses, but he saw the term as also covering "literary trends, problems and theories of 'general interest'" (Remak 1961: 15). Finally, he found none of these terms to be watertight as to overlap between them all, though he rather disliked "general literature" as too vague, and preferred more precise indications for the various things it covered, such as for instance "literary theory" (Remak 1961: 19). In this, he joined Wellek, who at the end of his own "The Crisis of Comparative Literature" had also called for a "reorientation toward theory and criticism" (Wellek 2009: 170).

As we now know, Wellek's call for theory was followed with a vengeance in the 1960s to 1980s in the United States with the successive waves of structuralism, phenomenology, poststructuralism, reader reception studies, deconstruction, dialogism, and new historicism succeeding, and often tumbling over, one another, more often than not sparked by the import of various European theories of French, German or Central and East European origin. In one sense, this signaled the triumph of comparative literature. In another sense, it also brought about the demise of comparative literature, because "theory," unlike works of literature themselves, was not thought to suffer in translation, and could therefore readily be accessed in English. In practice, this meant that theory rapidly became the province also of English departments, with comparative literature, because of its foreign language requirements, spurned as a "difficult" and untrendy subject.

In Europe, the newer insights found their way into what for a generation became the accepted handbook on comparative literature in France, Claude Pichois (1925–2004) and André-M. Rousseau's *La littérature comparée* (1967; *Comparative Literature*), and into Ulrich Weisstein's *Einführung in die vergleichende Literaturwissenschaft* (1968), translated as *Comparative Literature and Literary Theory* (1973) upon Weisstein's assuming the Chair of Comparative Literature at Indiana University. Earlier, François Jost, a Swiss, had published *Essais de littérature comparée* (1964), which became the basis for his very informative, fair and evenhanded *Comparative Literature* (1974), published while he was teaching at the University of Illinois. Pierre Brunel and Yves Chevrel edited a massive collection, *Précis de littérature comparée* (*Outline of Comparative Literature*), in 1989. Meanwhile, there grew up distinct practices of comparative literature in Europe again, struggling to reclaim a "scientific" basis for their endeavors. Such was the case with the reader reception theories of Hans Robert Jauss (1921–97) and Wolfgang Iser

(1926–2007), the empirical studies approach of S.J. Schmidt and Douwe Fokkema, the text linguistics, text grammar, discourse analysis and socio-critical discourse analysis approaches of János Petöfi, Teun A. van Dijk, and Marc Angenot, and the imagology of Hugo Dyserinck and Joep Leerssen. Most of these efforts were largely to be situated in the field of "general" rather than "comparative" literature, and in many continental universities the concomitant departments were consequently restyled as of "general and comparative literature" (Lernout 2006). All the while, there also flourished what Jost calls the "Russian school" of comparative literature, with Mikhail Bakhtin, Juri Lotman, and Boris Ouspensky, but which we perhaps better call the Central and East European school, as it also legiti-mately includes Dionýsz Ďurišin, in Slovakia, and earlier not only the Moscow but also the Prague school of structuralism – suffice to repeat here that as of the 1960s, ideas and theories originating from Central and Eastern Europe found their way into Western literary theory, and that René Wellek himself served as an early bridge between a particularly Czech theory of lit-erature, especially with regard to "literariness," and American literary theory and criticism.

René Etiemble

Serving as a bridge the other way, or at least being depicted that way in the foreword to the translation of his ground-breaking *Comparaison n'est pas raison: la crise de la littérature comparée* (1963), was the French com-paratist René Etiemble (1909–2002). As can be gauged from its title, Etiemble's little booklet was a reaction to Wellek's "The Crisis in Compara-tive Literature," and his translators Herbert Weisinger and Georges Joyaux consequently opted for the subtitle to Etiemble's original title for their 1966 translation. "Etiemble's book," they said, "must ... be seen as the rainbow of academic peace raised after the storm of scholarly controversy," for "French and American comparatists, as well as those of other lands, ought now to be able to agree that comparative literature is a series of methods of literary study held together by a common attitude of mind ... it seeks to establish the relations between literatures in as many different ways by as many different methods as can be devised; it limits neither the choice of subject nor the means by which it can be examined, and, indeed, it endeavors constantly to add to its store of objects of inquiry as well as to its arsenal of investigative techniques" (Etiemble 1966: ix). In fact, Etiemble became most famous for a provocative speech he gave at the Fourth World Congress of the International Comparative Literature Association held in Fribourg, Switzerland, in 1964. Published in 1966 in the proceedings of that Conference edited by François Jost, Etiemble's "Faut-il réviser la notion de *Welt-literatur*?" was an impassioned plea for extending world literature to really include all of the world's literatures, and not just a few major European literatures.

In the preface to his *Essais de littérature (vraiment) générale* (1975; *Essays in [Truly] General Literature*), in which his 1964 ICLA speech was included, Etiemble gave an example of how Japanese literature rendered void all theories of literature based on European examples, and he concluded that "any literary theory built only on European phenomena will not fare any better from now on" (Etiemble 1975, 14; toute théorie littéraire qui s'élabore a partir des seuls phénoménes européens ne vaudra pas mieux désormais). To be honest, Albert Guérard, though in a much less provocative way, had already (in 1940) lamented that in what commonly passed as the canon of world literature (his concrete example and point of departure had been a list drawn up by Sir John Lubbock in 1885 but he maintained that things had not really altered much for the better since then) "the East is woefully under-represented" (Guérard 1940: 34). In other words, Guérard said, "the term *World Literature* is an obvious exaggeration," though it might be retained "as the voicing of a distant hope" (Guérard 1940: 34). In the meantime, he suggested, it would be more accurate to call the field "*Western* World Literature: a literature for Westerners, wherever they may be, and for Westernized Orientals" (Guérard 1940: 34).

Re-thinking comparative literature in the United States

Etiemble was a polyglot, with an intimate knowledge of especially Arab and Chinese culture. When in the 1980s multiculturalism spread throughout the United States this ironically led to a yet increased Anglophone monolingualism, and much the same thing happened with the parallel onset of postcolonialism, once again favoring English departments over those of comparative literature. World literature seemed to have shrunk to only what happened in English. In 1987, when comparative literature was at an absolute low in the United States, Sarah Lawall, of the University of Massachusetts, organized a National Endowment of the Humanities Summer Institute on World Literature, which eventually resulted in the 1994 volume *Reading World Literature: Theory, History, Practice.* In her introduction Lawall insisted that the title of the volume should also be taken as "reading" the world, and that to this end the geographical, generic, and methodological reach of the essays was as wide as possible. She also stressed the specificity of the teaching, or "reading," of world literature in the United States, that is to say as a specifically American pedagogical practice. I will come back to this issue, and to Lawall, in Chapter 4.

A true comeback for world literature, though, and for comparative literature in the United States only happened with 9/11 and its aftermath, waking Americans up to a wider and multilingual world. Often, calls for a renewal of comparative literature went hand in hand with the revisiting of earlier practitioners, often even the pioneers, in the discipline. In the previous chapter I showed how Edward Said in *Humanism and Democratic Criticism* (2003), returning in his final work to his own earliest inspiration at the beginning of his career, invoked the example of Auerbach, and how Emily Apter in the opening pages to her *The Translation Zone: A New Comparative Literature* (2006) insists that the debacle of the Iraq war is at least partially due to a lack of knowledge of languages and foreign cultures on the part of Americans, and how she too calls upon the examples of Auerbach and especially Spitzer in Istanbul in the 1930s. Gayatri Spivak in *Death of a Discipline* (2003) calls for a renewal of comparative literature through an alliance with area studies.

David Damrosch's *What is World Literature?* (2003) echoes the call for a "littérature engagée" (launched by Jean-Paul Sartre (1905–80) after WWII in *What is Literature?* (1947)). Damrosch gives as his threefold definition of world literature that it "is an elliptical refraction of national literatures," that "it is writing that gains in translation," and that "it is not a set canon of texts but a mode of reading: a form of detached engagement with the world beyond our own place and time" (Damrosch 2003: 282). Further on Damrosch clarifies the first part of his definition as: "world literature ... is a double refraction, one that can be described through the figure of the ellipse, with the source and host cultures providing the two foci that generate the elliptical space within which a work of literature lives as world literature, connected to both cultures, circumscribed by neither one" (Damrosch 2003: 283). He recognizes that this poses the enormous problem of depth of knowledge versus breadth of knowledge for the comparatist. How can one know enough about either part of the ellipse, each of the two national cultures, that a work of world literature moves in? *A fortiori*, how can one know enough about all the different national literatures and cultures, or periods, works of world literature circulate in?

One possible solution, Damrosch suggests, is to work collaboratively, and he points to the ongoing series of histories of literature in European languages produced under the auspices of the International Comparative Literature Association. Discussing a multi-volume project for a world history of literature presently being coordinated in Sweden, Damrosch in a 2008 article in *New Literary History* also points to the possibilities offered by new media such as the internet. Amy J. Elias, writing in the same issue of *New Literary History*, wonders what would happen "if the wisdom of crowds were combined with a community of experts in an interactive online format ... enacted by a gated wiki" (Elias 2008: 718). In fact, she suggests, "the database itself might be a new kind of literature or a new kind of historical notation" (Elias 2008: 720). The fullest possible solution to the problem of how to avoid amateurism for the individual "doing" world literature, Damrosch suggests, is to learn more languages, and he laments that especially in North America a knowledge of foreign languages is not something that speaks for itself. Obviously, this is also where his seizing on Meltzl and his "principle of polyglottism" finds its origins. Beyond this, though, and if we do not want to forcibly limit our reach to the number of languages we know, we will have to learn how to do with translations, but we should learn how to use them judiciously. Finally, one should understand that the task of the comparatist doing world literature is not to provide the insider's or specialist's view on either one of the two foci contained in the ellipse that the work of world literature moves in; it is rather to bring out the strangeness of the work with regard to both these foci, thus offering a new and different perspective on the work, and in the process also dis-engaging the reader or student from his unconscious immersion in his own culture.

Franco Moretti in a 2000 article "Conjectures on World Literature" offered his solution to what he called the "problem"(Moretti 2004: 149) of world literature, that is to say: how to cope with the mass of information and reading that doing world literature on the basis of first-hand and close reading of texts poses. "Distant reading" (Moretti 22004: 151) is to rely on the work done by specialists in national literatures, genres, authors, and individual works to then draw more general conclusions from them. This is another form of collaboration, suggested this time not so much by the example of the humanities as by that of the social sciences. Moretti consequently also proposes to translate his data into the visual imagery customary to the social sciences and suggested by his book *Graphs, Maps, Trees* (2005). Comparative literature, he feels, should study world literature via comparative morphology (as elaborated by primarily the biologist Ernst Mayr): "take a form, follow it from space to space, and study the reasons for its transformations"(Moretti 2005: 90). And of course, he adds, "the multiplicity of spaces is the great challenge, and the curse, almost, of comparative literature: but it is also its peculiar strength, because it is only in such a wide, non-homogeneous geography that some fundamental principles of cultural history become manifest"(Moretti: 90). Curiously, Moretti here almost joins Etiemble in his call for the simultaneous study of the most diverse literatures on earth, and like Etiemble he does so from a decidedly leftist inspiration, albeit that with Moretti this does not so much take the form of ethical engagement as dedication to a certain methodology of what he unabashedly calls his "Marxist formation" (Moretti 2005: 2) under the influence of the Italian philosopher Galvano della Volpe (1895–1968), who advocated a scientific Marxism.

Djelal Kadir in 2004 reacted to Moretti's position with "comparative literature is neither a subject, nor an object, nor is it a problem … comparative literature is a practice. … it is what its practitioners do … comparative literature takes on its significance by what is done in its name and by how those practices become ascertained, instituted, and managed" (Kadir 2004: 1). Kadir calls for a radical re-thinking of comparative literature, and especially for what he sees as the discipline's possible complicity with hegemonic forms of power, and thus for the firm "worlding" of "world literature." The question then becomes, "who carries out its worlding and why?" (Kadir 2004, 2), because the result will always be "the interested outcome of those in a position to assume the subject agency of the verb 'to world' … [and] … the question for us as comparatists who are party to the resonant discourse on world literature, then, is what our own role might be in this worlding" (Kadir 2004: 8). Kadir powerfully revisited the issue in a 2006 article in which he called for a *negotiated comparative literature* that would "negotiate among cultural productions and discursive formations that arrogate to themselves the immunities of incomparability and the impunity of exceptionalism" (Kadir 2006: 133). Such a comparative literature also "would aim to negotiate the relationship between the reigning doxa of any given period and the discipline's apposite accommodation to that paradigm and its cultural *habitus* as *Realkultur*" (Kadir 2006: 135). In other words, such a comparative literature should constantly reflect on its own bases, and particularly on how at any given moment its own methods and pivotal concerns, such as for instance "world literature" right around the turn of the twenty-first century and even more specifically, at least in the USA, after 9/11, correlate to, or perhaps with, the often unspoken power assumptions of the cultures and societies in which they operate. Kadir powerfully returns to these issues in his *Memos from the Besieged City: Lifelines for Cultural Sustainability* (2011).

It seems as if by necessity, then, and not from idealism or choice, that Etiemble's 1960s call for including "the world" is being at last achieved: immediately so through the terrible events of 9/11, but more generally through the pressures of a changing world, the rise of the "global South", the shifting of centers of power to the East, especially China and India. While postcolonialism and multiculturalism were the first intimations of such shifts they were confined to intra-lingual "comparisons" between mother-country versus ex-colony literatures and therefore safely remained within the province of monolingualism, whether English, as initially, or later also French, but did not challenge the "Western" linguistic order. Even if Western linguistic orthodoxy can be said to have come under threat from for instance the creolization theories of Edouard Glissant, a writer and theoretician who is not by coincidence from the Caribbean, the first focus of colonial and later postcolonial interest, this did not necessarily reach beyond national literature departments, or beyond national literature studies or interests. With the 9/11 events and the paradigm shift in power relations in the world brought about by this; the Afghan and Iraq wars and what at first seemed the global reach of the United States as the last superpower, but quickly ushered in what may turn out to be its imminent demise; the capital crisis of 2008 further eroding the power of the US in the world economic market and hence also in the political and military balance, concomitant to, and also contributing to, the rise of Asian nations with a different state and economic model rivaling the US and almost certainly poised to overtake the latter within the near future; the need for other languages imposes itself again. This time, though, it is not European languages that matter but Asian ones. If there is a return, then, of comparative literature in the United States through a renewed interest in world literature this is certainly not the old form of the discipline. Comparative literature in the US now faces East and South rather than "back" towards Europe.

In Europe, meanwhile …

In Europe, meanwhile, comparative literature is involved in rethinking Europe's place in the world, both in terms of the continent's ongoing process of unification and its diminished weight in the world. Hinrich C. Seeba, in a 2003 article, rereads Ernst Robert Curtius as a post-WWII exponent of the return of world literature in the service of the unification of Europe. Seeing Curtius as the European counterpart to the "Americans" Wellek, Spitzer and Auerbach, Seeba claims that:

> The comparative analysis of the themes, motifs and structures of this world literature became the norm for a transatlantic school of literary hermeneutics that regardless of its self-declared ideological disinterest did not only serve to emphasize the immanence of literature: "The Europea-nisation of the historical picture," Curtius declares in the introductory chapter of his book, "is now a political requirement, and this not just for Germany." The aim was not only a new "world literature scholarship," but a new transnational world picture, that would make room in the European peace and unification process for the cultural tradition of the West threatened with extinction.

> (die vergleichende Analyse der Themen, Motive und Strukturen dieser Weltliteratur wurde zur Norm einer transatlantischen Schule der Werk-interpretation, die trotz ihres erklärten Ideologieverzichts nicht nur die literarische Immanenz im Auge hatte: "Europäisierung des Geschichts-bildes," so erklärt Curtius im einleitenden Kapittel seines Buchs, "ist heute politische Erfordernis, und nicht nur für Deutschland." Sie zielte nicht nur auf eine "Weltliteraturwissenschaft," sondern auf ein neues übernationales Weltbild, das die Kulturtradition des vom Untergang bedrohten Abendlandes in die europäischen Friedens-un Einigungsprozess einbringen sollte.)

> (Seeba 2003: 532)

Lucia Boldrini, in 2006, finds that comparative literature in Europe is engaged with "the necessary redefinition of a European comparative literature (a comparative literary re-thinking of what is Europe and what is European at the beginning of the twenty-first century): our role, the role of our discipline, at the present moment, is to rethink Europe, its internal and external bound-aries, how we have historically selected and defined them and how we do so today ... to understand the boundaries we have created and those we have elided, the equivalences we have assumed; how we wish to open Europe up to what constitutes it and what is outside it, opening it to new forces that would be meaningless, today, to call 'other'; and to confront the otherness of the languages that we have traditionally considered to be ours" (Boldrini 2006, 22). If in what Spivak called the "old comparative literature," the one for which she – I think rather gleefully – tolled the death knell in 2003, European literature equaled world literature, Europe's comparatists now are busy (re-) inventing their own "new" comparative literature, returning to their own "pioneers," re-"worlding", to use that term once again, their own discipline, their own literatures, and "European" literature. And there is nothing wrong with that, of course – after all, this merely repeats Goethe's own first thinking of *Weltliteratur* as a corollary to the changes *his* world was undergoing.

Conclusion

- World literature and comparative literature have developed concurrently, sometimes in intimate and sometimes in distant relationship with one another.
- Comparative literature for the first century of its existence has been mostly a European, and even primarily a French discipline, with especially as of the turn of the twentieth century an emphasis on actual comparisons between works, genres, authors, literatures; in this period world literature was considered a rather utopian horizon for comparative literature instead of a feasible proposition.
- After WWII the United States becomes dominant in comparative literature studies; this brings with it a shift of attention to broader issues having to do with what we now call theory of literature, and also to literatures from beyond Europe.
- Since the turn of the millennium the renewed and intense interest comparative literature in the United States has shown in world literature has propelled the discipline to the forefront of literary studies; a large part of this has to do with the reevaluation of America's position in the world after 9/11.
- In the meantime comparative literature in Europe is doing its own re-thinking of itself and of world literature in function of Europe's changing role in the world.

4 World literature as an American pedagogical construct

Overview

In the United States world literature has, since the beginning of the twentieth century, been taught at university level. The reasons for this are to be sought in the specific organization of US secondary and higher education. World literature courses were seen as furnishing new university students with some basic knowledge of their European cultural and literary heritage – knowledge it was found these students were lacking, at variance with their European counterparts. Especially in the first half of the century, such courses often took the form of "Great Books" courses. Although courses in world literature and in Great Books originated with comparative literature departments, they quickly, and for reasons connected with the pressure of numbers, migrated to English departments. All reading in world literature classes was in translation. World literature courses remained at an introductory level. They typically relied on massive anthologies, arranged along chronological or thematic lines, and often gathering numerous short works or excerpts from longer works. For all these reasons world literature classes eventually came to be looked down upon by comparative literature departments. This was especially the case after WWII. During the 1980s and the so-called "culture wars" in the United States, academic world literature courses came under heavy attack because of their historical bias toward European literature. This eventually led to major changes in the material included in world literature courses, and in the anthologies serving them. At the end of the twentieth century, and very explicitly after the turn of the millennium, world literature was reclaimed by comparative literature departments, but its teaching, both as to content and method, led to heated debate. The latter focused most explicitly on whether world literature courses inherently served to confirm and project American hegemony around the world, or whether they might serve to relativize it.

Higher education in the United States

The one question to emerge clearly from Haun Saussy's 2004 American Comparative Literature Association Report published, along with a number of reflections on and responses to it, as *Comparative Literature in an Age of Globalization* in 2006 is, according to the noted American comparatist and structuralist scholar Jonathan Culler, "how comparative literature should deal with 'world literature'" (Culler 2006: 90). "The question is not," he insists, "whether we should study all the literatures of the world, but about the stakes in the construction by comparative literature departments in the United States of 'world literature,' as displayed most concretely in world literature courses. (I suspect that this issue is addressed in quite different ways in other countries)" (Culler 2006: 90).

In fact, until relatively recently what Culler calls an "issue" in the United States would not have been an issue at all for the rest of the world – as Sarah Lawall put it succinctly in 1988: "Courses in world literature are a uniquely American institution. ... world literature exists elsewhere as a scholarly topic or as the subject of ambitious global histories, but it is not an academic institution ... only in the United States do we find a systematic attempt to encompass the 'world' (however defined) in literature courses" (Lawall 1988: 53). Why this is so has to do with the peculiar position of foreign language and literature teaching in United States academe.

In the previous chapter I mentioned that comparative literature in its orthodox definition and in Europe, or at least in Continental Europe, until well past the middle of the twentieth century largely remained the hunting ground of scholars who almost self-evidently possessed the multiple language skills necessary to its practice, and for whom European literature in its major languages was in practice equivalent to world literature. Not so in the Anglophone world. In fact, although the first handbook of comparative literature was written by an Englishman, Hutcheson Macaulay Posnett's 1886 *Comparative Literature*, in England the interest in the discipline has always remained marginal at best. A. Owen Aldridge, in his 1986 *The Reemergence of World Literature*, reported that at the time of his writing there were only three Comparative Literature departments in all of England (Aldridge 1986: 41).

In the US, as in fact in most of Europe, the actual study and teaching of foreign – that is to say mostly Western European – languages only became a matter of concern in the first half of the nineteenth century. When they did, though, scholars such as Henry Wadsworth Longfellow (1807–82), Smith Professor of Modern Languages at Harvard, who qualified himself in a variety of European languages and literatures by several years abroad, can also be said to have been in practice, if not in theory or by the name, comparatists or world literature scholars. However, not all American colleges, or scholars, could afford such luxuries. Moreover, as the nineteenth century wore on and higher education became more generally institutionalized across an increasingly far-flung nation, which toward the end of the nineteenth century also adopted a pattern all of its own when it came to that higher education, there sprang up a peculiarly American division of labor between world literature and comparative literature.

Henry Wadsworth Longfellow (1807–82) was an American poet and scholar, Professor of Romance Literatures at Harvard. He translated Dante's *Divine Comedy*. With the larger public he was popular primarily for longer poems such as *Evangeline* (1847), *The Song of Hiawatha* (1855), and "Paul Revere's Ride" (1861). Longfellow conducted a gigantic correspondence with writers all over Europe and the Americas, and was very popular also abroad. For a long time Longfellow was disparaged as merely having imitated European models, but his reputation has been rising again since the end of the twentieth century.

Toward the end of the nineteenth century American higher education gradually adopted an organizational model that differentiated between research-oriented and more teaching-oriented institutions. The former eventually mostly came to call themselves universities while the latter often retained the appellation of a "college." Colleges typically offered, and often continue to offer, especially when they are so-called "liberal arts colleges," a general four-year undergraduate education roughly equivalent to what in Europe usually already (and at least partly) was offered at high school or secondary education level. The term "college" in Europe actually originally applied to institutes of "higher" learning for fifteen- to eighteen year-olds, or in other words roughly equivalent to the age bracket today covered by "high school" in the USA. In Europe over the course of time some of these colleges grew into universities or university departments; others remained what are now "high schools" in America. To make matters even more confusing, in most Germanic countries, the equivalent to "high school" – that is to say, *Hochschule* (German), *Hogeschool* (Dutch) or *Höjskol* (Danish) – in the nineteenth century came to stand for what we now call universities. With the creation of Prussian-style research universities in the course of that same nineteenth century the term *Hochschule* etc. then became restricted to what in most Romance countries such as France, and also in England, came to be called *Ecoles Polytechniques* or Polytechnics – that is to say, institutes geared to more practical technical learning, whereas "University" (*Universität, Universiteit, Universitet*) became the proper term for research-oriented institutions.

When the United States also adopted the concept of the German-style research-oriented university at the end of the nineteenth century it did so with a difference. In (most of) Europe, students immediately entered a specialized course of studies leading to a marketable specialization, usually after four years of study. Beyond these four years they could do a doctorate or PhD, but very few actually did so. The US opted for a system whereby the first four years of college or university, as in the British system (even though there it often only involved a three-year course of studies), were given over to a broad course of study leading to a more general BA or BS. Specializations in medicine or law only became available as graduate studies, as did study leading to a doctorate in all other disciplines. These graduate degrees in the US comprised, and continue to comprise, a compulsory component of course work. In Europe specialization in one's discipline was considered complete after the first four years and only a dissertation was further required for a doctorate, no course work. In more recent years things have gotten more complex in Europe, largely as a result of the so-called Bologna reform, named after the Italian city in which a number of European ministers of education in 1999 signed a protocol aimed at harmonizing all of Europe's higher education along a three-year BA followed by a two-year MA program.

Why is it necessary to go into such detail on higher education systems in the US and in Europe? Because the widely divergent fortunes of world literature in the US and in Europe are precisely due to this difference in higher education systems. In essence, the US had its BA and BS courses of study do what in Continental Europe (truly or supposedly; I will not get into that) already happened at the level of secondary education, especially at elite schools giving immediate access to university such as gymnasia in Germany, The Netherlands, or the Scandinavian countries, or the *lycées* and *athénées* of the Romance-language countries. The curriculum at such institutions always comprised a certain (and sometimes a fair) amount of foreign language training next to courses in the classics (Greek and Latin), philosophy, history, religious instruction, and the sciences.

In the US, especially away from the Eastern seaboard, such knowledge of languages was not so easy to commonly come by. This was due in part to the widely disparate levels of schooling in the US. It was also due to that country's more democratic (at the time we are speaking of here) attitude toward access to higher education which resulted in a less culturally homogeneous student body than in Europe. Undoubtedly, a working knowledge of foreign languages was for self-evident reasons also felt to be of less importance in the US. Even for the sons of the social and cultural elite, then, foreign languages as a rule were harder to come by in the US than in Europe, and they were not a natural part of one's upbringing, even if Latin and Greek were taught at high school level, and even if some knowledge of French and German, at least passively, may not have been exceptional within certain circles. We might conclude the latter from a brief article entitled "World Literature" that Thomas Wentworth Higginson in 1890 published in the general circulation periodical *The Century*.

Higginson quoted passages in German and French in the original. As Higginson strongly advocated foreign language teaching in the US, though,

Thomas Wentworth Higginson (1823–1911) was an American protestant minister, journalist, author, and fervent abolitionist. He fought for the Union in the Civil War. He also advised Emily Dickinson on her poetry in a series of letters they exchanged.

he may have been only putting his ideals in practice in this particular article. John Pizer (2006) points out that in the same year in which he published his article on "World Literature" Higginson had also published a biography of Margaret Fuller. Fuller was a member of the Transcendentalist Circle around Ralph Waldo Emerson and eventually developed into one of the most influential nineteenth-century US literary critics. In 1839 she was the first to bring out a selection from Eckermann's conversations with Goethe in English translation. Pizer credits Fuller's early acquaintance with Goethe's ideas on world literature for her, at least in America at that time, unusually cosmopolitan outlook on literature. Higginson, then, obviously took his cue from Fuller, and from Goethe, when he called for the teaching of World Literature courses to impart, in Pizer's words, "to students those general values, ideas, and structures he finds at the root of all *belles lettres*" (Pizer 2006: 88). Higginson saw foreign language and literature courses at undergraduate level as a necessary first step in this direction.

Margaret Fuller (1810–50) was an American feminist, journalist, and literary critic. She published *Woman in the Nineteenth Century* (1845), and translated (and abridged) Eckermann's *Conversations with Goethe* (1838).

However, the specific situation the USA found itself in at the turn of the twentieth century did not favor the realization of Higginson's ideals. The US between the middle of the nineteenth century and WWI was undergoing an unprecedented wave of mass immigration. Most of these newcomers were of very different stock than the hitherto dominant British and West-Europeans. Their linguistic and cultural diversity only emphasized the role of English as a necessary agent of acculturation and cohesion in the country. But knowledge of the language was not enough. The need was also felt to actively promote, to quote Pizer again, "general values, ideas, and structures," but not so much those that lay at the root of *belles lettres*, as Higginson had wished; rather those that lay at the root of American culture as perceived by those who considered themselves its guardians. At the university level, this led to courses that introduced the students to "their" cultural heritage. This cultural heritage was thought to be embodied by a number of "Great Books" from the past. These, however, were not restricted to Higginson's *belles lettres* or "literature" proper, but ranged from philosophy over literature to the sciences. Given that these courses were seen as primarily introductory, and hence geared to incoming university students in their first or second year of studies (in American parlance: freshmen or sophomores), and given prevailing language conditions in the US, such courses were inevitably given in English, and with all reading material in English translation. What must have been one of the first, if not the very first, such course was offered in 1901 at Berkeley (Graff

1987: 134). Still, it was only after WWI that Great Books courses became widespread in US higher education.

Richard Moulton

It is against this background that Richard Green Moulton in 1911 published *World Literature and Its Place in General Culture*, the first book-length publication on the subject in English. Moulton was an Englishman who had become first Professor of English and later, as of 1901, Professor of Literary Theory and Interpretation, and Head of the Department of General Literature at the University of Chicago. Before his removal to the USA, though, he had been active in university extension lecturing in England. In his book on world literature he systematized what he had been doing for his working class audience in England also for his US audience, thinking that what was needed in both cases was an introduction to the literatures of the world – read: Europe – as a shorthand for instilling in them a sense of their own nation's culture at the top of Western Civilization. In a sense this was complementary on the home front to what the British had been doing in India over the nineteenth century (Viswanathan 1989). There, following the historian and politician Thomas Babington Macaulay's advice in his 1835 *Minute on Indian Education*, English was introduced as the language of instruction as of the sixth year of schooling. Moreover, the teaching of British literature at both high school and university levels was to instill in the colonial subjects (or at least the more intelligent and more ambitious, but therefore also the potentially more dangerous ones) the right civic – read British – virtues and attitudes. For Macaulay this was entirely to the benefit of the Indians themselves, as the English language and English literature were more useful, and therefore more valuable, to them than their own languages and literatures. As Macaulay famously put it in his *Minute*, "I am quite ready to take the Oriental learning at the valuation of the Orientalists themselves. I have never found one among them who could deny that a single shelf of a good European library was worth the whole native literature of India and Arabia" (Macaulay 2011).

In fact, British literature was taught as a university subject in India before it was taught in Britain itself, where Greek and Latin continued to dominate the humanities curriculum. As of the mid-nineteenth century British literature, through the kind of extension lecturing that Moulton engaged in, was also taught at so-called Working Men's Institutes in Britain itself, partially as a means to instill also in the rising working class the right virtues and attitudes, and this according to the ideas of Matthew Arnold, inspector of schools, poet and social critic. After WWI, as a corollary to growing democratization, the study of English, and to a lesser extent of modern languages and literatures, gradually came to take the place of the classics for a growing student body increasingly recruited from (relatively) lower social levels in England. During and immediately after WWI the American (later English) modernist poet T.S. Eliot engaged in extension lecturing in London. The emphasis on Arnold's 1869 injunction in *Culture and Anarchy* to make "the best that has been thought and known current in the world everywhere" (Arnold 1978: 70) would eventually lead the English critic F.R. Leavis (1895–1978) to effectively cast a selection of four English-language writers (Jane Austen, George Eliot, Henry James and Joseph Conrad; Leavis later added Charles Dickens) as something akin to "world literature" in his *The Great Tradition* (1948).

Moulton's book aimed at the same audience as the "Great Books" courses, and so he too had to rely on translations rather than on works in the original. Moreover, though Moulton bravely began the title of his book with "World Literature," its continuation "and Its Place in General Culture" indicates that what Moulton had in mind was in fact not too far removed from what "Great Books" courses had already started doing in the US by then. In his Preface he says that his book "presents a conception of World Literature, not in the sense of the sum total of particular literatures, but as a unity, the literary field seen in perspective from the point of view of the English-speaking peoples" (Moulton 1921: v). In the main body of his book he follows up on this with the statement that world literature will be "a different thing to the Englishman and the Japanese" (Moulton 1921: 7) and therefore, as an Englishman, he will "trace the Literary Pedigree of the English-speaking peoples" (Moulton 1921: 9). Or, as he puts it later on, "whatever of universal literature [by which he means all literature from all the world], coming from whatever source, has been appropriated by our English civilization, and made a part of our English culture, that is to us World Literature" (Moulton 1921: 297). Though Moulton's insistence that his choice of material is based on "intrinsic literary interest" (Moulton 1921:8) or "intrinsic literary value" (Moulton 1921: 9) indicates that he wanted to set his enterprise apart from the Great Books courses in which the emphasis was on ideas rather, his claim that world literature is "nothing less than the Autobiography of Civilization" (Moulton 1921: 56) reveals that his "World Literature" too amounts to a form of "cultural heritage" for the use of "English-speaking peoples."

Building on Matthew Arnold's ideas about the Hellenic and Hebraic origins of European civilization as well as on then current theories about the linguistic and racial relationships of Europeans, and especially the English, to the rest of the world's peoples, Moulton divides the world's literatures into a number of categories dependent on their relevance to the literatures of the "English-speaking peoples" at the beginning of the twentieth century. In a general introduction Moulton first singles out the two "civilizations" that he saw as directly feeding into the culture of the English-speaking peoples via their Hebraic and Hellenic components: the "Semitic" and "Aryan" civilizations. Next, he lists as "extraneous" a number of civilizations, such as the Chinese and Japanese, that he deems not to have had any influence on English literary culture.

In the main part of his book Moulton first distinguishes a number of works that are so important that he dubs them "Literary Bibles" and to each of which he devotes a full chapter. The first of these, not surprisingly, is the Holy Bible itself, followed by "Classical Epic and Tragedy," "Shakespeare," "Dante and Milton: The Epics of Medieval Catholicism and Renaissance Protestantism," and "Versions of the Story of Faust," – the latter focusing on works by the Englishman Christopher Marlowe, The Spaniard Pedro Calderón de la Barca, and especially Goethe. One chapter deals with what Moulton calls "Collateral World Literature," by which he means works from the Semitic and Aryan civilizations that have contributed elements towards European, and particularly English, literature. Here Moulton discusses a.o. the Quran, the *Arabian Nights*, the Persian poet Omar Khayyam, James McPherson's (pseudo)Celtic *Ossian*, the Norse epic of Sigurd, and the Finnish *Kalevala*. Then there is a chapter on "the comparative reading that instinctively draws together similarities and contrasts from different parts of the literary field" (Moulton 1921: 408). One such instance of comparative reading across time and space he adduces is that grouping together the *Bacchanals* of the ancient Greek playwright Euripides, *Ecclesiastes* from the Bible, Omar Khayyam's *Rubaiyat*, the second book of the sixteenth-century English poet Edmund Spenser's *The Fairie Queene*, and "The Vision of Sin" by the nineteenth-century English poet Alfred Tennyson on the grounds that they all deal with "moral chaos" (Moulton 1921: 374). Then there is a chapter on "The Literature of Personality: Essays and Lyrics," and one on "Strategic Points in Literature," defined as "points in the literary field which are especially valuable for their bearing on the survey of the field of literature as a whole" (Moulton 1921: 408). Basically, he here includes a number of authors and works that he considers not quite important enough to figure into any one of his "Literary Bibles," but too important to pass over without mention: the ancient classical writers Plato, Lucretius, and Aristophanes; the medieval *The Romance of the Rose*, *Reynard the Fox*, and *Everyman*; Thomas Malory's *Morte d'Arthur* and Chaucer's *Canterbury Tales*; Spenser's *Fairie Queene*, the medieval French Froissart's *Chronicles,* Cervantes' *Don Quijote*; the Renaissance philosophers Desiderius Erasmus and Francis Bacon; the seventeenth-century French playwrights Molière and Racine; the nineteenth-century historical novelists Walter Scott and Sienkywicz; French writers Rabelais, Balzac and Victor Hugo; and the nineteenth-century English Romantics Byron and Wordsworth. In his next to last chapter Moulton draws a parallel between national literature and world literature in the sense that if national literature is, as "is generally recognized" (Moulton 1921: 429), a reflection of the national history of the country in question, so "World Literature is autobiography in the sense that it is the presentation of civilization in its best products, its most significant moments emphasized as they appear illuminated with the highest literary setting" (Moulton 1921: 437). Precisely because it is the "Autobiography of Civilization," *their* civilization, Moulton argues in his "Conclusion," world literature should be part of American students' general education, "not to be considered as an option that may be taken late, but as an essential in the foundation stage of education, part of the common body of knowledge which makes the election of optional studies intelligent" (Moulton 1921: 447).

Albert Guérard, in his 1940 *Preface to World Literature*, resurrects Moulton's "Literary Bibles." However, instead of making Goethe's *Faust* one of several works by various authors on the same figure, he opts for a generous selection from the principal works of Goethe as his Fifth Bible. Two more Bibles are meant to offset one another: that of *Romance*, from the medieval French writer Chrétien de Troyes to the American poet Edwin Arlington Robinson, and of *Ironic Nationalism*, from the *Romance of the Rose* and Chaucer over Cervantes to the twentieth-century English novelist Aldous Huxley's *Eyeless in Gaza*. Finally, there is what Guérard calls the *Bible of Social Pity*, from the early writings of Victor Hugo over Charles Dickens, the great Russians Fyodor Dostoevsky and Leo Tolstoy, and the French naturalist Emile Zola and his German counterpart Gerhart Hauptmann to the American John Steinbeck's *Grapes of Wrath*.

The Great Books

Moulton's recommendation to make world literature an integral part of the early stages of American university education found ready application, but his valiant effort to imbue such foundational courses with an almost exclusively literary content would have to wait a while yet. For the time being it was the more orthodox Great Books courses that carried the day, and not world literature courses. In the aftermath of WWI the concern to introduce students to the Western heritage probably outweighed that of turning them into critical readers of that heritage. With large numbers of soldiers returning from Europe and being entitled to educational benefits, along with an increased ambition for upward mobility through advanced education on the part of the fast growing middle class, American higher education became increasingly democratized. Most of these aspiring undergraduates had no foreign language skills or training whatsoever, nor did they have any training in the classics. John Erskine (1879–1951), Professor of English at Columbia University, during WWI had taught the equivalent of Moulton's extension lecture courses to US soldiers, and on his return to Columbia he proposed, and in 1920 got accepted, the introduction of a General Honors Course teaching the classics in English translation to all undergraduates. Eventually this developed into a two-course two-semester core curriculum. One course, called "Contemporary Civilization," concentrated on philosophical works. The other course became the famous "Humanities A" course, and concentrated on literary masterpieces. Comparable courses were instituted at the University of Chicago in 1931 and at Stanford in 1935, and from then on in countless US universities. As Herbert Lindenberger notes, these courses at least initially often went by the title of "Western Civilization" (Lindenberger 1990: s.l.).

Erskine's Great Books course (though he himself never called it by that name, nor did or does Columbia University), and others like it, were tailored to set students on a minimal common cultural footing firmly anchored in the Western tradition. Some of Columbia's most famous faculty members, such as for instance Lionel Trilling (1905–75), for many years taught "Humanities A." It continues today under the title "Literature Humanities" and comprises perennial classics – that is to say, works that have never left its list of required reading – such as Homer's *The Iliad*, Aeschylus' *Oresteia*, Sophocles' *Oedipus the King*, Dante's *The Inferno*, and William Shakespeare's *King Lear*, while works by, for instance, Augustine, Montaigne, and Virginia Woolf, as well as the Bible, have rotated on an off. That the aims of "Lit Hum," as it is commonly called, continue to reflect some of the ideas underlying the original Great Books courses appears from the description of the course on Columbia's website as "designed to enhance students' understanding of main lines of literary and philosophical development that have shaped western thought for nearly three millennia." Lest we should think that at the beginning of the third millennium things have not moved on from the early twentieth century, however, the next sentence hastens to add that "much more than a survey of great books, Lit Hum encourages students to become critical readers of the literary past we have inherited" (http://www.college.columbia.edu/core/lithum; accessed 11/10/10). That Lit Hum left a great impression on Columbia students can be gauged from David Denby's *Great Books: My Adventures with Homer, Rousseau, Woolf, and Other Indestructible Writers of the Western World* (1996). Denby re-attended the Lit Hum course at Columbia in 1991, thirty years after he had first attended it as a freshman. He had become enraged by how politicized the debate on literary canons had become during the so-called "culture wars" raging in the United States during the 1980s and 1990s. Therefore he decided to go and ascertain for himself what this debate was all about in a course that centered, precisely and deliberately so, upon the Western canon.

World literature courses

Courses that went by the label "World Literature," and that more closely resembled what Moulton had in mind at least as far as their content was concerned, were pioneered in the late 1920s by Philo Buck, Professor of Comparative Literature at the University of Wisconsin. One difference between world literature and Great Books courses was that the former concentrated on works of the imagination or literature proper while the latter concentrated on the ideas contained in a number of works of varied provenance. A further difference, Pizer (2006: 101) contends, is that a Great Books course concentrates on just a few major and unabridged works while a world literature course typically is built around an anthology that comprises a multitude of shorter works and passages from longer works in an effort to achieve some representative historical and geographical coverage. Surely this is what we would deduce from the *Anthology of World Literature*, based on his class teachings, that Buck brought out in 1934 and that Lawall (Lawall 2004: 59–60) labels "the first single-volume academic anthology to attempt global scope." Buck, as Moulton advocated, focused on the European tradition, although he also included some Indian, Persian, and Arab materials while, again like Moulton, excluding works from China and Japan on the grounds that their "vital influence upon the European tradition has been negligible or very recent" (Buck 1934: v). In later editions he did add some Chinese works. However, and at variance with Moulton's recommendations, Buck included no English-language works in his anthology.

As we have seen in the first chapter, Buck's not including English-language works in his *Anthology of World Literature* was not unprecedented. It was not unusual to see world literature as complementary to one's national literature, and Buck too may have been seeing his enterprise, and the course in world literature he gave and which his anthology served, as complementary to courses in English and American literature. What may also have played a role is the traditional "turf war" between university departments. This certainly came to the fore after WWII, when world literature courses rapidly became the province of English departments rather than, as with Buck and in the initial stages of their introduction, comparative literature departments. There are a number of reasons for this, but prime among these is the further round of democratization of American higher education brought about by WWII. Indicative in this regard may be the brief remark by the West Virginia educator and superintendent of schools Oliver Shurtleff who in 1947 was quoted as having said to the *West Virginia School Journal* that "if I were to be asked to add a subject to the curriculum of high schools and colleges, I should add World Literature ... At this very time in the history of our world, this addition, it seems to me, would be quite pertinent" (Shurtleff 1947: 5).

Next to answering to a genuinely felt need to open more "windows on the world," to use David Damrosch's phrase (Damrosch 2003: 15), now that the US – because of WWII – had not only come out of the relative isolation into which it had withdrawn in the period between the two world wars but also actually found itself to be the strongest nation on earth, the rapid popularization of world literature courses focusing on works of the imagination rather than on "ideas" as in Great Books courses was probably not unrelated to the parallel rise to dominance of the so-called "New Criticism" in the US. This critical and educational movement, primarily centered in English departments, focused on the intrinsic qualities of the literary work as artifact and structure rather than on the historical and biographical details of its creation. When in many places world literature courses became compulsory for undergraduates, the traditionally small comparative literature departments that before and immediately after WWII had started offering such courses simply could not cope with the rapidly swelling student numbers. Moreover, many comparative literature professors were reluctant to teach what they considered as degraded versions of what they really should be teaching.

Indeed, while Higginson, Moulton, Erskine, and Buck were diligently plugging away at promoting Great Books and world literature courses in English translation and for undergraduates, "real" Departments of Comparative Literature swore by courses on which literature was read in the original. In practice, this meant that they limited themselves to graduate teaching, as American students in general needed their undergraduate years to work up the necessary language skills to even be considered for enrollment in a comparative literature program or department. The combined result was that when the crunch came, world literature, being taught as it was in English and via translations into English, rapidly migrated to the biggest language department around, which invariably happened to be the English department anyway.

The New Critical paradigm, moreover, did away with – at least in theory and often in practice – any real need to have an intimate knowledge of a work's historical or linguistic background, or its author's biography. Given the supposedly low degree of specialization required to teach these courses, then, they often were assigned to junior faculty members. As these were almost invariably trained in English literature themselves, world literature courses rapidly came to be seen as at least partially a preparation for the study of English and even American literature, providing students with a minimal knowledge of Western literature as a prelude to their engagement with what really mattered (Brown 1953). In fact, Sarah Lawall, who over the last twenty years or so (and mainly on the basis of her general editorship of the more recent editions of the *Norton Anthology of World Literature*) has been one of the most influential commentators on the anthologizing of world literature, narrates that back in the mid-1970s when she first became involved with what was then still called the *Norton Anthology of World Masterpieces* she had never seen the anthology before because "teaching French, Francophone, and comparative literature" she functioned in a "curricular framework that did not include world literature – the course was 'owned' by the English department" (Lawall 2004: 69).

The crisis of world literature

This state of affairs led to a major standoff between world literature and comparative literature at the end of the 1950s. At a Conference on "The Teaching of World Literature" held at Philo Buck's University of Wisconsin in April 1959, the Swiss-American comparatist Werner Friederich, Professor of Comparative Literature at the University of North Carolina in Chapel Hill, humorously but also scathingly rehearsed all that was wrong with world literature courses from the point of view of "legitimate" comparative literature departments. They promised more than they could deliver – in a famous diatribe he proclaimed that "sometimes, in flippant moments, I think we should call our programs NATO Literatures – yet even that would be extravagant, for we do not usually deal with more than one fourth of the 15

NATO-nations" (Friederich 1960: 14–15). They were taught in translation, laying them open to the accusation of amateurism. They used anthologies that because of the brevity and multiplicity of passages included confused the students. Finally, they were mostly taught by younger faculty members who were not really up to a job that would have been daunting even to experienced professors skilled in various foreign languages next to English (Friederich 1960: 14–18). In short, Friederich argued, such courses threatened the integrity of the discipline of comparative literature. Therefore, he advocated that world literature courses taught to freshmen and sophomores really be Great Books courses focusing on only a few major works or authors: "the true giants in literature – Aeschylus, Virgil, perhaps Petrarch, Molière, Schiller, Dostoevski," and that they be used to illustrate "the basic meaning of Antiquity, Middle Ages, Renaissance, Classicism, Romanticism, Realism, Naturalism" (Friederich 1960: 17.) In another version of the same article/speech Friederich replaced Petrarch with Chaucer (Friederich 1970: 31). These courses should then be followed by "Foreign Literature in English Translation" courses covering a given foreign literature or a cluster of such literatures, and, given by specialists in the literatures concerned, they should be resolutely restricted to the undergraduate level.

Such a set of courses, Friedrich felt, would provide "a truly liberal education" for "a businessman, a physician, or a professor of English" (Friederich 1970: 35). If given well, Friederich hoped, such courses might even lead talented undergraduates to pursue graduate study in comparative literature proper, reading and studying literary works not in translation but in the original. At that graduate level, though, he also pleaded for extending the reach of comparative literature beyond its traditional European domain to embrace the cultures of Latin America, Asia, Africa, and Oceania. With its mixture of races and cultures, its history of migration, its geographical location, and its world leadership in matters military, economic and political, Friederich concluded, the US was uniquely well placed to take the lead in matters cultural too, and part of such leadership would be a greater opening to the world beyond Europe and the US itself. Yet, just a few years earlier, in 1954, Friederich, along with David Henry Malone, had published an *Outline of Comparative Literature: from Dante Alighieri to Eugene O'Neill* that stayed well within the framework of the world literature courses he so critically scrutinized in 1959. Offering "a new panorama of Western literature" Friederich and Malone aimed to present "the constant flow of forms and ideas across national borders and the dissemination of cultural values among neighboring countries" as showing "the essential oneness of Western culture and the stultifying shortsightedness of political or literary nationalism" (Friederich and Malone 1954: Preface).

The Wisconsin Conference where Friederich spoke followed closely after the ICLA Conference at his own University of North Carolina in Chapel Hill where René Wellek had denounced "the French School" for "The Crisis in Comparative Literature." Friederich's rather triumphant statements with regard to the future of comparative literature in American academe reflected the already widely accepted belief, at least in the US, that "America had more than caught up with the leadership of France in the field of Comparative Literature" (Friederich 1960: 18). Given the strict separation between undergraduate and graduate teaching Friederich advocated, and given also that world literature courses largely remained under the wings of English literature departments, it took a while before the new wind that was felt to blow in US comparative literature departments also was felt in world literature teaching. Moreover, as sketched in the previous chapter, the turn to theory comparative literature departments took in the years after the Chapel Hill conference led them away from the concerns with the larger world as expressed by Friederich.

Ironically, it was a French scholar, René Etiemble, who most vocally took up these concerns (Etiemble 1966). Even more ironically given Wellek's denunciation of the French school of comparative literature, the theory US comparative literature departments turned to was largely French again. The first to arrive was phenomenological criticism as practiced by the so-called Geneva School (Lawall 1968). Main adherents in the US were the early J. Hillis-Miller along with the Belgian Georges Poulet (1902–91), who taught at Johns Hopkins in the 1950s. Shortly thereafter Paul de Man (1919–83; another Belgian) was instrumental in disseminating the thought of Jacques Derrida (1930–2004) in the US. In the 1970s De Man was one – many would say *the* – leader of the so-called Yale school of deconstructionism. As of the 1970s English departments also entered the age of theory, with the fervor of various waves of structuralism, poststructuralism, deconstructionism, new historicism, multiculturalism and postcolonialism rapidly succeeding each other. Most of this, though, primarily applied to graduate study and research. World literature meanwhile kept quietly bubbling along as an undergraduate course.

Anthologizing world literature: the "Norton"

In fact, the proliferation of World Literature courses in the US led to the creation, in the mid-1950s, of a working instrument tailored to the new conditions – that is to say, a major anthology that combined Buck's focus on foreign literature with Moulton and Guérard's inclusion of English-language literatures in their surveys. Norton's *World Masterpieces: Literature of Western Culture* appeared in 1956. In line with the by then well-established practice for world literature courses to be taught within an English department, the Norton's general editor was a specialist in English literature: Maynard Mack (1909–2001). Mack had a particular interest in Early Modern to Augustan literature, and strongly promoted New Criticism in the English department he led for many years at Yale University. The other editors were drawn from English again, as well as from Classics, Italian, French, Slavics, and comparative literature. Many of them taught at Yale, among them René Wellek. Through its third edition, in 1973, the anthology went under the same title as the original edition. The fourth edition carried the title *The Norton Anthology of World Masterpieces: Literature from Western Culture*. The fifth and sixth editions, from 1985 and 1992 respectively, dropped the subtitle. An *Expanded Edition* appeared in 1995. In 2002 this expanded edition turned into *The Norton Anthology of World Literature*, Second Edition. In the meantime there was also a seventh edition of *The Norton Anthology of World Masterpieces*, this time subtitled *The Western Tradition*.

The name changes the Norton underwent are of course not arbitrary or coincidental. Most immediately, they reflected the changes affecting the study of English and American literature as of the late eighties. This is the moment that multiculturalism, in American studies, and postcolonialism, in English studies, took over from "pure" theory as the leading paradigms. Predictably, this led to loud calls for a much expanded canon (hence the 1995 Norton *Expanded Edition*) comprising generous selections of works by minority writers in the case of American literature, and by writers from the former British colonies for English literature. The ensuing so-called "Culture Wars" also led to the then current core curriculum undergraduate courses in Western literature being increasingly challenged as to their continuing relevance for a rapidly changing and increasingly diverse American student body, as well as for an equally rapidly changing world. Most famous in this respect became the struggle in 1988 over Stanford's Western Culture course, the then descendant – with a brief hiatus in the late 1960s and 1970s – of the 1935 Western Civilization course. Lindenberger (1990: s.l.) lists this course as comprising: "Hebrew Bible, Genesis; Homer, major selections from *Iliad* or *Odyssey* or both; At least one Greek tragedy; Plato, *Republic*, major portions of Books I–VII; New Testament, selections including a gospel; Augustine, *Confessions*, I-IX; Dante, *Inferno*; More, *Utopia*; Machiavelli, *The Prince*; Luther, *Christian Liberty*; Galileo, *The Starry Messenger* and *The Assayer*; Voltaire, *Candide*; Marx and Engels, *The Communist Manifesto*; Darwin, selections; Freud, *Outline of Psychoanalysis* and *Civilization and Its Discontents*." Inclusion of the *Aeneid*, selections from Thomas Aquinas, Hobbes's *Leviathan*, Goethe's *Faust* and *Werther*, and a nineteenth-century novel to be chosen by the instructor, were "strongly recommended." These works formed the common core to a number of tracks that allowed considerable variety in reading and contextualization. Still, after complaints from a number of minority groups on campus and after long debates in the University Senate, the Western Culture core course was replaced with a new one called "Cultures, Ideas, Values" that did not require a fixed set of common texts but the contents of which would be democratically decided upon from year to year by the faculty members teaching the course that particular year. It was stipulated, though, that each track around this core course must "include the study of works by women, minorities, and persons of color" and must study "at least one of the non-European cultures that have become components of our diverse American society" (Lindenberger 1990: s.l.). The changes to the Stanford program made the national headlines, and became a battleground between political and cultural conservatives, such as Allen Bloom and the then Secretary of State for Education William Bennett, and more generally left-wing progressives. One party lamented that Stanford was selling out "American" culture by debasing and diluting its cultural heritage. The other party upheld that the "old" canon had been restrictively and unjustifiably male, white, and Eurocentric.

While earlier editions of the Norton anthology had also already responded to claims, for example from feminist quarters, for wider representation, it is clear that the changes in the name and contents of the Norton anthology as of the fourth edition were increasingly determined by the claims of multi-culturalism and postcolonialism. The *Expanded Edition* of 1995 basically added an equal number of pages of non-Western texts to the earlier exclusively Western edition. The Norton until the *Expanded Edition* indeed was (almost) exclusively Western. That is also why from the late 1980s and early 1990s on it came under attack by proponents of change. It was also the most successful anthology of its kind until then, to the point even of seeming to define the field in its "old" dispensation, and that is undoubtedly why it also became the foil against which all newcomers in what was suddenly perceived as a different market reacted. As Sarah Lawall, who had joined the Norton editorial team as of the 1979 Fourth Edition, and who became the general editor with the 1999 seventh edition, felt obliged to remark in 2004, when at least three major competitors had appeared on the market: "many critics (especially those connected with new anthologies) seem to believe that the world literature anthology began in 1956 with the first edition of *The Norton Anthology of World Masterpieces* and that the future consists solely in reacting to the presumed origin" (Lawall 2004: 63). Not only was there a well-established and flourishing tradition of earlier world literature anthologies, including Buck's mentioned earlier, she argues, but by the middle of the twentieth century there had also sprung up a "consistent set of beliefs and practices that would shape – and continue to shape – anthologies of 'world literature'" (Lawall 2004: 62). These included an almost exclusive concern for a literary work's cultural status but "little or no concern for analysis or pedagogy," an orientation toward "the generic-American-English-speaking student," an "educational mission to give this generic student a perspective on human evolution from barbarism to civilization, with special emphasis on Western tradition as the foundation of twentieth-century America," and an unspoken understanding that "the writers are male and, for the most part, European" (Lawall 2004: 62).

The 1956 Norton *World Masterpieces: Literature of Western Culture*, Lawall says, broke with these assumptions in the following ways: "The encouragement of critical thinking and literary analysis instead of prescribed outlines of cultural history; a focus on imaginative literature instead of the transmission of Great Books; a preference for complete works instead of myriad extracts; and – aimed specifically at classroom teaching – an unprecedented amount of information about the texts: analyses of works, textual annotations, and individual bibliographies" (Lawall 2004: 63–64). In fact, because it went so blatantly against then current practice it proved very difficult to find a publisher for what eventually became "the Norton." Prentice-Hall and Harcourt Brace, two of the biggest players in the American textbook market, turned the project down after initially having declared an interest in it. Finally, the anthology was taken on board by W.W. Norton and Co., a smaller publisher willing to take a risk. In other words, Lawall stresses, the Norton anthology was innovative in its day, and continued to be so, for instance including already in its 1985 edition a section "Contemporary Explorations" that made room for non-Western voices. Not by coincidence she claims some merit for the introduction of this particular innovation herself. Although not with so many words again, it is evident that she claims the same kind of merit for the transformation of the *Expanded Edition*, the last to appear under the general editorship of Maynard Mack, and which she calls unwieldy for a number of reasons, into the dual *Norton Anthology of World Masterpieces: The Western Tradition* and *Norton Anthology of World Literature* from the moment she took over as general editor in the late 1990s. Undoubtedly, although again she never explicitly alludes to it as such, Lawall, who was herself Professor of Comparative Literature at the University of Massachusetts, Amherst, also sees herself assuming the general editorship leading to the modernization of the Norton as reclaiming the territory of world literature from the English departments where for the longest time it had lingered. For all these reasons she is obviously not very happy with what she calls "a tendency to mystify 'the Norton' that is ultimately not very useful when examining theoretical or practical issues of anthology making or the persistent shaping power of certain historical and analytical habits; moreover, such mystification obscures the way that many of these habits persevere – if in more sophisticated form – today" (Lawall 2004: 63).

The Norton's competitors

One of the critics connected with a more recent anthology that Lawall has in mind is no doubt David Damrosch. Damrosch, like Lawall, is Professor of Comparative Literature, at Columbia University until 2008, and at Harvard since then. He served as contributing editor to the 1994 *HarperCollins World Reader* under the general editorship of Mary Ann Caws and Christopher Prendergast. He also served as consultant on the Mesoamerican additions to the Norton *Expanded Edition* of 1995. Most importantly, though, he authored a major theoretical study of the field, *What is World Literature?* in 2003 and served as general editor himself for the 6-volume *Longman Anthology of World Literature* published in 2004 (Second Edition 2008–9). In a 2000 article, reprinted in Di Leo 2004, Damrosch had severely criticized both the Norton *Expanded Edition* and the *HarperCollins World Reader*. The *Harper-Collins World Reader*, he found, "proceeds essentially by exploding the 'old world,' making room for a vivid gallery of snapshots of the 'whole world,' yet the result is fragmentary, inconsistent, a disorienting series of abrupt leaps from one brief selection to another" (Damrosch 2004: 41). The Norton *Expanded Edition* he found lacking in integration between the "old" and "whole" world parts. Drawing a line from some early twentieth-century anthologists to the HarperCollins and Norton anthologies he claimed world literature to have oscillated between extremes of assimilation and discontinuity: "either the earlier and distant works we read are really *just like us*, or they are unutterably foreign, curiosities whose foreignness finally tells us nothing and can only reinforce our sense of separate identity" (Damrosch 2004: 44). Instead of acquiescing in having to choose between what he calls "a self-centered construction of the world" and "a highly decentered one," Damrosch proposes "an *elliptical* approach" in which contemporary America will "logically be one focus of the ellipse for the contemporary American reader, but the literature of other times and eras always presents us with another focus as well, and we read in the field of force generated between these two foci" (Damrosch 2004: 44). The ideas he presented in this article, and which he had already defended also in earlier publications, likewise provided the groundwork for his 2003 *What is World Literature?*

Whereas the *Norton Anthology of World Literature*, like its other Norton predecessors, is strictly chronological in organization, both the *Bedford Anthology of World Literature*, edited by Paul Davis, Gary Harrison et al (2003), and the *Longman Anthology of World Literature*, while still adhering to chronology for their overall organizing principle, also introduce thematic units that cut across chronology. In the Longman anthology, for instance, a number of selections feature "resonances." The ancient Greek Homer's *Odyssey* is thus followed by the early twentieth-century Austrian-Czech-Jewish Franz Kafka's story "The Silence of the Sirens," the mid-twentieth-century Greek poet George Seferis's poem "Upon a Foreign Verse," and selections from Derek Walcott's late twentieth-century Caribbean epic *Omeros*. All of these, of course, refer to (events in) the *Odyssey*. In this particular case the three works resonating with the "original" are all themselves works of the imagination, from the same period (the twentieth century), and although written in three different languages (German, Greek, English, though the latter with the input of French Caribbean "créole"), they also come from what we could roughly define as "the West," although again of course this could be contested with regard to Wallcott and his *Omeros*, which is an icon of postcolonialism and as such can be seen as dissenting from the Western tradition. In other instances, though, the resonances can be critical reactions to an original, can come from different periods, and from both West and "non-West." This is the case with (a passage from) Kuntaka's "The Life-force of Literary Beauty," Goethe's "On *Shakuntala*," and (a passage from) Rabindranath Tagore's "Shakuntala: Its Inner Meaning," all of them relating to the original play *Shakuntala* by the classical Sanskrit writer Kalidasa. Next to these "resonances" the Longman also features "perspectives," units that gather material on a specific topic. An example is the "perspective" on "Tyranny and Democracy" with texts by the ancient Greeks Solon, Thucydides and Plato. Both the Norton and the Longman carefully list already in the table of contents in which language a text was originally written, and they list the translator. Both anthologies also take care to let chronology decide on sequence, with in many cases sections on non-Western literatures preceding those on Western literatures. Thus all possible care seems to be taken to offer as evenhanded a survey of "world literature" as possible.

Yet Lawall, writing in 2004, after the publication of her own *Norton Anthology of World Literature* in 2002, and obviously feeling that Damrosch's critique of 2000 is no longer warranted, implicitly takes both the *Bedford Anthology of World Literature* and Damrosch's *Longman Anthology of World Literature* to task for basically reverting to an approach that she has just been at pains to demonstrate that the original 1956 Norton was precisely designed to transcend – that is to say, a focus on cultural rather than literary issues, and dispersal over a wide range of shorter extracts rather than concentration on fewer complete works. While praising the newer anthologies for their "viable approaches to cultural complexity" and for including "a wide range of valuable material," Lawall also finds that by doing so they "shift attention to a higher, combinatory level while minimizing the time spent on rereading individual texts"(Lawall 2004: 83). Instead, she argues, the Norton continues to follow "a work-centered approach using a wide variety of texts and with the study of aesthetic structures as a way to elucidate the intersecting paths of meaning ... that situate a text" (Lawall 2004: 85). Indeed, she even somewhat defiantly suggests that the *Norton Anthology of World Literature* deliberately courts unpopularity because of its consistently aesthetic approach to literature in an age when "'aesthetic'. ... has a bad press" (Lawall 2004: 85).

Worlding world literature

One thing that is clear from Culler's statement cited at the beginning of this chapter, and from world literature anthologies published since 2000, is that the initiative has passed again from English departments to departments of comparative literature. With the exception of the Bedford anthology, the four editors of which are all professors (sometimes emeriti) at the University of New Mexico, both the general editors and a significant number, if not the majority, of the subsidiary editors of the Norton and the Longman hail from comparative literature departments. Ideally, this should facilitate opening up world literature to the world beyond that covered by English-language literature. Here, however, the importance of Culler's remark that what is presently at stake is how comparative literature departments in the US construct "world literature" in their world literature courses comes to the fore. In a number of recent articles on comparative and world literature Djelal Kadir, has referred to this as "worlding" (Kadir 2004, 2006, 2010). What he means is that the comparatist talking of world literature should be aware of "where she is coming from" so as to avoid unconsciously reproducing the hegemonic unbalances of power in the world that she professes to correct by furthering the cause of "world" literature over any form of national literature. For Kadir the "compelling question" is "who carries out [world literature's, TD] world-ing and why," and "the inevitable issue is the locus where the fixed foot of the compass that describes the globalizing circumscription is placed" (Kadir 2004: 2).

This, then, is where we have to utter some reservations as to all recent anthologies of world literature, and where we have to at least partly concur with Lawall as to the continuation, albeit it in a more sophisticated form, as she put it, of habits that date back at least to the middle of the twentieth century. Let me hasten to add that it would seem very difficult to change these habits anyway, which only goes to show to what an extent they are part and parcel of the teaching of world literature in the United States. To begin with, even though as I have just mentioned the Norton and the Longman have a cast of editors that is largely drawn from comparative literature, by far the majority of these – there are very few exceptions indeed – is American or at least teaches at an American university. Perhaps one will object that this is only normal as the US seems to be the only country where world literature courses are being taught. It is hard to see, though, how the relatively homo-geneous provenance of these teams of editors would not influence their choi-ces and, perhaps more importantly still, their stance toward these choices. Inevitably, there emerges an American view on world literature. Second, there is no denying that the HarperCollins, Bedford, and Longmans anthologies are geared towards what Lawall called the generic American student. In line with changing demography and expectations of political correctness, of course, that generic American student is now no longer seen as predominantly white and male, but rather as inherently multicultural, with perhaps even a bias in favor of the former minorities as far as representation of non-Western works is concerned, but also with regard to works from the Western tradition. Still, the emphasis remains on the American-English-speaking student in that all material is presented in English translation and, at least if we are to believe Lawall's evaluations of the Bedford and the Longman anthologies as earlier summarized, is selected and arranged so as to provide that student with a comprehensive idea of his or her "cultural heritage," however much expanded that heritage may be as compared to the previously exclusive emphasis on the Western cultural heritage. For all these reasons all these anthologies – and I would include the Norton now – always remain skewed with regard to the rest of the world, as Gayatri Spivak implies in her 2003 *Death of a Discipline*, when she expresses her suspicion of contemporary world literature antholo-gies in English translation. She implies that such anthologies, while aiming initially at the US academic market but in practice pre-empting that of the entire world, linguistically, presenting and hence reducing all the world's

literatures to "in English" literature, and culturally, by "U.S.-style world literature becoming the staple of Comparative Literature in the global South,"
project the world as "American" to Americans and "America" as the world to
non-Americans (Spivak 2003: 39). Notwithstanding the best of intentions,
then, American proponents of world literature always risk turning the practice
of what they are doing against their avowed aims, thus perhaps unconsciously
and almost against the grain upholding a cultural hegemony they consciously
profess to be combating.

Two considerations here impose themselves. The first has to do with the
issue of translation. This has always been a contentious issue in world literature, and I will return to it in a later chapter. Suffice it here to say that
translation has very much become a focus of attention in literary studies, and
specifically in comparative literature, over the last fifteen years. There are
two solutions to the threat of a basically self-confirming "world projection"
inherent in the presentation of the literatures of the world exclusively in
English (American) translation. The first, as was the proposal already of
Friederich, is to study all materials in the original. This is obviously not a
viable possibility given the multiplicity of languages involved and the
nature of American undergraduate education. The second and more feasible
option is to adopt what to Goethe was the highest form of translation – that
is to say, a translation that preserves the strangeness, the foreignness of the
original and thus, literally, brings home to the reader, in this case the student,
that she is stepping into an "other" world. This is a world that can be rendered comprehensible but that can never be completely apprehended, that
cannot, so to speak, be "domesticated" to the point where the student starts
to feel familiar with it. In other words, it is a world that never can be made
her "own."

This brings me to the second consideration. Even with the best of
anthologies available, a course in world literature can only cover a limited
part of the wealth of material offered in any anthology. What gets taught,
then, and how it is taught in final instance depends upon the individual teacher, or at best (or sometimes worst) a team of teachers. Earlier I mentioned
that Damrosch proposes the figure of the ellipse as an appropriate metaphor
for what he sees as an ideal approach for world literature. The constant
shifting between the two foci in the ellipse – that of the reader's time and
place and that of the text's – leads to what Damrosch calls a "detached
engagement" on the part of the reader with "worlds beyond [her] own place
and time" (Damrosch 2004: 281). This detached engagement is pretty close to
the kind of estranged reading brought about by the form of translation briefly
proposed in my previous paragraph; in fact, such detached engagement can
be greatly helped by this form of translation. As mentioned, though, in the
final instance it will be the task of the teacher to make sure that the two foci
of a Damroschian ellipse are kept "in focus" in order to bring out the desired
detached engagement on the part of the student. This is also what Kadir sees
as the task of "worlding" a text, but it is only part of that task. The further

part consists in making the student aware of the simultaneous act of appro-priation and distancing she is engaged in, and of its implications for the relationship between her place and time and that of the text, a relationship that, as we saw just a few paragraphs ago, is almost always one of power.

In essence, what Kadir calls for is a meta-stance with regard to the very process of "doing" world literature. Another such call comes from John Pizer (2006). Pizer emphasizes the similarities between the world Goethe found himself in, in an age after the break-up of the Napoleonic empire that for a moment had threatened to bring all of Europe under its sway, but also an age that saw the quickening of commerce and of communications, and the world we have found ourselves in after the fall of the Berlin Wall in 1989 and the quickening of globalization. Therefore, he advocates including as inalienable part of a world literature course a reflection on the very history of what he calls the "Goethean" paradigm so as to make the students see the rationale of their enterprise – rather than worlding a particular reading, then, Pizer is here worlding the very course "world literature" itself.

Conclusion

- Because of the specific structure of higher education in the United States, and because of the relative lack of knowledge of foreign languages there, world literature courses in translation in one guise or another came to be part of the university curriculum in the USA from early on.
- Over the course of the twentieth century there developed a tension between the proponents of "Great Books" courses, which concentrated on the ideas contained in the works read and also included non-literary works, and those of world literature courses, which focused on literary works and on aesthetic issues.
- For most of the twentieth century world literature courses were the province of English departments; only recently have comparative literature departments taken the relief, leading to decisive shifts in the content and methodology of such courses.
- World literature courses in American academe rely heavily upon anthologies in English translation; the nature, form, and arrangement of these anthologies has been, and continues to be, the subject of heated debate.
- World literature has become an issue in the current debate on the position of the United States in a fast-changing world.

5 World literature as system

Overview

Goethe often spoke of world literature in metaphorical terms related to the domain of trade and of the exchange of goods. So did Marx and Engels when, in their 1848 *Communist Manifesto*, they mentioned world literature. In their wake there have sprung up a number of systemic approaches to literature, and to world literature, stressing not the intrinsic literary value of such or such a work, author, genre, or any such thing, but examining the circulation of literary works, genres, and authors within a transnational and even a global context. Two recent such approaches are those of Pascale Casanova, interpreting all of world literature as centered upon Paris as of the end of the Renaissance, and of Franco Moretti, tracing the emergence, growth, and spread of the novel as a world literature genre. Both of these approaches have run into severe criticism, but the amount of debate they have engendered, and its heat, are in themselves proof of the centrality of world literature to contemporary literary studies.

The "free trade" of literature

Eckermann records that on Sunday 15 July 1827 Goethe, in the context of a conversation on Thomas Carlyle's *Life of Schiller* remarked that, "It really is a very good thing that with this close intercourse between Frenchmen, Englishmen and Germans we have a chance of correcting each other's errors ... this is the great advantage that world literature affords, one which will in time become more and more obvious" (Strich 1949: 249). The English "intercourse" here stands for the German "Verkehr," which, as Jonathan Arac reminds us, translates in "a standard dictionary" as "*traffic, transportation, communication, commerce, intercourse* in its sexual as well as other senses, and *communion*" (Arac 2004: 96). We might add to that the term "circulation." Elsewhere, Arac quotes a passage from Goethe's 1830 preface to the German translation of Carlyle's biography of Schiller to the point that, "Goethe argued that world literature arose because the Napoleonic Wars had forced all the combatant nations into 'aware[ness] of much that was foreign,' producing 'intellectual needs that were previously unknown' [and that] to assuage these needs required 'free intellectual trade relations (*freien geistigen Handelsver-kehr*)'" (Arac 2008: 755). Many commentators have pointed out the almost seamless analogy Goethe here establishes between the circulation of ideas and that of goods. In fact, of course, ideas also traded as goods, that is to say in the form of "material" books and periodicals. While Goethe was imaginatively moving from the free exchange of intellectual goods to the trade in actual material goods in his use of analogy, with Karl Marx and Friedrich Engels the vector goes the other way in their *Communist Manifesto* (1848).

Karl Marx (1818–83) and **Friedrich Engels** (1820–95) are the authors of the *Communist Manifesto* (1848). Though both Marx and Engels came from relatively wealthy families they both became social revolutionaries. Marx's most famous work, next to the *Communist Manifesto*, is his massive *Capital* (*Das Kapital*, 1867–94), in which he interpreted history from a materialist perspective and which provided the theoretical underpinnings for the social and political movement known as Marxism in the twentieth century.

The relevant passage, which I quoted in full in Chapter 1, has often been explained, especially after the Russian Revolution of 1917 and by Soviet literary critics, as Marx and Engels investing "world literature" with a utopian dimension, as the future realization in the realm of culture of the erasure of boundaries they also conceived of as the ultimate goal of a classless society. In reality, the German scholar Peter Gossens contends, the use of the term in the *Communist Manifesto* of 1848 signals the end of the idea of *Weltliteratur* as "utopian model for society" (Gossens in press: 7; geschellschaftsutopisches Modell). For a number of younger writers the concept of *Weltliteratur* had, between Goethe's death and the socially driven revolutions of 1848 that shook all of Europe, and partially based on a utopian reading of Goethe's *Wilhelm Meisters Wanderjahre*, been enlarged from the literary to the social realm, especially in the orbit of early social-democratic thought. With the failed revolutions of 1848, however, such utopianism had lost all credibility. Hence, Gossens argues:

The passage in the manifesto where Marx ... refers to world literature is at best double-faced, because in one sense it situates itself in the context of a national understanding of culture that sees in the accumulation of [national] literatures a model for world literature and hence has left behind the era in which peoples were united as only people. On the other side the thought of world literature for Marx is not revolutionary in the socialist sense, but as a strategy fueled by the bourgeoisie that, along with the free trade that Marx criticizes at the same time, in the final analysis serves imperialist and colonialist ends in the sense of a "free development of capital."

Die Passage des Manifestes, in der Karl Marx ... sich auf die Weltliteratur bezieht, ist bestenfalls janusköpfig ... denn zu einen steht sie argu-
mentativ in der Nachfolge eines nationalisierten Kulturverständnisses, das
in der Addition der "Literaturen" ein Modell von Weltliteratur entdeckt und
damit den Völker verbindenden Gestus der Frühzeit hinter sich gelassen
hat. Ausserdem, und das is die andere Seite der Medaille, ist der Gedanke
der Weltliteratur für Marx nicht revolutionär im Sinne des Sozialismus,
sondern eine von der Bourgeoisie angestossene Strategie, die, wie der zur
gleichen Zeit von Marx bekritisierte Freihandel, letzlich imperialistische
und kolonialistische Ziele im Sinne einer "freie[n] Entwicklung des
Kapitals" ... verfolgt.

(Gossens in press: 9)

To bring out the full import of Marx and Engels's remarks, the passage that
immediately follows upon that which I earlier referred to should also be
quoted:

The bourgeoisie, by the rapid improvement of all instruments of production, by the immensely facilitated means of communication, draws all,
even the most barbarian, nations into civilisation. The cheap prices of
commodities are the heavy artillery with which it batters down all Chinese walls, with which it forces the barbarians' intensely obstinate hatred
of foreigners to capitulate. It compels all nations, on pain of extinction, to
adopt the bourgeois mode of production; it compels them to introduce
what it calls civilisation into their midst, i.e., to become bourgeois themselves.
In one word, it creates a world after its own image.

(Marx and Engels 2010: 16)

In Chapter 1 we saw that Goethe himself was not completely at ease with the
implications of the already ongoing commercialization of literature in his
time, and especially in the twentieth century philosophers, theoreticians, and
critics of a more generally progressive or left-leaning bent have tended to
follow him in this. The Hungarian Geörgy Lukács (1885–1971), the German
Theodor Adorno, and the American Fredric Jameson have all expressed their
deep suspicion, or sometimes their outright condemnation, of what they saw
as the "popular," that is to say the commercially driven in culture in general
and in literature in particular. The irony, of course, is that they often found the
popular to be quite a different thing. For Lukács, after his early *The Theory
of the Novel* (1974 [1916]) and his turn to Marxism, only instances of true
realism qualified as valid literature in a pre-Marxist or communist society.
They did so because they depicted their characters as in a dialectical, and
hence critically positive, relation to their world (Lukács 1983 [1937], 2001
[1938]). This kind of realism Lukács recognized in the works of Sir Walter
Scott, Honoré de Balzac, Maxim Gorky, and Thomas Mann. In contrast,
works written for entertainment could only pretend to be realist, because their

characters were implicitly in alignment with the dominant tenets of their society. Modernist works of any kind disqualified themselves in Lukács' eyes because they followed the market logic of capitalism in responding to fast-changing fashions as embodied in the successive-isms in European literature since the middle of the nineteenth century. Adorno, heavily influenced by Lukács, criticized the culture industry for its "commodity fetishism" and hence its complicity with an alienating power structure (Adorno and Horkheimer 1988 [1944], 1969 [1951], 2003 [1966]).

Geörgy or **György Lukács** (1895–1971) was a Jewish-Hungarian literary theoretician, critic, and philosopher. He was a staunch defender of realism in literature, and developed important theories about the history of the novel, and especially of the historical novel, in Europe. Though an adherent of the Communist Party for most of his life, Lukács regularly got into trouble with the Party because of his dissident views.

The leading neo-Marxist American critic and literary theoretician Fredric Jameson, himself heavily influenced by Adorno, directs his critique specifically against postmodernism and instead defends the continuing oppositional relevance of the avant-garde along Modernist lines (Jameson 1984, 1991). With this stance Jameson is close to the German philosopher Jürgen Habermas, who upheld a similar position in his "Modernity, an Unfinished Project" (Habermas 1982), and the equally German writer and philosopher Walter Benjamin who in his "Six Theses on History" (1940) had argued the necessity to continuously re-think history from an oppositional perspective, oppositional that is to dominant power. In all this, of course, Lukács, Adorno, Jameson, and Benjamin subscribe to the role of the politically committed intellectual as a rootless and alienated individual, in the Marxist sense, in his (bourgeois or industrial capitalist) society. Benjamin and Adorno, along with Max Horkheimer (1895–1973), were leading figures of the so-called Frankfurt School at the Institute for Social Research of the University of Frankfurt in Germany. Habermas still is. Because they were inspired by Marxist thought but wanted to apply this in a critical spirit and not subject to the doctrinaire interpretations of orthodox communism as it had come to power in the Soviet Union and later in most of Eastern and Central Europe after WWII, they are usually referred to as neo-Marxists or Western Marxists. Their work has been very influential for the development of more recent cultural studies approaches.

While a PhD student at Yale University in the mid-1950s, Jameson studied under Auerbach, who in his essay "Philology and *Weltliteratur*" of 1952 had voiced suspicions similar to those of Adorno and Horkheimer with regard to "a standardized world" with as ultimate possible consequence "a single literary culture, only a few literary languages and perhaps even a single literary

Theodor Adorno (1903–69) was a German philosopher, one of the founders of the so-called Frankfurt School of social theory. He was also a gifted musicologist. Like many Jewish intellectuals Adorno had to flee Germany during the Hitler years. After a brief period in England he moved to the United States, first to New York, and then to California. He spent WWII in Los Angeles, along with fellow exiles Max Horkheimer, Thomas Mann and Bertolt Brecht. One of his most important works, *Dialectic of Enlightenment* (*Dialektik der Aufklärung*, 1944), written with Horkheimer, was composed in LA. After the war Adorno returned to Germany.

language," as "herewith the notion of *Weltliteratur* would be ... at once realized and destroyed" (Auerbach 2009 [1952]: 127). However, as he saw such a homogenization of world literature as not immediately imminent, Auerbach gives over most room to discussing the need to find a point of departure, what he called an *Ansatzpunkt*, from which to synthesize the overwhelming wealth of material world literature lays out before the researcher or literary historian. Damrosch (2003) and Apter (2006), and from other perspectives altogether Wai-Chee Dimock (2006a and 2006b) and Djelal Kadir (2011) have taken Auerbach's lesson to heart. Damrosch (2003) finds his *Ansatzpunkt* in his elliptical or triangulated reading of the past and the distant or the present and the near. Apter (2006) finds it in translation. Dimock (2006b) finds it in American literature as world literature. Kadir (2011) finds it in looking for a number of literary, philosophical and academic exiles and wanderers making up a loose network of precursors to the eventual discipline of comparative literature. Both Apter and Kadir make Auerbach himself into an *Ansatzpunkt* when they cast him as the subject of one of their chapters. For all four, however different they otherwise might be, the method pursued is basically philological in that it consists of a close study of the texts analyzed. In a very loose sense we could also say that notwithstanding all their differences all four of them stay close to a typically American paradigm, hallowed since the New Criticism, of close reading.

Systemic world literature

The answers some other would-be historians of world literature have come up with, though, are very different. Whereas the approaches to world literature discussed in the previous paragraphs, and chapters, mostly argued from an ideational base implicitly assuming the value of "high" literature and of the literary works they dealt with, it is clear that in the *Communist Manifesto* Marx and Engels are arguing literature from a materialist point of view – that is to say, as operating in and under market conditions. In other words, what is in call here is not the aesthetic value of one work over another, but rather which works "circulate" better in terms of that other possible translation of "Verkehr" we alluded to earlier. In the second half of the twentieth century, particularly, there have emerged a number of approaches – most of them influenced in one way or another by Marxist principles – that concentrate on the circulation of literature rather than on making distinctions in terms of literary value. In the words of the Belgian comparatist José Lambert (1987) these are "systemic" approaches in that they study literature as system and not as isolated instance. In other words, with them the question is not which work is to be more highly rated but which work *has been* more highly rated, or more widely disseminated, at which moment in time and where and why.

Three such approaches are Yuri Lotman's cultural semiotics, Dionýsz Ďurišin's theory of interliterary processes, and Itamar Even-Zohar's poly-system theory. Of these three only Ďurišin (1929–97) ever explicitly worked on world literature himself, presenting the synthesis of his thoughts on the subject in his 1992 book *Čo je svetová literatúra?* (*What Is World Literature?*). Because of his untimely death, just before the renewed interest in world literature in the United States and Western Europe, as well as for the specific reasons discussed by Domínguez (2011), Ďurišin's theories have remained almost unknown in the West, and particularly so in the United States (Swiggers 1982, Bassel and Gomel 1991). As such they have played no role in the current debate on world literature, at least not on the level at which the leading interlocutors in that debate operate. In Italy and in Spain, though, Ďurišin has had some influence (Domínguez 2011). Even-Zohar's influence has been most marked in translation studies, and I will deal with him in the relevant chapter. Lotman (1922–93), like Ďurišin, died before the renewed interest in world literature. However, his "cause," so to speak, has been picked up by Ilya Kliger in reaction to two more recent systemic theories. Also in reaction to these same theories, Alexander Beecroft has developed an approach to world literature based on the social systems theory of the German sociologist Niklas Luhmann (1927–98). The two theories in question, formulated by Pascale Casanova and Franco Moretti, respectively, can in fact be said to have galvanized, rejuvenated, and re-oriented the discussion on World Literature at the turn of the third millennium.

Yuri Lotman (1922–93) was a Jewish-Estonian semiotician, structuralist, and cultural critic. For most of his life he taught at the University of Tartu. Many of his books and essays remain unavailable in English translation. His best-known works available in English are *Analysis of the Poetic Text* (1976), *The Structure of the Artistic Text* (1977), and *Universe of the Mind: A Semiotic Theory of Culture* (1990).

Pascale Casanova and the world republic of letters

Casanova, in her *République mondiale des lettres* (1999), published in English translation as *The World Republic of Letters* in 2004, starts from the theories of the French sociologist Pierre Bourdieu (1930–2002). As her *Ansatzpunkt* Casanova refers to Fernand Braudel's injunction in his *Civilisation matérielle, économie et capitalisme* (1979; *Civilization and Capitalism*) to describe the world "from a certain vantage point" (Casanova 2004: 4). Casanova observes "world literary space as a history and a geography" (Casanova 2004: 4). The structures of this worldwide literary space, she claims, have been consistently obscured by two generally accepted customs. The first is to look upon the writing of literature as an act of pure creation. The second is to look at literature within the framework of national literatures. Both of these could be termed as being part of the literary "habitus" with the term used by Bourdieu for a set of mind that has become interiorized to the point of seeming "natural" to those that operate in what Bourdieu again called a certain "field," in this particular case the field of literature. In reality, Casanova argues, literature does not, or does not exclusively, play itself out within the confines of a national literature; nor is it an act of pure creation. In fact, she reminds us, a number of writers, and not the least among them, have themselves hinted at this truth, but the "field" – and here we can think of the realm of literature itself as well as the academic field concerned with the study of literature – has consistently, out of habitus, ignored this.

As instances upholding her views she cites the passage from Goethe quoted earlier in this chapter. She finds further support with the early twentieth-century French writer Paul Valéry who repeatedly talks of civilization as "a form of capital whose increase may continue for centuries" and of culture as "a form of capital" (Casanova 2004: 91–10). And she approvingly cites Antoine Berman that the emergence of a *Weltliteratur* runs parallel with that of a *Weltmarkt* (Casanova 2004: 14; Berman 1984: 90). Just as for Marx the world and its history formed a battleground for power between the classes, so with the literary world for Casanova: "Its history is one of incessant struggle and competition over the very nature of literature itself – an endless succession of literary manifestos, movements, assaults, and revolutions ... these rivalries are what have created world literature" (Casanova 2004: 12). And just as on the Stock Exchange the value of shares and bonds rises and falls, so she says, approvingly citing Valéry (1960 [1939]) once again, on "the bourse of literary values" (Casanova 2004: 12).

Paul Valéry (1871–1945) was a French poet, critic and philosopher. An important public intellectual in the years between the two world wars, Valéry was a member of the Académie Française, and a frequent speaker at public occasions. Valéry's most famous poem is "Le Cimetière marin" ("The Seaside Graveyard", 1920).

On Casanova's literary stock exchange literary works, and the national literatures to which they belong, are valued according to their cultural or symbolic capital, to use another term from Bourdieu's sociological arsenal. The older and the more universally recognized a work is, and the more "classics" a specific literature counts, the higher their stock. Other assets of what Casanova calls the "literary patrimony" or "capital" of a culture or country are a well-developed literary establishment consisting of publishers, translators, critics, literary journals, bookstores, libraries, universities, and academies providing the necessary "volume" of trade and bestowing literary "credit" upon the works circulating in the culture or country in question. A major asset is the language in which a writer publishes or a literature lives: obviously, some languages are more valuable than others because of their seniority, their historical importance, and/or the number of their speakers, and, indeed, their literary capital accumulated over the ages. The latter also explains why the languages with the greater number of speakers are not necessarily the more important or "richer" ones on the literary stock exchange. The more literary capital accrues to a specific language the higher that language's "index or measure of literary authority" (Casanova 2004: 20):

> Such an index would incorporate a number of factors: the age, the "nobility," and the number of literary texts written in a given language, the number of universally recognized works, the number of translations, and so on. It therefore becomes necessary to distinguish between languages that are associated with "high" culture – languages having a high degree of literary value – and those that are spoken by a great many people. The former are languages that are read not only by those who speak them, but also by readers who think that authors who write in these languages or who are translated into them are worth reading. They amount to a kind of license, a permit of circulation certifying an author's membership in a literary circle.
>
> (Casanova 2004: 20)

First on a European scale and more recently on a world scale, Casanova sees literatures and writers battling it out for pre-eminence. Before the thirteenth century in Europe there is no rivalry on the European literary scene, at least not between separate literatures, as there is only one literary system using only one language: Latin. There is, of course, Greek being used in the Byzantine empire, but literary contacts between that empire and the rest of Europe always remained very limited. And equally self-evidently, within the non-Byzantine part of Europe and within the one literary system prevalent there, authors may still vie with one another for greater recognition. It is only with the emergence of literature in the vernacular, though, that we see an opposition shaping up between the dominant system and a rival one. This first happens in Italy, with Dante, Petrarch and Boccacio challenging the hegemony of Latin by creating, "inventing" so to speak, a powerful vernacular literature. This is not to say that Latin immediately disappears as a literary language nor, and even less so, as the language of authority, in religion and in science. In fact, in religion Latin would preserve its dominance until the sixteenth century, and then only lose it to the vernacular where Protestantism eventually gained the upper hand, while remaining dominant until the middle of the twentieth century where Catholicism continued to reign. In science Latin remained dominant until the seventeenth century, and only gradually gave way to the vernaculars after that. In fact, it is from the challenge to Latin as the language of science in Joachim Du Bellay's *Deffence et illustration de la langue francoyse* (*Defense and Illustration of the French Language*) of 1549 that Casanova dates the establishment of France, and more particularly Paris, as the center of the literary world. Even if Italian predates French as a vernacular literary language, it is in France that there first arises a truly "national" literature in the vernacular, and centered upon a single major center, that is to say Paris. Whereas French, and a French literary system, spring up in rivalry with Latin and the Latin-dominated European-wide system, henceforth other "national" systems in Europe will emerge in imitation of, and in rivalry with, French and the French system. Implicitly, therefore, French literature continues to function as the fixed point from which, and against which, all other literatures measure themselves; that is also why Casanova metaphorically calls Paris "the Greenwich meridian of literature" (Casanova 2004: 87).

Parallel to this Casanova sees "literature," and this very much along the lines developed by Bourdieu with regard to the various professional and other fields he distinguishes as operating within modernity and modern society, as assuming the character of an autonomous domain, irrespective of nation or state. In fact, it is the existence of a semi-independent so-called "Republic of Letters" in the sixteenth to eighteenth century, loosely uniting writers and thinkers across Europe, who moreover often kept in contact by means of "letters," first using Latin and later French as their means of communication, that inspired Casanova for the title of her book. Paris, then, becomes and remains the literary center of this autonomous domain, functioning as the great clearing-house for works, writers and literatures that aspire to recognition beyond the purely national or local level. Casanova sees this system as continuing to function until at least the 1960s, and even beyond. It does so by serving as the point where foreign works are being translated, reviewed, praised (or damned), and from there on disseminated into the wider world. In essence, Casanova is here claiming for Paris, and for the French language and the French literary system, what Goethe had suggested might be the role of German as privileged mediator for first Europe's and later the world's literatures. Even Goethe, though, had recognized the pre-eminence of Paris in matters of culture and literature, or its greater "literary authority" in Casanova's term.

Criticism of Casanova

Many objections and questions can be raised with regard to Casanova's views in general, and to her resolute and absolute focus on Paris as *the* center of the world literary system in particular. One of the earliest, most closely reasoned and forceful attacks came from Christopher Prendergast, who objects that much of what Casanova is doing is grounded in metaphors and anecdotes rather than in "a more theoretically robust explanation" (Prendergast 2004: 8). Although he expresses admiration for Casanova's drawing upon a wide-ranging set of examples to illustrate her theory, he also questions her choice of examples, arguing that the hypotheses from which she starts necessarily "skew the picture, such that the inclusions and omissions, as well as the distribution of emphasis in the discussions, constantly return us in one way or another to the shores of the *Vieux Continent*" (Prendergast 2004: 9). Moreover, Prendergast contends, Casanova's prioritizing of the categories of "nation" and "literature" to mount her construction of world literature as an inter-national competition leads her to completely misinterpret, in the case of "nation," some of her prime examples, among whom Kafka, Joyce and Beckett, and in the case of "literature," the realities of how texts, and indeed oral materials, function in societies other than the (West-)European. Casanova's exclusive concentration on the struggle between nations, according to Prendergast, also leads her to grossly misread developments that may be internal to national literatures as steered or provoked by inter-national competition.

Helena Buescu (2011) argues that Casanova completely by-passes the historical notion of the Republic of Letters. The latter, she reminds us, was also, and indeed primarily so, concerned with "letters" in a much broader sense than Casanova's narrow concentration upon "literature" in the sense of "belles-lettres." Moreover, Buescu adduces, the historical Republic of Letters antedates the rise of national literatures, so for Casanova to ground her theory about the development of a "World Republic of Letters" in what she conceives as the struggle between national literatures is an anachronism. Like Prendergast, Buescu too questions Casanova's brushing aside of the Italian precedence in the use of the vernacular for both literary and other purposes, and her not mentioning any other European vernaculars if not as pre-dating then at least as paralleling the emergence of French as a national literary language. She points out, for instance, that the use of Portuguese by several centuries antedates that of French for some of the purposes Casanova sees the latter as fulfilling as of the sixteenth century, and that Spanish and Portuguese grammarians of the late fifteenth and early sixteenth centuries were already concerned with the role of European vernaculars in colonial settings.

Mads Rosendahl Thomsen has proposed the existence of "shifting focal points" for an international canon as a corrective to Casanova's exclusive concentration upon Paris (Thomsen 2008: 33). Although his concept of such "focal points" does not quite correspond to what Casanova means when she talks of Paris as the ultimate authority-holding and recognition-conveying center of world literature until the 1960s, we could pick up on Thomsen's suggestion by, as he does, pointing to the at least temporary emergence of rival centers to Paris. As Casanova herself intimates, this is certainly the case with London and New York as of the 1960s, parallel to the loss of prestige and usage of French as *the*, and over the last few decades indeed even as *an* international language of trade, diplomacy and culture. But we could argue that similar shifts occurred for instance around the turn of the twentieth century with the rise of Berlin and Vienna as potential alternatives for Paris as the literary centers of Europe, and that it is only political vicissitudes that have cut short that rise. Berlin, indeed, might actually be re-emerging as such at the beginning of the twenty-first century, if not on a world scale then at least on a European one, with both Paris and Berlin having to cede first place on the world scale to English-language centers. But we could also argue that Weimar, or perhaps rather Goethe himself, at the time of his writing about world literature occupied a similarly central position within "European, in other words, World Literature" (Strich 1949: 351). After all, Goethe for "all the world," that is to say Europe, himself stood as the ultimate arbiter of literature in the first third of the nineteenth century.

Criticism of Casanova on a more fundamental level perhaps is expressed by Jerome McGann, who asks:

> What if we decide that the center/periphery map has been drawn Under Western Eyes only and that it gives poor service in a truly globalized world? What if– going further still – we were to propose, to theorize, that in such a world, this myth [of literature as an aesthetically autonomous system] resembles less a map than a kind of equilibrium device, a cultural gyroscope for maintaining cultural status quo? It seems to me, looking from my marginal American position, that such thoughts are now common among non-Euro-Americans.
>
> (McGann 2008: 651–52)

And David Damrosch scathingly sums up much of the early criticism of Casanova when in a footnote to his own 2003 *What is World Literature?* he condemns *La République mondiale des lettres* for its "implicit triumphalism" and suggests that it might have been better titled "*La République parisienne des lettres*" (the Parisan republic of letters) because it is "an unsatisfactory account of world literature in general" yet "actually a good account of the operation of world literature within the modern French context" (Damrosch 2003: 27).

Still, on the same page that he indicts Casanova Damrosch himself admits that "for any given observer, even a genuinely global perspective means a perspective from somewhere, and global patterns of the circulation of world literature take shape in their local manifestation" (Damrosch 2003: 27). Therefore, he asserts, he himself in his book will be concentrating "particularly (though not exclusively) on world literature as it has been construed over the past century in a specific cultural space, that of the formerly provincial and now metropolitan United States" (Damrosch 2003: 27–28). By referring to the USA as "metropolitan" Damrosch perhaps has in mind the distinction that Prendergast also invokes in his critique of Casanova, and which he borrows from Anne Querrien (1986). Prendergast sums up Querrien's views as follows:

> The capital is a political and cultural "centre," with the power and the authority to dominate a wider "territory," to keep in place a "social hierarchy" and to "subjugate a population ... to a common heritage". A metropolis on the other hand "is not a centre and has no centre," it "has no identity to preserve," it "begins with the slightest desire to exchange," is "made up of networks," puts "an incongruous mix of beings into circulation" and is the place where migrants find their socially predetermined destination.
>
> (Prendergast 2004: 20)

For Prendergast, twentieth-century Paris is both capital and metropolis, serving different and even partially antithetical functions, one for the nation, the other for "the world." This also suggests the possibility of two different literary systems co-existing in one singular place and of the national system, instead of serving as the arbiter for the world, actually re-aligning itself along "world" lines generated elsewhere rather than the other way around. Perhaps we can even speculate that this is what has been happening over the last two decades or so with French literature, as Casanova suggests, becoming more "postcolonial." The publication in 2007 of the manifesto "Pour une littérature-monde" in Paris but arguing for a world literature in French not rooted in "l'hexagone" (the hexagone, shorthand for continental France) would then go to support this view.

Be all this as it may, we may wonder whether Damrosch's own 2003 book does not reveal at least a residual American bias, even if packaged much more subtly than Casanova's French equivalent. Damrosch, in his triangulated readings, from the epic of Gilgamesh and pre-Columbian Mexican incantations to the "Zairean" (now again: Congolese) Mwbil Ngal's novel *Giambatista Viko*, and from ancient Egyptian poems over Mechtild von Magdeburg, Franz Kafka and P.G. Wodehouse to Rigoberta Menchú and Milorad Pavič's *Dictionary of the Khazars*, demonstrates how the cultures of the globe can be made intelligible and accessible to his American readers. These readers are, in the first instance, American undergraduate students, and, to a lesser extent, graduate students of comparative literature. Consequently, Damrosch's main concern, in line with the typical American approach to world literature as I discussed it earlier in this book, is essentially didactic or pedagogic. As I also suggested earlier, it therefore follows the more generally American didactic preference for detailed readings of singular texts. In contrast, Casanova's book, as Louis Menand put it in a joint review of *The World Republic of Letters* and James English's *The Economy of Prestige* (2005), is "simply [an] effort ... to understand literature sociologically" (Menand 2005). The same point is taken up by Frances Ferguson in one of the most spirited defenses of Casanova so far. Against Damrosch's and Prendergast's complaints that Casanova misses the subtleties of such-and-such an author (Kafka is Prendergast's example), Ferguson objects that Casanova writes as a sociologist of literature and can therefore dispense with close reading. Contrary to what Casanova has often been charged with, Ferguson argues, she does not write from a personal, because a chauvinistically French and Parisian, stance. "We should not mistake her argument about the centrality of Paris in the world republic of letters for an expression of personal partiality cloaking itself in the language of system," Ferguson reprimands Damrosch and Prendergast (Ferguson 2008: 665). "Casanova's discussion," Ferguson maintains, "is methodologically unified, in that she identifies the way inequality operates in the literary field and can thus provide a fresh sense of how the linguistic materials of literature function in the unequal distribution of literary capital" (Ferguson 2008: 669). It is certainly not a coincidence that it is two critics and academics of a decidedly "leftist" or neo-Marxist bent, Perry Anderson in *The London Review of Books* and Terry Eagleton in *The New Statesman*, who wrote some of the most positive reviews of Casanova's book upon its appearance in English in 2004.

Damrosch simply finds himself in the opposite corner to Casanova's systemically informed investigation of the mechanics of (admittedly, a particular cross-cut of) world literature. And while his approach, at first sight, might be more "open" than Casanova's, his own admittance that any take on world literature is always going to be a perspective from somewhere basically repeats Moulton's similar assertion in the very first book on world literature. Obviously, Damrosch's perspective is more circumspectly phrased and is less directly and unabashedly unilateral than Moulton's. Waïl Hassan has argued that "the pedagogical application of the concept of 'world literature' in the United States since [the] Second World War has developed in step with the political, economic, and strategic remapping of global relations, sometimes in subtle ways that tend to mask its affiliations with power" (Hassan 2000: 38). However, he also notes, "there are ... other non-hegemonic conceptions of difference that self-consciously historicize their understanding of world cultures and literatures while maintaining 'critical vigilance' (to use Gayatri Chakravorty Spivak's term) toward their own affiliations with power" (Hassan 2000: 40). While Damrosch is clearly engaging in such self-conscious historicization, one still cannot fail to wonder whether Damrosch's perspective is not just as intimately related to a particular mapping of global relations as is Casanova's. The bottom line then seems to be that Damrosch and Casanova are simply "writing" different "world literatures."

Franco Moretti conjectures on world literature

In a statement that has become famous, and also much reviled, Franco Moretti in 2000 declared that, given the multiplicity of the world's languages and the overwhelming number of texts written in those languages, "world literature is not an object, it's a *problem*" (Moretti 2004: 149). He proposed to solve that problem by what he calls "distant reading" (2004: 151). This basically involves not the close reading of literary texts themselves but what literary historians have said about them, and especially about the regularities found in larger aggregations of texts. These regularities are then interpreted with a combination of methods drawn from the social and the biological sciences. More specifically, Moretti combines evolution theory and world systems theory as developed by the economic historian Immanuel Wallerstein. World systems theory posits the unity of the world's economic system (and in its wake, or concomitant with it, also other systems such as the military and political ones) as of the sixteenth century, with a core (Western Europe), a semi-periphery (the rest of Europe), and a periphery (the rest of the world) in a relationship of exchange. These exchanges can be charted according to volume, intensity, kind of products, and so on. The same thing can be done for literature, both in the form of actual material goods, such as the trade in books, or in translations, and in that of the ideas and forms embodied in those books: genres, styles, motifs, etc. Moretti published the results of a research program carried out along such lines in his *Atlas of the European Novel, 1800–1900* (1998). Having been inspired from the very beginning of his studies at the University of Rome under Galvano della Volpe by the latter's scientific Marxism, the study of literature according to world systems theory principles made Moretti realize the basic inequality at work in the world literary system.

Immanuel Wallerstein (1930–) is an American social and economic historian and sociologist. He is mostly known for his world systems theory, which he elaborated in three volumes on *The Modern World System* (1974–89). Wallerstein sees the entire world starting to function as one overall economic system of exchange with the voyages of discovery, and particularly with the discovery of the Americas. In this system, Western Europe occupies the center, with other regions and continents functioning as peripheries or semi-peripheries.

Although couched in different terms, and elaborated according to a different methodology, then, Moretti's starting position at least is very close to Casanova's. His study of the European novel between 1800 and 1900, for instance, led him to discern a system with Paris and (to a slightly lesser degree) London at the core, a number of countries immediately surrounding France along with Scandinavia as a semi-periphery, and most of Central and Eastern Europe as the periphery. Moretti quotes Itamar Even-Zohar, applying polysystem theory rather than world-systems theory, as having reached largely similar conclusions about the power relationships obtaining between core and more peripheral literatures (Moretti 2009a: 402). "The study of world literature is – inevitably –," Moretti says, "a struggle for symbolic hegemony across the world" (Moretti 2004: 158).

In his 1998 book and his 2000 article, Moretti distinguishes between the model of the tree, which he takes to stand for "the passage from unity to diversity," and that of the wave, which he sees as "uniformity engulfing an initial diversity" (Moretti 2004: 160). The tree he associates with national literatures developing and distinguishing themselves from one another over time; the wave he links to market forces radiating out from a core. For the study of what he calls the "comparative morphology (the systematic study of how forms vary in space and time)" (Moretti 2004: 158) of world literature, Moretti deploys graphs, maps, and trees in a combination of evolution and world-systems analysis (Moretti 2005). He had already used evolution theory in one of his early books, *Modern Epic* (1996), while world-systems analysis, as we just saw, largely inspired his 1998 book on the European novel. Now he combines the two into one model for world literature, although active in different historical times. Evolution, leading to divergence, or the tree-metaphor, pertained before (roughly, and as Moretti himself says, oversimplifying things) the eighteenth century. World-systems analysis, or convergence, modeled along the maps and graphs metaphors, applies from the eighteenth century onwards. When elements emanating from the core and diffusing themselves into the periphery meet with local forms, the resulting combination can – and does – lead to new original forms. Moretti's example is the diffusion of the novel in the nineteenth and twentieth centuries.

Radiating out from a core in Western Europe centered on Paris and London, the novel, when it reaches semi- and full peripheries, retains the plotlines exported from the center but adopts indigenous characters and styles. The result, as Moretti puts it, is "a hybrid form," but one that, rather than amalgamation, produces "dissonance, disagreement, at times a lack of integration between what happens in the plot, and how the style evaluates the story, and presents it to the reader" (Moretti 2009a: 406). In other words, what we have is "form as struggle," a struggle "between the story that comes from the core, and the viewpoint that 'receives' it in the periphery," and the fact that the two are not "seamlessly fused is not just an aesthetic given ... but the crystallization of an underlying *political* tension" (Moretti 2009a: 406). Finally, he sums up the situation with regard to world literature, and particularly with regard to the fact that apparently "we still do not know what [it] is," as follows; perhaps, he says, this is because

> we keep collapsing under a single term two distinct world literatures: one that precedes the eighteenth century – and one that follows it. The "first" *Weltliteratur*, a mosaic of separate, "local" cultures; it is characterized by strong internal diversity; it produces new forms mostly by divergence; and is best explained by (some version of) evolutionary theory. The "second" *Weltliteratur* (which I would prefer to call world literary system) is unified by the international literary market; it shows a growing, and at times

stunning amount of sameness; its main mechanism of change is convergence; and is best explained by (some version of) world-systems analysis.

(Moretti 2009a: 407)

The "intellectual challenge posed by *Weltliteratur* in the twenty-first century," then, Moretti concludes, is to learn "to study *the past as past* ... and *the present as present*" (Moretti 2009a: 407).

Against Moretti

If anything, Moretti's views on world literature have occasioned even more reactions than have Casanova's, and even more piqued reactions from American comparatists. The large amount of attention Moretti's initial articles on world literature generated undoubtedly also has to do with the fact that they started appearing already in 2000, whereas Casanova's book, although in its original French version predating Moretti's very first article on the subject, remained untranslated until 2004, and only then really started being noticed beyond France. Jonathan Arac, in 2002, admitted that Moretti's 2000 "Conjectures on World Literature" made him uneasy because it so patently went against what in American academe had been the rule for at least some decades, that is to say the actual reading and analysis of specific texts. This is an issue that has continued to rankle in American academe, as the "preface" to a 2009 *SubStance* issue on close reading reveals. Beyond this, however, Arac also has more fundamental questions with regard to some of Moretti's claims. One question has to do with Moretti's positioning of France and England, or Paris and London, as the core of a world system of literature, and his description of the meeting between what emanates from the core and what it finds in the periphery as resulting in a "compromise." I described the mechanism earlier. Arac points out that Henry Fielding's *Joseph Andrews* (1742) "defines itself as a 'comic epic in prose, *written after the manner of Cervantes*'", and that consequently "Moretti's modern core itself has arisen by adaptation from what, by a later date, had become the periphery" (Arac 2002: 38).

Moreover, Arac contends, in the model that Moretti adopts, that is to say Wallerstein's world-systems analysis, "the relation between core and periphery is synchronic – only its relation to the periphery allows the core to be core, and the two together define the system at a given point in time" (Arac 2002: 38). With Moretti, "the centre's relation to the core operates by 'influence' ... that is, the centre is earlier than the core: what in Wallerstein is spatial becomes, in Moretti, temporal; and the result comes closer than Moretti might wish to the old priorities of Western comparatism" (Arac 2002: 38). Finally, Arac notes, Moretti's "distant reading" seems to eliminate the necessity for the scholar or student of world literature to know any but one dominant language, that is to say English, as it does not require any direct contact with literary texts themselves, but only with "second hand" literary history, criticism and theory, most or all of which may be available in English. The danger, Arac implies, is that this may reduce the actual material, even second hand, used to draw up Morettian large scale analyses of world literature to material written in English, thus in practice restricting "the world" of world literature to what is written about it in what is arguably the dominant or even hegemonic world language of what is equally arguably the world's hegemon. Arac wrote his article in 2002, when such a view of the US may have been more self-evident than has been the case more recently.

In a later article, on William Dean Howells and the languages of American fiction, Arac tempered his "suspicions" with regard to Moretti's "distant reading." Arguing that "philological criticism is not just the same as close reading," he pointed to the examples of Mikhail Bakhtin and Edward Said as evidence that "philological care for language and the work of language in human life may operate in the study of discourse practices and patterns that cross the bounds of individual works, even as those patterns are discerned and delineated through scrupulous attention to particular textual moments" (Arac 2007: 1). "Yet," he pursued, "sometimes even this may be too close," so "despite [his] suspicions of Franco Moretti's 'distant' reading, [his] essay pursues a case where distance seems the right path" (Arac 2007: 1).

Critical noises similar to Arac's initial "suspicions" were made by Emily Apter, who finished off Moretti with the remark that his approach "favors narrative over linguistic engagement, and this, I would surmise, is ultimately the dangling participle of Moretti's revamped *Weltliteratur*" (Apter 2003: 256). A more whole-scale condemnation came from Gayatri Spivak, who, with reference to Arac's 2002 article, dismissed Moretti and Moretti-like endeavors because the world-systems theorists they relied upon she found to be "useless for literary study – that must depend on texture – because they equate economic with cultural systems" (Spivak 2003: 108). Spivak also objected to Moretti's ambition to treat those scholars in the periphery who did pay attention to the "texture" of literary works, in this case the novel, as "native informants" (Spivak 2003: 108).

A different kind of doubt was raised by Efraín Kristal (2002) with regard to Spanish American literature, in which, he argues, not the novel but poetry and the essay were the dominant genres until the middle of the twentieth century, and unless or until Moretti's analyses can account for that it can hardly be called a "world system of literature." Francesca Orsini (2002) voiced pretty much the same objections with regard to the Indian subcontinent. Wai Chee Dimock chimed in with the by then familiar objections to Moretti's "distant reading" when she cautioned "against what strikes me as his over-commitment to general laws, to global postulates operating at some remove from the phenomenal world of particular texts" (Dimock 2006a: 90). More recently, Nirvana Tanoukhi (2008) questioned the applicability, and the lingering Eurocentric aspects, of Moretti's theories with regard to the African postcolonial novel. Earlier we saw that Frances Ferguson abounds with praise for Casanova. She is considerably more reserved about Moretti. Most importantly, the difference to her seems to reside in that Casanova attempts to elaborate a complete theory of world literature while Moretti stops at a partial one, thereby truncating the reach of his explanatory models. As Ferguson puts it:

> Moretti's desire to use graphs, maps, and trees to make the history of the novel more perspicuous points to the novel's loneliness and vulnerability even in its triumph. For the story of the survival of the novel is also very much the story of the disappearance of other narrative forms – the disappearance of painting and sculpture that could tell the story of Narcissus and Echo or the stories of Jonah and Noah, the movement of drama into the margins of public life, and the death-by-preservation of oral narratives that exist as their own fossil remains within the pages of books. Any study of the evolutionary history of any representational form, in other words, needs to incorporate into itself an account of its own nature – the things it is made of.
>
> (Ferguson 2008: 677)

Moretti himself answered his critics in 2003 with "More Conjectures." Systematically countering their criticisms he concluded that, "the way we imagine comparative literature is a mirror of how we see the world. ... 'Conjectures' tried to do so against the background of the unprecedented possibility that the entire world may be subject to a single centre of power – and a centre which has long exerted an equally unprecedented symbolic hegemony" (Moretti 2003: 81). In the work he has done since then Moretti has equally systematically elaborated on his earlier proposals (Moretti 2005, 2006, 2009b, 2010).

Other world literature systems

Reactions to Casanova and Moretti's proposals have also come from proponents of the other systemic theories I mentioned at the outset of this chapter. These reactions have tended to stress that what Casanova and Moretti are doing can also be done, and done better, by these other systemic theories. A good example is a 2010 article by Ilya Kliger, in which he argues that Yuri Lotman's cultural semiotics operates "with categories – such as boundary, translation, centre, periphery – that turn out to be crucial for some major recent attempts to formulate a methodology for the study of literature as a world system" (Kliger 2010: 259). One advantage of confronting a Lotmanian approach with those of Casanova and Moretti, according to Kliger, would be that it offers a "geopolitically different perspective," diffferent from that of Western scholars who until now have dominated the conversation on the subject, and that we might thus gain "something like a second-world, or (semi-)peripheral, view of world literature to complement the view from the 'centre'" (Kliger 2010: 259). This would help us see that, in Lotman's terms, ideas and theories about world literature are also "geopolitically, or 'semio-spherically' conditioned" (Kliger 2010: 259). Specifically, Kliger sees the Western conceptualizations of world literature as conditioned by the culture industry, and by a will to see, as Arac also noted, the relation between center and (semi-)periphery not only, and perhaps not even primarily, as spatial but rather as temporal. This implies the primacy of the center, in this case the West, or Moretti's Paris and London, Casanova's Paris, over the periphery, and also that whatever is "original" always originates from the center, with the periphery passively and incompletely absorbing what radiates from the center. "A less linear temporality, as well as a more tangled geography," Kliger concludes, "underlies the centre-periphery relations as Lotman conceives of them in his late essays on the semiotics of culture" (Kliger 2010: 263). Specifically, Kliger claims, Lotman's theories leave more room for innovation from the periphery, or in the exchange between the center and the periphery, and they construe that relation on a more even basis. The centre-periphery relation in Lotman is a *"functional* one," Kliger argues, "between centripetal and centrifugal forces of signification, the former producing totalizing narratives and universal models and norms while the latter generates incongruities, accidents, chance encounters and semiotic lacunae" (Kliger 2010: 266).

Niklas Luhmann (1927–98) was a German sociologist and pioneer of systems theory. In Luhmann's view all human society is ruled by communication between individuals but also between groups of different compositions and levels of intricacy, hierarchy and organization. All these function within a total system of communication. Some of his many publications are *Social Systems* (*SozialeSysteme: Gundriß einer allgemeinen Theorie*, 1984) and *Ecological Communication* (*Ökologische Kommunikation*, 1989).

Alexander Beecroft has critiqued both Casanova and Moretti on the grounds that their theories are unable to overcome the chronological limitations they have set themselves, and which with Casanova do not go farther back than the sixteenth, and with Moretti, at least as far as his work on the novel is concerned, than the eighteenth century. Instead Beecroft proposes a six-mode model of literature across time inspired upon the systems theory of the German theoretician Niklas Luhmann, and specifically the latter's *Ecological Communication* (1989). Each of these modes is linked to a specific form of social organization stretching from the most simple to the most complex, and to that organization's relationship to the environment. His theory, Beecroft claims, "will recognize the multiple centres and systems of cultural power in operation across human history, and in addition will affirm that profound theoretical insights can and must come from the study of diverse literatures, rather than from the study of a core tradition or from the work of a dedicated class of theoreticians exempted from the cultural labour of textual analysis. ... in sum, it will be a theory of 'world literature' rather than 'world-literature', focused on the production of verbal art and its relationship to its environment as a genuinely universal phenomenon in human culture" (Beecroft 2008: 91).

Below are the six modes that Beecroft distinguishes.

1 The *epichoric* is a mode of literary production in which literature is produced within the confines of a local community.
2 The *panchoric* refers to literary texts and systems of circulation operating across a range of epichoric communities, united to some degree in language and culture, but generally fragmented politically.
3 The circulation of literature within a *cosmopolitan* literary system is distinct from that encountered in a panchoric system, partly because cosmopolitan literary languages can be used by groups speaking a variety of mother tongues and partly because cosmopolitan literatures tend to represent themselves as agents of an ideology of universal rule, whether or not that ideology is seen as practiced or practicable (Beecroft cites Sanskrit, Greek, Persian, and Latin as examples). Where a panchoric literary language allows literature to circulate among a set of political entities sharing a native language (but likely not a political regime), a cosmopolitan literary language creates a cross-cultural system, in which speakers of many languages share a common literary idiom.
4 Texts circulating in the *vernacular* but not yet in a
5 *National* context, when the history of a given literature, and its contemporary practices, are mapped onto the history and contemporary status of a particular political state.
6 *Global* literature. This category, still more conjectural than real, consists of literatures whose linguistic reach transcends national, even continental, borders. In some senses, a global literature resembles a cosmopolitan literature, except that (at least at this time) global literatures continue to represent themselves as systems of national literatures to an extent that cosmopolitan literatures do not. They are in that sense inter-national rather than extra-national.

(Beecroft 2008: 92–98)

At various points Beecroft sees the theories of Casanova and Moretti intersecting with his own categories, but his approach, he argues, is not hampered by the same chronological or generic limitations. Therefore he proposes, "rather than a division of labour in which national-literature specialists produce raw data for processing by world-literature scholars ... a sharing of labour by which, say, specialists in Persian literature find useful theoretical and practical insights in the work of Sinologists, or Anglo-Saxonists in the work of specialists of Old Kannada" (Beecroft 2008: 100). Such an approach, he believes, holds out "the possibility of world literature, unhyphenated, as a coherent field of study; taking as its object not a world-literary system which maps roughly onto Wallerstein's world system, but rather, and simply, the literature – the verbal artistic production – of the world" (Beecroft 2008: 100).

Conclusion

- From the very beginning word literature has been conceived of as a system of exchange of ideas, motifs, structures, and genres, as well as of the material carriers of all these things.
- Marxist and neo-Marxist critics have tended to prefer realist or modernist strategies as appropriate for a world literature in the service of the worldwide spread of socialism.
- Around the turn of the millennium two systemic approaches, by Casanova and Moretti respectively, have attempted to explain the world circulation of litera- ture by positing Paris, in the case of Casanova, and Paris along with London, in the case of Moretti, as the center or centers of a world literary system.
- Casanova and Moretti have been severely criticized, especially by American scholars; more often than not, though, Casanova and Moretti are faulted not for doing what they themselves claim they set out to do, but for not doing what their American colleagues think they should have done.
- Most recently, attempts are being made to also construct world literature approaches on the basis of other European systemic theories of literature.

6   World literature and translation

Overview

Goethe himself was a prodigious translator, and he considered translation a necessary instrument for the spread of world literature. In fact, he thought that the German language and German literature had a great task ahead of them in serving as mediators, through translation, for world literature. Most commentators on world literature after Goethe have likewise recognized the importance of translation. For the early twentieth-century German writer and philosopher Walter Benjamin, translation was even the most important means for a work of literature to survive its own period and gain a meaningful afterlife. In the final quarter of the twentieth century a number of scholars, building on the polysystem theory of Itamar Even-Zohar, have elaborated an approach to translation that makes the latter, instead of a handmaiden to "real" literature, the engine of change in literature. Towards the end of the century there have even been calls that translation studies would replace comparative literature as the central discipline in the transnational study of literature.

The indispensable instrument

"The indispensable instrument" is what Albert Guérard calls translation in his 1940 *Preface to World Literature*. Indeed, the question of translation forms an inevitable part of any discussion on world literature. As long as world literature in practice was restricted to the traditional and inevitable comparatist trinity of French-English-German, with perhaps Italian and Spanish thrown in for good measure, along with the classical languages that until roughly the 1960s would have been considered an inalienable part of the high school education of anyone (at least in Europe) aspiring (or rich enough) to pursue university studies, and on top of that some "minor" language (usually the comparatist's mother tongue when he or, less frequently she, originated from one of Europe's smaller countries), insistence on reading in the original could be said to have been a reasonable, even if already fairly demanding, requirement. Beyond this, though, and certainly in the American situation sketched in Chapter 4, translation is inevitable, even if perhaps regrettable. Certainly Posnett (1886), writing at the dawn of the systematic study of comparative literature, at least in English, feels that translation, even if necessary, is always a poor choice, especially when it comes to poetry. He pointedly quotes Shelley, from the *Defence of Poetry*, on "the vanity of translation; it were as wise to cast a violet into a crucible that you might discover the formal principle of its colour and odour, as seek to transfuse from one language into another the creation of a poet" (Posnett 1886: 47–48).

Moulton, on the contrary, is much more sanguine on the subject. "It is obvious," he says, "that the study of literature as a whole is impossible without a free use of translations" (Moulton 1921: 3). For many, he admits, reading literature in translation is only a "makeshift" and smacks of "second-hand scholarship" (Moulton 1921: 3). Yet, he points out, many creative writers, and some of the greatest among them, men such as John Dryden and Alexander Pope, were prodigious translators. For sure, he admits, literature in translation suffers a loss, but think also of what one gains: "one who accepts the use of translations where necessary secures all factors of literature except language, and a considerable part even of that ... one who refuses translations by that fact cuts himself off from the major part of the literary field" (Moulton 1921: 4). And he approvingly quotes the nineteenth-century American writer-philosopher Ralph Waldo Emerson to the effect that the latter "rarely read any Greek, Latin, German, Italian – sometimes not a French book – in the original which [he could] procure in a good [English] version" (Moulton 1921: 4).

With the democratization of higher education in the USA as of WWI, and in Europe as of WWII, the almost complete erosion of the classics in high school education in Europe and the Americas, the multiculturalization, postcolonization and globalization of literary studies, and the concomitant call for an ever greater multiplicity of languages and their literatures to gain access to "world literature" in the anthologizing and educational sense, any requirement, or even expectation, of reading all in the original is obviously illusory. Equally obviously, even prior to 1960 the language combination theoretically expected of an "orthodox" comparatist would have been beyond the reach of most actual practitioners of the discipline, and far beyond the reach of most "ordinary" readers of "world literature." The latter is why as of the beginning of the twentieth century there have appeared, at least in most or many European languages, popular anthologies in translation either of world literature in the broadest sense or of specific genres, usually poetry, or book series specifically, or at least partly, dedicated to such translations.

In English one could think of the Penguin Classics, with an inaugural volume in 1945 of a translation of Homer's *Odyssey*, and later the Penguin Twentieth-Century/Modern Classics series. Both these series also contain works originally in English. Like all other Penguins, the Classics and

Modern Classics series were first published by Allen Lane, but since the 1970s have formed part of the Pearson Longman Company. In the United States the Modern Library of (originally) Boni and Liveright started publishing what was then modern European literature in English translations in 1917. In Portugal Portugália Editora in Lisbon published a series "Antologías Universais" from 1942 until the 1970s. In Copenhagen Hasselbachs Kulturbibliotek has been publishing both classics and more modern works of world literature in Danish translation since before WWII. Albert Bonniers Forlag, in Stockholm, brings out its Klassiker series with both Swedish and foreign works in Swedish translation. In Dutch the publishing house De Wereldbibliotheek makes good its name, "The World Library," by publishing both Dutch and foreign works of world literature in Dutch translation. At the beginning of the twentieth century there also sprang up a series of world literature in translation in China, under the guidance of the man who became China's most celebrated writer of the twentieth century, Lu Xun, and his brother Zhou Zuoren.

The grandfather of all these enterprises is the *Universal-Bibliothek* or "library of world literature," which, since 1867, has been published by Reclam Verlag, originally in Leipzig and since 1945 in Stuttgart. This series publishes works in German next to works in other languages and bi-lingual works. On the occasion of the sixtieth anniversary of their *Universal-Bibliothek* in 1927 Reclam commissioned an essay from the then best-selling German author Herman Hesse. In 1929 it appeared in the *Universal-Bibliothek* in a slightly expanded version as a little booklet under the title *Eine Bibliothek der Weltliteratur.* For Hesse, collecting a good library containing the basic works of world literature is an essential part of *Bildung,* the German ideal of a well-rounded education, and akin to making sure that your body is in excellent shape, the so-called *Körperkultur* eagerly practiced in the Weimar Germany of the 1920s and early 1930s. While allowing for personal preferences which will make each person's selection at least slightly different from anyone else's, when it comes to drawing up his own list Hesse actually includes most of what we would still regard as classics today, although obviously some of his choices are steered by either period or national considerations. However, he stipulates, many of the works he lists would be unavailable to most of his readers if it were not for translation. Fortunately, he says "we Germans have the good luck to possess an extraordinarily rich treasure of good translations from foreign and dead languages" (Hesse 2008: 5; wir Deutsche [haben] das Glück über einen ausserordentlichen reichen Schatz an guten Übersetzungen aus fremden und toten Sprachen zu verfügen). Regardless, Hesse feels that much is still lacking on this score, and moreover each translation, however good, is only an approximation (Annäherung) of the original (Hesse 2008: 11). As language changes over time, finally, new translations of older works become necessary, and he points to the Bible, which he feels is no longer really accessible in Martin Luther's sixteenth-century translation.

Hermann Hesse (1877–1962) was a German-Swiss author, primarily known for his novels *Siddhartha* (1922), *Steppenwolf* (1927), *Narcissus and Goldmund* (*Narziß und Goldmund,* 1930), and *The Glass Bead Game* (also known as *Magister Ludi, Das Glasperlenspiel,* 1943). Hesse won the Nobel Prize in 1946. Most of his works explore a character's inner journey towards auto-cognition and fulfillment. Hesse's novels were very popular between the two world wars, and again in the 1960s and 1970s, during the so-called flower-power years.

Walter Benjamin and translation

Hesse wrote his Reclam essay not long after the publication of one of the most famous texts in translation studies, Walter Benjamin's 1923 "The Task of the Translator," an introduction to a translation of the *Tableaux parisiens* of Baudelaire. Hesse's text, although in much simpler language, in many ways reverberates with Benjamin's. For Benjamin too, "while a poet's words endure in his own language, even the greatest translation is destined to become part of the growth of its own language and eventually to be absorbed by its renewal" (Benjamin 2000: 18). In other words, whereas the original endures as is, even though its meaning may change as the language changes, a translation because of this very same fact, but also because its own language changes too, always is overtaken by time, and, as is Hesse's argument with regard to Luther's Bible translation, needs re-doing in time. Benjamin's essay also contains the important insight that the afterlife of a work lies in translation, while at the same time the translation only becomes relevant because of the work's afterlife. If we translate this into world literature terms, we can take this to mean that a work stops being "world literature" when it is no longer *being* translated or, in Damrosch's term, but in fact this is also the term used by for instance Guillén (1993: 40), when it no longer "circulates" beyond its language and culture of origin.

Walter Benjamin (1892–1940) was a German-Jewish author, philosopher, historian and social critic. A prolific writer, Benjamin published major essays on Baudelaire and Paris in the nineteenth century, translating parts of Baudelaire's *Flowers of Evil* (*Les Fleurs du Mal*). He also wrote on Goethe and Proust, and on many other writers, as well as on social and cultural issues. Famous essays are "The Task of the Translator" (1923) and "The Work of Art in the Age of Mechanical Reproduction"(1936). Fleeing Nazi Germany Benjamin established himself in Paris in 1933. Upon the German invasion of France Benjamin fled to Spain, but fearing extradition to Germany he committed suicide. Benjamin's work gained wide popularity in American academic circles in the 1960s and 1970s, especially through the intervention of Hannah Arendt, herself a refugee from Nazi Germany and by then an influential philosopher and political scientist in the USA.

Finally, Benjamin also discusses the difference between bad and good translations. He first makes a detour to discuss the various degrees of "translatability" of an original. Contrary to common expectation, for Benjamin it is those texts that are to the highest degree purely informative that are the most untranslatable. Such texts, he argues, are completely hidden in translation because the only thing that matters is their content, and that can be perfectly rendered in translation. Consequently, they read in translation as if they were originals and all sense of their foreignness is lost to the reader. As such they also pose no challenge to the translator. On the contrary, "the higher the level of a work, the more does it remain translatable even if its meaning is touched upon only fleetingly" (Benjamin 2000: 23). "Content," then, is not what matters. "The task of the translator," for Benjamin, "consists in finding that intended effect [Intention] upon the language into which he is translating which produces in it the echo of the original" (Benjamin 2000: 19–20). It should be remembered that Benjamin always writes with "the true language" of Holy Writ in mind, in which there is no gap between language and truth, as there is no mediation of meaning: revelation simply is what it is. In such a case, Benjamin writes, "Translations are called for only because of the plurality of languages ... just as, in the original, language and revelation are one without any tension, so the translation must be one with the original in the form of the interlinear version ... the interlinear version of the Scriptures is the prototype or ideal of all translation" (Benjamin 2000: 23). Although overlaid here with both messianic and Heideggerian overtones, Benjamin's ideas on translation also echo Goethe's. In fact, Benjamin hails Goethe's Notes to the *West-Östlicher Diwan*, along with some observations by Rudof Pannwitz in the latter's *Die Krisis der europäischen Kultur* (1917; *The Crisis of European Culture*), as "the best comment on the theory of translation that has been published in Germany" (Benjamin 2000: 22).

Goethe himself translated from many languages, including a number he himself was not directly conversant with, but which he worked through mediation of other translations or translators, a practice later also taken up by for instance Ezra Pound in his translations from the Chinese. Birus (2000) stresses that the extensive knowledge of, and intercourse with, foreign literatures that Goethe's concept of *Weltliteratur* presupposes likewise presupposes extensive translational activity. Though he thinks that Berczik (1963: 288) exaggerates when the latter claims that, for Goethe, "world literature ... is nourished foremost by translations; more, it is almost identical to the art of translation" (Birus 2000: 5), Birus still approvingly quotes Goethe himself, in his review of Carlyle's *German Romance*, as stating that, "Whatever one may say about the shortcomings of translation, it nonetheless remains one of the most important and most worthy activities in the business of this world" (Birus 2000: 5). In this sense, Birus concludes, "Goethe regards the process of development of world literature as profoundly bound up with the medium of literary translation, over and above our striving for the widest possible direct knowledge of the various literatures, and over and above the lively interaction among Literatoren (that is poets, critics, university teachers, etc.)" (Birus 2000: 5).

In the Note on "Uebersetzung" (translation) Goethe appended to the *West-Östlicher Diwan*, he outlined the three "Arten" or kinds of translation he discerned. The first kind is that which "acquaints us with the foreign according to our own lights, a simple prose translation is most suitable here" (Goethe 1819: 526; macht uns in unserm eigenen Sinne mit dem Auslande bekannt; eine schlicht-prosaische ist hiezu die beste). Translation here is a purely "functional" exercise; the only thing that matters is the content of the original without bothering about style, versification or other matters. The second stage or "Epoche" is "where one is concerned with entering into the foreign situation, but really only with the intent of appropriating to one-self the foreign and to refashion it according to one's own lights" (Goethe 1819: 527; wo man sich in die Zustände des Auslandes zwar zu versetzen, aber eigentlich nur fremden Sinn sich anzueignen und mit eignem [*sic*] Sinne wieder darzustellen bemüht ist). Here the translator "naturalizes" the original within his own literary target system. Finally, there is the third stage: "A translation that aims to identify itself with the original finally approaches the condition of an interlinear version and much furthers understanding of the original, it leads us back to the original text, stronger, it forces us back to that text, and thus finally the circle is closed in which the foreign and the native, the known and the unknown move closely together" (Goethe 1819: 532; Eine Uebersetzung die sich mit dem Original zu identificiren [*sic*] strebt nähert sich zuletzt die interlinear-Version und erleichtert höchlich den Verständniss des Originals, hiedurch wirden wir an der Grundtext hinangeführt, ja getrieben, und so ist denn zuletzt den ganzen Zirkel abgeschlossen, in welchen sich die annäherung des Fremden und Einheimischen, des Bekanntenn und Unbe-kannten bewegt). This third kind of translation, then, does not strive to nat-uralize the original in the target language but instead aims to preserve the former's strangeness, its foreignness. This is also what Pannwitz, in the book Benjamin refers to, expresses when he says that "the basic error of the trans-lator is that he preserves the state in which his own language happens to be instead of allowing his language to be powerfully affected by the foreign tongue ... he must expand and deepen his language by means of the foreign language" (Benjamin 2000: 22).

The rise of translation studies

It is not surprising that Homi Bhabha seizes upon Benjamin's essay, and precisely also upon the latter's citation of Pannwitz, in his own essay "How newness enters the world: Postmodern space, postcolonial times, and the trials of cultural translation" (Bhabha 1994). It is precisely in the making foreign one's own language in the act of translation that the possibility of newness enters the world for the postcolonial, migrant, diasporic or other minority author: by making the present not the transitional moment between the inevitability of a future issuing from a teleological past but rather a moment where time stops and re-direction is possible. Cultural translation, in other words, becomes the site for Bhabhian in-betweenness, hybridity, and third-space.

In truth, what Bhabha was militantly, almost oracularly, certainly spectacularly, putting forward as a revolutionary program for postcolonial cultural translation was not different from what practicing writers had been aware of at least since Cervantes in the early seventeenth century passed off his *Don Quijote* as translated from the Arabic. Almost concurrently with Bhabha's writing on translation, moreover, the then emergent discipline of translation studies had been describing Bhabha's translational "newness" as commonly practiced in most actual literary translation. The term "translation studies" was coined by James S. Holmes in 1972 (Holmes 2000) in an article that constituted one of the first really systematic attempts to map the rapidly growing proliferation of approaches, research, and theories having to do with "translation" in the widest sense of the word. Susan Bassnett, in 1980, consolidated much of these trends in her still widely used and several times updated primer *Translation Studies*. Specifically with regard to literature, what Bassnett, and with her the so-called Tel Aviv-Leuven-Amsterdam school of translation studies picked up on was literary polysystem theory as elaborated by Itamar Even-Zohar in a number of articles in the early and mid-1970s, largely while he was on a research stay in the Low Countries, and in close conversation with James S. Holmes and a number of scholars at the universities of Amsterdam, Antwerp and Leuven. At the same time Even-Zohar also closely collaborated with his colleagues Benjamin Hrushovski and Gideon Toury at the Porter Institute for Poetics and Semiotics of Tel Aviv University in a tradition inspired by various schools of structuralism.

Itamar Even-Zohar (1939) is an Israeli cultural and literary theoretician. Starting from structuralist premises Even-Zohar as of the 1970s came to see society, and culture, as multi-layered, with a number of sub-systems operating within a larger system. This led to his polysystem theory in which systems dynamically interrelate with one another, thus leading to continuous transformation. Even-Zohar's insights strongly influenced literary studies, and were particularly influential in the rise and development of translation studies.

As far as their interest in translation was concerned, Even-Zohar and Toury worked both in what Holmes had termed descriptive translation studies. Even-Zohar was particularly concerned with the function of translated literature within his more comprehensive view of all literature as an interlocking "polysystem" composed of central and peripheral sub-systems (such as genres, but also such as translated literature versus literature in the

original) battling it out for supremacy. Toury concentrated rather on estab-
lishing the norms that ruled actual translations. For a description of these
norms he drew upon, and refined, the terminology of "shifts" between original and translation that for instance the linguist J.C. Catford had also developed in an influential 1965 book. In earlier approaches such shifts, on both
the micro (words, sentences, nuances) and macro levels (the structure of the
text as a whole, including its arrangement in chapters or other forms of ordering,
prefaces, notes, and other so-called paratextual features), would have been
evaluated in terms of "equivalence" – or not – between original and translation, or between "source" and "target" text. Some such shifts might be
deemed inevitable because of insuperable differences between source and
target language or culture, others were simply deemed "failures" on the part
of the translator, whose highest "norm" was always supposed to be the
greatest possible fidelity to the original. In all fairness it should also be said
that much of the earlier terminology, and the emphasis on "equivalence,"
derived from research and theorization primarily pertinent to non-literary
translation, and in the context of the translator-training institutes that as of
the 1950s started to appear all over Europe.

Now, however, scholars working on literary translations have adopted this
very same terminology, coupled with the insights of Even-Zohar and Toury,
not to "find fault" with the work of literary translators, but to study what
shifts they made as part of the process, or the strategy, of adapting the
translated work to the receiving culture. The title of a collection of essays
edited by Theo Hermans in 1985 is a fair indication of this shift of emphasis:
The Manipulation of Literature: Studies in Literary Translation. Probably the
best-known exponent of this approach is André Lefevere, who eventually
came to see translation as only one form of what he called the "refraction" of
literature, next to for instance criticism and historiography. In one of his best-
known articles, "Mother Courage's Cucumbers: Text, System and Refraction
in a Theory of Literature" (2000 [1982]), Lefevere showed how what at first
sight are blatant distortions in the American translations of the German
playwright Bertolt Brecht's play *Mutter Courage und ihre Kinder* are in fact changes effected because of constraints upon what was acceptable to an American
public, possible because of political conditions, and presentable according to
an American "horizon of expectations," at the moment of production of these
translations.

According to Lefevere, a translation always represents "a compromise
between two systems," the originating and the receiving one (Lefevere 2000:
237.) "The degree of compromise in a refraction," Lefevere adds, "will
depend on the reputation of the writer being translated within the system
from which the translation is made," while "the degree to which the foreign
writer is accepted into a native system will, on the other hand, be determined
by the need that native system has of him in a certain phase of its evolution"
(Lefevere 2000: 237). Lefevere is here expressing on the level of an individual
author what Even-Zohar had put in more general terms when he said that

"through the foreign works, features (both principles and elements) are intro-duced into the home literature which did not exist there before," and that "the very principles of selecting the works to be translated are determined by the situation governing the (home) polysystem: the texts are chosen according to their compatibility with the new approaches and the supposedly innovatory role they may play within the target literature" (Even-Zohar 2000: 193). According to Even-Zohar there are three situations in which a literature may be particularly receptive to such "import" via translation: "when a literature is 'young,' in the process of being established," "when a literature is either 'peripheral' (within a large group of correlated literatures) or 'weak,' or both," and "when there are turning points, crises, or literary vacuums in a literature" (Even-Zohar 2000: 194).

Translation, postcolonialism and feminism

Susan Bassnett (1993) emphasizes the enabling role of translation for post-colonialism and feminism. For the former she draws a parallel with the work of the Brazilian *antropófagos*, specifically that of the brothers Haroldo and Augusto de Campos, who, after the poet Oswald de Andrade's 1928 *Manifesto Antropófago*, developed a theory and a practice of translation in which Brazilian authors would appropriate, devour, or cannibalize, European ancestors and models to digest them and transform them into something entirely Brazilian. For the latter she adduces the work of a number of Cana-dian feminist translation studies scholars. What both these Brazilians and Canadians have in common, she argues, is "the aim of celebrating the role of the translator, of making the translator visible in an act of transgression that seeks to reconstruct the old patriarchal/European hierarchies" (Bassnett 1993, 157). In fact, both groups can also be seen as answering to some of Even-Zohar's different kinds of situations in which translations can, and usually do, play an important role in a particular literary system. The case of the Brazi-lians is that of a still relatively young literature that until the 1920s, notwith-standing such exceptions as the late nineteenth-century novelist Machado de Assis, had always felt itself at the same time also as "peripheral" to the lit-eratures of Europe. *Antropofagismo* allows the Brazilians to both import from European literature what they can use and at the same time, at least meta-phorically, transcend the stage of imitation or dependence by reversing the customary role between source and target literatures, casting the latter now as the active, possessive partner in the transaction rather than the passive, receptive one.

Haroldo de Campos (1929–2003) was a Brazilian poet, critic and translator. Together with his brother **Augusto de Campos** (1931–), Haroldo de Campos started the concrete poetry movement in Brazil in the 1950s.

Bassnett makes a point of how such metaphors were also used for the traditional roles between the sexes, and how feminist translation theory therefore also implies a subversion or reversal not only of these same metaphors but also of real gender relationships in society. That such feminist translation studies should have arisen in Canada, and primarily in French-speaking Canada, has therefore everything to do with the likewise relatively "young" status of Canadian literature, and certainly Canadian literary theory, in general at the time, and the even younger status of French-Canadian literature, which found itself doubly peripheral as a "minor" literature in what was itself a "peripheral" culture. At the same time the influence of women writers, with Margaret Atwood, Margaret Laurence, Alice Munro, Mavis Gallant, and Carol Shields on the English-language side, and Anne Hébert and Nicole Brossard on the French-language side, and all of them with a more or less markedly feminist inclination, was particularly strong in Canadian literature. Especially a group around Nicole Brossard has been instrumental in elaborating a feminist translation studies.

In both the Brazilian and the Canadian case, then, as Bassnett quotes Lefevere (1992), "Translation is not just 'a window opened on another world,' or some such pious platitude ... rather, translation is a channel opened, often not without a certain reluctance, through which foreign influences can penetrate the native culture, challenge it and even contribute to subverting it" (Bassnett 1993: 159). This is very different from Damrosch's view in *What is World Literature?*, where he describes "world literature," at least in one of its manifestations, and as enabled by translation, as exactly such a "window" (Damrosch 2003: 15). As Bassnett puts it: "Writing does not happen in a vacuum, it happens in a context and the process of translating texts from one cultural system into another is not a neutral, innocent, transparent activity ... translation is instead a highly charged, transgressive activity, and the politics of translation and translating deserve much greater attention than has been paid in the past" (Bassnett 1993: 160–61).

World literature and translation

For world literature, the point that Bassnett and Lefevere, drawing out the implications of Even-Zohar's polysystem theory, can be seen to be making is that one and the same "world literature author" may fulfill completely different functions in different literary systems. If I take an example I am fairly familiar with, and look at Dutch literature of the nineteenth and twentieth centuries, we can see how, for instance, Byron, Yeats, and T.S. Eliot have played very different roles there from those they played in a number of other contexts, and from those that now usually make for their inclusion in world literature anthologies, especially in the United States. Byron was quite frequently translated into Dutch during the period 1825–45, but it was a fairly narrow selection from his works, mostly the so-called "oriental tales," lyrical pieces, and isolated passages from the longer poems. Byron, as the poet of

Romantic nationalism and revolt, never found favor with his Dutch translators or with the Dutch public. This was mostly because the Belgian revolt of
1830 against the Dutch (what is now Belgium having been incorporated into
a Kingdom of the United Netherlands in 1815 by the Congress of Vienna)
made the Dutch particularly unreceptive to revolutionary feelings of nationalism, at least on what they considered their own soil. Moreover, the majority
of Byron's translators were students, or young men, while working on their
translations. They almost all went on to become Protestant ministers and
staunch upholders of a Dutch variant of petit-bourgeois or *Biedermeier* culture. Not surprisingly, they all came to repudiate Byron as altogether too fri-
volous and morally dangerous. The versatilities of Byron's poetry left no
impression upon Dutch poetry except in the form of a parody that turns
Byron's *Don Juan* inside out to preach good morals to upstanding young
men. In short, Byron served as a negative catalyst for the Dutch literary
system of the mid-nineteenth century, and both the selection of what was
translated from him and the contemporary discourse pertaining to it show
this (D'haen 1990: 2005).

Translations of W.B. Yeats were mainly the work of one man, the Dutch
poet Adrian Roland Holst, who repeatedly returned to translating Yeats over
the course of a very long poetic career spanning the 1910s to the 1970s.
Again, though, the Yeats of Roland Holst is not the Modernist Yeats we
know from our contemporary anthologies or literary histories; nor is he the
postcolonial Yeats of Edward Said in *Empire and Culture* (1993). Because of
the selection Roland Holst makes from Yeats, and because of the interpretation he puts upon his own work and life, and upon Yeats, the latter emerges
as almost exclusively the poet of the Celtic Twilight. Within the Dutch literary system, however, Roland Holst needed the example of a foreign
authority to escape the overbearing influence of Herman Gorter, a leading
Dutch poet around the turn of the century, and a close friend of Roland
Holst's family. Although once considered one of Holland's major poets,
Roland Holst now has largely faded, as his poetics are considered old-fashioned
and dated even by the standards with which we now measure the early twentieth century. In fact, whereas Yeats continues to sound fresh in English,
Roland Holst in his Yeats translations, and indeed in a great part of his own
production, sounds predictably and artificially "poetical" and stale (D'haen
1991 and 2006).

In contrast, the Dutch poet mainly responsible for translating T.S. Eliot,
Martinus Nijhoff, has increasingly emerged as the real leading poet of that
same early twentieth century, mostly because of two long poems that rather
resemble Eliot's *The Love Song of J. Alfred Prufrock* and *The Waste Land*,
although these are precisely the poems by Eliot that Nijhoff never tackled. In
fact, Nijhoff translated primarily a number of shorter poems by Eliot and,
probably towards the end of his life, some plays. Therefore, the Eliot we have
in Dutch translation is once again a very selective and partial one, though his
own poetic practice shows that Nijhoff was very well acquainted also with the

rest of Eliot's *oeuvre*. Whereas Roland Holst and Nijhoff both resorted to translation to fashion their own poetics, Roland Holst, like the Dutch Byron translators of the nineteenth century, did not finally bring "newness" to the Dutch literary system. Nijhoff did, and the generation of poets following him looked back to him and not to Roland Holst. At least, that is how things look now. Of course, there is nothing to prevent future poets eventually going back to Roland Holst and developing a wholly new poetics from him and from his translations of Yeats. The irony in all this is that Nijhoff probably himself seized upon Eliot as his example to evade the overbearing influence of Roland Holst, who, slightly older than Nijhoff, certainly looked formidable at Nijhoff's debut, and in fact throughout most of the latter's career (D'haen 2009).

In all this, the fact remains that, as Lefevere says, "the refraction ... is the original to the great majority of people who are only tangentially exposed to literature" (Lefevere 2000: 246). In other words, to the Dutch reader Roland Holst's Yeats *is* Yeats, and so with Byron, and with T.S. Eliot. In truth, this is a tenuous point, as in fact there would be few Dutch readers of Yeats, Byron or Eliot in translation that would not also be sufficiently conversant with English to at least be able to get a fairly good idea of the original in the original. The matter would be very different, of course, for the translations from the Chinese, specifically Li-Po, by another early twentieth-century Dutch poet, J.J. Slauerhoff, by way of Arthur Waley. Likewise, in other cultural contexts, such as for instance that of the United States, translation might be the only access to any or almost any foreign literature. Still, the fate of Byron and Yeats in Dutch translation may explain why these two poets have never had much of an "afterlife" in The Netherlands, and therefore may not loom very large in a hypothetical Netherlands-generated "canon of world literature."

A different case of afterlife occurs in the numerous postcolonial rewritings of European classics, all of them forms of the kind of cultural translation that Bhabha also explores in the article referred to above, and as example of which he uses Wallcott's *Omeros* rewriting Homer. Well-known other cases are Jean Rhys in *Wide Sargasso Sea* re-writing Charlotte Brontë's *Jane Eyre*, Maryse Condé in *La migration des coeurs* doing the same with Emily Brontë's *Wuthering Heights*, and J.M. Coetzee grounding *Foe* in Daniel Defoe's *Robinson Crusoe*. Shakespeare's *The Tempest* and Joseph Conrad's *Heart of Darkness* have been the subject of numerous rewritings from both a feminist and a postcolonial point of view (Zabus 2002; Farn 2005). Arguably, to many contemporary readers Bertha Mason is not the crazy murderess from *Jane Eyre* but the duped French-créole Antoinette from *Wide Sargasso Sea*.

In all these cases we could see similarities with the *antropófagismo* of the Brazilians discussed before: the "original" work disappears after having been consumed by its "afterlife." Or, for the reader that does go back to the "original", the latter has been utterly changed by its "translation." If, as Bassnett argues, "the new notion of translation confer[s] new life on the source text"

(Bassnett 1993: 152), this is not to be taken as a simple continuation of the latter's former life but rather as an "updated" version, giving it new meanings, tying it to new locales, different times.

Translation studies and the "new" comparative literature

In 1993, Susan Bassnett concluded her *Comparative Literature: A Critical Introduction* with a chapter entitled "Towards Translation Studies," in which she gave a very upbeat and militant prognosis as to the future of translation studies. Until then translation studies had been considered a branch, and for the longest time a minor branch, of comparative literature. However, she posited, "cross-cultural work in women's studies, in post-colonial theory, in cultural studies has changed the face of literary studies generally," and given the importance of translation in all of these, "we should look upon translation studies as the principal discipline from now on, with comparative literature as a valued but subsidiary subject area" (Bassnett 1993: 161). Since the time of Bassnett's writing, the study of translation certainly has gained in importance, but instead of becoming a major discipline of its own, its evident success, like that of "theory" with comparative literature in the 1970s and 1980s, rather seems to have led to its dissipation into all kinds of adjacent disciplines. At present it undoubtedly is one of the major foci of interest in the most recent comparative literature update paradigm of world literature studies, thus sharing the fate of the discipline Bassnett once thought it would replace.

In fact, the re-emergence of world literature as of the early years of the twenty-first century has spawned fresh reflections on the role of translation. In a 1992 article entitled "The Politics of Translation," Spivak had already, albeit in the context of a reflection on Third World feminism and not on world literature, argued that "in the act of wholesale translation into English there can be a betrayal of the democratic ideal into the law of the strongest ... this happens when all the literature of the Third World gets translated into a sort of with-it translatese, so that the literature by a woman in Palestine begins to resemble, in the feel of its prose, something by a man in Taiwan" (Spivak 2000: 400). Her reproach here very much resembles that she earlier made of Foucault and Deleuze when in "Can the Subaltern Speak?" she accused these French philosophers of mistaking the Western working class man as representative for all the oppressed in the world, and of their own discourse as empowered to speak for all discourses on oppression. In *A Critique of Postcolonial Reason* (1999) Spivak extends her remarks to literature. In yet more recent work, branding the recent interest in world literature in the United States as "the arrogance of the cartographic reading of world lit. in translation as the task of Comparative Literature" (Spivak 2003: 73), Spivak vehemently opposes "U.S.-style world literature becoming the staple of Comparative Literature in the global South" (Spivak 2003: 39). Instead, and this in both her 1992 article and her 2003 book, she advocates learning and teaching local languages and gaining an intimate knowledge of the local cultures. When translation is necessary, it should "make visible the import of the translator's choice"(Spivak 2003: 18.). She propounds a "new Comparative Literature" where a "joining of forces between Comparative Literature and Area studies" (Spivak 2003: 20) would "persistently and repeatedly undermine and undo the definitive tendency of the dominant to appropriate the emergent"(Spivak 2003: 100). This can only be done by close textual analysis, looking for what Spivak calls signs of "planetarity" (Spivak 2003: 81) by-passing the necessarily hegemonously localized geographies of "globalization" and "world literature" in any of its present, and particularly its most recent US comparative literature, avatars. Spivak's impassioned plea seems triggered by the same fear that led Erich Auerbach, in his "Philology and World Literature" of 1952, to lament that "man will have to accustom himself to existence in a standardized world, to a single literary culture, only a few literary languages and perhaps even a single literary language ... and herewith the notion of *Weltliteratur* would now be at once realized and destroyed" (Auerbach 2009: 127).

Obviously taking up Spivak's call for a "new Comparative Literature," and drawing on the writings of Jacques Derrida, Edward Said and Leo Spitzer, Emily Apter boldly proposes to reground the discipline in "the problem of translation" (Apter 2006: 251). "A new comparative literature," she professes, "would acknowledge [the] jockeying for power and respect in the field of language" and hence "seeks to be the name of language worlds characterized by linguistic multiplicity and phantom inter-nations" (Apter 2003: 244–45). In a 2008 article Apter seems to be at the same time echoing and questioning Spivak's concerns about the hegemonic dangers of English for new postnational paradigms (such as world literature) when she feels that "Postnationalism can lead to blindness toward the economic and national power struggles that literary politics often front for, while potentially minimizing the conflict among the interests of monocultural states and multilingual communities (as in current U.S. policy that uses an agenda of cultural homogeneity to patrol 'immigrant' languages and to curtail bilingual education)" and that "though planetary inclusion may be the goal of new lexicons in contemporary comparative literature, they often paradoxically reinforce dependency on a national/ethnic nominalism that gives rise to new exclusions" (Apter 2008: 581). After a brief discussion of new names given to postnationalism in literature – world literature, cosmopolitanism, planetarity, etc. – Apter then turns to possible solutions for handling such transnational constellations as offered by translation studies, and particularly by investigations of "untranslatability" figuring in two collaborative undertakings: the *Vocabulaire européen des philosophies: Dictionnaire des intraduisibles* (*Vocabulary of European Philosophy: A Dictionary of Untranslatables*) under the general editorship of Barbara Cassin, and *The Novel*, the five-volume Italian version of which appeared in 2001–3, and the two-volume condensed version of which in English dates from 2006, both with Franco Moretti as general editor.

I will not go into Apter's discussion of Cassin's project here, but will concentrate instead on that of Moretti's. Apter, like many other commentators of Moretti's, is particularly intrigued by Moretti's conjecture, in his 2000 article, that the spread of the European novel retains the plotlines exported from the center but adopts indigenous characters and voice. Almost echoing Bhabha on how "newness" enters the world, Apter, putting things in translation terms, wonders whether "new genres [are] made by virtue of translation failure?" and whether "the lack of a common ground of comparison [is] a spur to literary evolution?" (Apter 2008: 293). "Is a genre's travel the measure of its aliveness," she asks, and "its drift the gauge of force required to break open the bounds of a closed world-system?" (Apter 2008: 293). Taking up while at the same time countering Spivak's 2003 call for a combination of language-learning and area studies to resist the hegemonic cartographies projected by a world-literature-in-translation studies US-style, Apter marshalls translation for a "translational humanities responsive to fluctuations in geopolitics, and which intersects with but is not confined to national language frontiers" (Apter 2008: 297). Offering Cassin's vocabulary of European philosophy and Moretti's study of the novel as examples, Apter posits the collective authorship both these projects imply as, "like multiple language learning and off-site academic immersion," "one of the more viable ways of experiencing 'in-translation' or '*un*translatability' as explosive conceptual practices capable of limning new cartographies of the present" (Apter 2008: 297).

Finally, Lawrence Venuti, in his piece on "World Literature and Translation" for the *Routledge Companion to World Literature*, amplifies upon Lefevere's earlier remark that for most readers the translated version is the only one they know of a particular work not written in their own native language by advancing that "for most readers, translated texts constitute world literature" (Venuti 2011: 23). Summarizing a lot of recent discussions on the role of translation in literary studies, and referring amongst others to Casanova (1999, 2004) and Moretti (2000), Venuti concludes that, "To understand the impact of translation in the creation of world literature, we need to examine the canons developed by translation patterns within the receiving situation as well as the interpretations that translations inscribe in the source texts" and that "to be productive, to yield the most incisive findings, this sort of examination must combine distant and close reading of translations to explore the relations between canons and interpretations" (Venuti 2011: 23).

Ann Steiner nuances Venuti's remark on translation patterns in the sense that she sees translation as part of what she terms "the economy of literature," along with "sale systems, publishing traditions ... government support, [and] taxes" (Steiner 2011: 316). These mechanisms, along with other factors such as the hegemonic or peripheral position a certain culture or language occupies in the world order of things, explain the uneven flows of translation between languages, cultures, and literatures. Certain cultures, such as for instance the American, translate very little themselves from foreign literatures while their own literature is widely and massively translated into other languages. Other cultures, such as most West-European ones, translate almost exhaustively from English, but not necessarily on any comparable scale between each other's literatures. Moreover, the works actually translated differ widely as to their status, with, next to a number of perennial classics such as the Bible, or Shakespeare, a preponderance of works in popular genres. The latter typically have a short life span, both in the original and in translation. Yet the translation patterns they are subject to, and the mechanisms these patterns are themselves subject to, certainly also deserve attention in the context of world literature studies. Of course, the Danish critic Georg Brandes in his 1899 article "World Literature" had already argued as much.

Conclusion

- The study of world literature has always recognized the importance of translation.
- The systematic study of translations as influencing the national as well as transnational development of literature has really only come into its own in the latter half of the twentieth century.
- An author or a literary work may occupy quite different positions in different literatures as a result of translation.
- Some influential contemporary critics warn of the potentially unwittingly homogenizing consequences of feeding students world literature in translation, thereby dulling the real differences between languages, literatures and cultures, and in practice reducing all literature to literature in the language of translation; rather than introducing students to a world beyond their own culture this naturalizes the world for them as their own.
- Translation studies has become an inalienable part of comparative literature, and of present-day world literature studies.

7 World literature, (post)modernism, (post)colonialism, littérature-monde

Overview

In the early 1990s the well-known postcolonial critic Homi Bhabha proposed that postcolonial literature might be the new world literature. For him the literature of the displaced, the exiled, the uprooted, the marginalized, more accurately reflected the state of the present-day world than the postmodern literature produced by so-called mainstream literatures in the West. In reality, the division between postcolonialism and postmodernism is not so clear-cut. In fact, many contemporary writers may be seen to fit both categories. Moreover, most of the writers that would fit Bhabha's postcolonial category write in the language of the former colonizer or the present-day hegemon. This raises the question whether the postcolonial as commonly conceived of in present-day literary studies, rather than an alternative to "Western" literature, is not simply one more projection of that same Western hegemony in matters literary, theoretical as well as practical. If such issues have increasingly come to the fore in Anglophone literary criticism, they have been much less debated in other languages. Very recently, though, the issue has erupted also in French-language literature with a much-noted manifesto in a leading Parisian daily, followed by a collective volume.

Postcolonial literature as world literature

In his introduction to *Locations of Culture* (1994) Bhabha cites Goethe's remarks in the latter's introduction to Thomas Carlyle's *Life of Schiller* (1830) that through the Napoleonic Wars nations had become aware of "much that was foreign" and conscious of "spiritual needs hitherto unknown" (Strich 1949: 351; Bhabha cites another, older translation, viz. that by Joel Spingarn [1921], which gives the same passages as "many foreign ideas and ways" and "previously unrecognized spiritual and intellectual needs," Bhabha 1994: 11). Goethe goes on to say that this has led to "a sense of relationship as neighbors" (Strich 1949: 251; Spingarn as quoted by Bhabha: "the feeling of neighborly relations," Bhabha 1994: 11). Bhabha, however, wrenches this in another direction by posing the question what would happen if such "needs" as Goethe refers to would "emerge from the imposition of 'foreign' ideas, cultural representations, and structures of power" (Bhabha 1994: 12). With a reference to Goethe as an "Orientalist who read Shakuntala at seventeen years of age" (Bhabha 1994: 11), and who in his autobiography referred to the Hindu monkey God Hanuman as "unformed and over-formed," Bhabha (1994: 12) suggests that world literature might be based not on the recognition of what is common in all literatures, as has often been the interpretation put upon Goethe's *Weltliteratur*, but rather rooted in "histor-ical trauma" (Bhabha 1994: 12). As Bhabha puts it: "The study of world lit-erature might be the study of the way in which cultures recognize themselves through their projections of 'otherness'" (Bhabha 1994: 12). Hence, he proposes, "where, once, the transmission of national traditions was the major theme of world literature, perhaps we can now suggest that transnational histories of migrants, the colonized, or political refugees – these border and frontier conditions – may be the terrains of world literature" (Bhabha 1994: 12).

> **Homi Bhabha** (1949–) is an Indian-born literary theoretician who has made his career first in England and since the late 1980s in the US, teaching at Princeton, the University of Pennsylvania, Dartmouth, The University of Chicago, and, since 2001, at Harvard. Often regarded, together with Edward Said and Gayatri Spivak, as one of the most influential theoreticians of postcolonialism, Bhabha has introduced and popularized notions such as "mimicry" and "hybridisation." Most of his essays have been collected in *The Location of Culture* (1994).

Bhabha's suggestion that the literature of migrants, and by extension that of postcolonialism, might be the new world literature, has been taken up again and again in the 1990s and in the early years of the twenty-first century. In her position paper on the 1993 Bernheimer report on "Comparative Lit-erature in the age of Multiculturalism," Emily Apter directly refers to Bhab-ha's introduction to *The Location of Culture*, quoting the sentences immediately preceding those I just cited. Reading the history of post-WWII American comparative literature as a succession of, and a dialogue among, exilic voices, and primarily those of Wellek, Spitzer and Auerbach, Said, Spivak and Bhahba, Apter is of the opinion that "translating the discursive maneuvers of unhappy consciousness characteristic of postwar criticism into a politicized, multicultural critical idiom, postcolonialism is in many respects truer to the foundational disposition of comparative literature than are more traditional tendencies and approaches ... with its interrogation of cultural subjectivity and attention to the tenuous bonds between identity and national language, postcolonialism quite naturally inherits the mantle of comparative literature's historical legacy" (Apter 1995: 86). The Bernheimer report itself, and especially the reactions to it, Apter reads as "crude generational/cultural warfare over Eurocentrism" and "a contest for the title of who lays claim to the exilic aura of comparative literature's distinguished past" (Apter 1995: 94). Echoing Bhabha's reference to "border and frontier conditions," Apter recasts the debate as a "border war, an academic version of the legal battles and political disputes over the status of 'undocumented workers,' 'illegal aliens,' and 'permanent residents'," and concludes that "postcolonialism will claim its place whether Continental comparatism likes it or not" (Apter 1995: 94–96). What is important, and even "imperative," she argues, is "to continue reinventing world literature with a concern not to warehouse theoretical culture," because, and again echoing Bhabha's statement above, she feels that this "'dissensual' confusion of First and Third World critical perspectives" gives cohesion to the field of comparative literature and that moreover "the exilic melancholy of theory is profoundly in sync with the narrative movement of comparative literature and comparative culture" (Apter 1995: 94). Mads Rosendahl Thomsen seems to follow up on Apter's suggestion when he proposes that "it is hard to overlook the fact that the most significant thinker related to the post-colonial discourse, Edward W. Said, was at the same time a strong proponent of world literature ... he translated Auerbach on world literature, and kept returning to the idea of it, ... was this the paradigm for which he really hoped, rather than the establishment and fortification of a dichotomy between centre and periphery?" (Thomsen 2008: 25).

Although Apter frames her remarks as if postcolonialism at the time of her writing still had to do battle to conquer its place under the comparative literature sun, by the mid-1990s such was surely no longer the case in English departments in the USA and the UK. In the mid-1980s, when postcolonialism indeed was still struggling to gain a firm footing, Fredric Jameson had anticipated upon things to come. As Vilashini Cooppan reminds us, Jameson's "Third-World Literature in the Era of Multinational Capitalism," published in 1986, quickly became "notorious for its claim that all third-world texts are necessarily national allegories," but is "largely forgotten for what it has to say about *Weltliteratur*"(Cooppan 2004: 17). Indeed, Jameson had almost presciently started off his article with "in these last years of the century, the old question of a properly world literature reasserts itself" before going on to say that "today the reinvention of cultural studies in the United States demands the reinvention, in a new situation, of what Goethe long ago theorized as 'world literature'," and to then assert that "any conception of world literature necessarily demands some specific engagement with the question of third-world literature [...]" (Jameson 2000: 318). Jameson's specific suggestion that all third-world literatures are necessarily allegorical quickly drew heavy critical fire, and under postcolonialism proper became almost completely discredited. Still, Jameson's insistence on linking the literary works produced in what was then, before the fall of the Berlin Wall and the implosion of the "second" world of the communist nations, still called the Third World to economic, and in their wake social and political, conditions pertaining in the nations concerned as well as to their position in the wider scheme of world economics, especially as ruled by late capitalism, did find some ready echoes, though most often elaborated along lines very different from those pursued by Jameson himself.

Amitava Kumar, in his introduction to a 2003 volume called *World Bank Literature*, quotes Jameson on the need for "the reinvention, in a new situation, of what Goethe long ago theorized as 'world literature'," and then wonders whether "World Bank Literature" could be "a new name for post-colonial studies?" (Kumar 2003: xx). Kumar argues that present-day expositions about world literature routinely by-pass the economic issues at the back, or at the heart, of the texts in question, and equally routinely select texts on the basis of so-called universal values. Instead, he argues, what we should do is pay attention to how literature comprises and reveals local or national economic realities of dominance, suppression, oppression and exploitation in a global context, or in the context of globalization:

> The focus on the World Bank, as an agent and a metaphor, helps us concretize the "wider context" of global capitalism. As we witnessed during the protests on the streets of Seattle or Washington, D.C., Davos, or Quebec City, the opposition to the World Bank, the IMF, and the WTO is both widespread and collective. On that basis alone, the analytic shift from the liberal-diversity model of "World Literature" to the radical paradigm of "World Bank Literature" signals a resolve not only to recognize and contest the dominance of Bretton Woods institutions but also to rigorously oppose those regimes of knowledge that would keep literature and culture sealed from the issues of economics and activism.
>
> (Kumar 2003: xix–xx)

As examples Kumar cites Arundhati Roy's *The God of Small Things*, Pankaj Mishra's *The Romantics*, Amit Chaudhuri's *A New World*, and Jhumpa Lahiri's *Interpreter of Maladies*, all of which show how economic globalization affects the lives of Indians, whether in India itself or when moving to the US. All of these would also squarely fit the postcolonial mold, and in Chaudhuri's and Lahiri's cases also the multicultural one. If, in 1995, Apter then still found it necessary to defend the inclusion of postcolonialism as a legitimate discourse in comparative literature thinking about world literature, in 2003 Kumar apparently already sees the need to dissolve the term in favor of a more fitting one to better respond to the conditions of globalization.

Cooppan argues that for Jameson, in his 1986 essay, "even as nationalism, 'that old thing,' is more or less sublimated in America into the placeless form of global postmodernism, 'a certain nationalism is fundamental in the third world'," (Cooppan 2004: 17). For Bhabha, on the contrary, "the currency of critical comparativism, or aesthetic judgment, is no longer the sovereignty of the national culture" conceived as Benedict Anderson's "imagined community" (Bhabha 1994: 6). Rather, Bhabha envisages new "modes of cultural identification and political affect that form around issues of sexuality, race, feminism, the lifeworld of refugees or migrants, or the deathly social destiny of AIDS" (Bhabha 1994: 6). In this new "geopolitical space," Bhabha argues, "the Western metropolis must confront its postcolonial history, told by its influx of postwar migrants and refugees, as an indigenous or native narrative *internal to its national identity*" (Bhabha 1994: 6). Where Jameson and Bhabha meet, I think, is in the dialectic between postmodernism and postcolonialism that both their arguments imply. For Jameson postmodernism is a mode expressive of America's inner reality, which he sees as "epistemologically crippling, and reduc[ing] its subjects to the illusions of a host of fragmented subjectivities, to the poverty of the individual experience of isolated monads, to dying individual bodies without collective pasts or futures bereft of any possibility of grasping the social totality" (Jameson 2000: 336). In third-world culture, on the contrary, he maintains, "the telling of the individual story and the individual experience cannot but ultimately involve the whole laborious telling of the experience of the collectivity itself" (Jameson 2000: 336).

Postcolonialism and postmodernism

For Bhabha, the popular use of the "post" in "postmodernity, postcoloniality, postfeminism" only makes sense "if [the latter] transform the present into an expanded and ex-centric site of experience and empowerment" (Bhabha 1994: 4). Concretely, he proposes, "if the interest in postmodernism is limited to a celebration of the fragmentation of the 'grand narratives' of postenlightenment rationalism then, for all its intellectual excitement, it remains a profoundly parochial exercise" (Bhabha 1994: 4). "The wider significance of the postmodern condition," he continues, "lies in the awareness that the epistemological 'limits' of those ethnocentric ideas are also the enunciative boundaries of a range of other dissonant, even dissident histories and voices – women, the colonized, minority groups, the bearers of policed sexualities ... for the demography of the new internationalism is the history of postcolonial migration, the narratives of cultural and political diaspora, the major social displacements of peasant and aboriginal communities, the poetics of exile, the grim prose of political and economic refugees" (Bhabha 1994: 4–5). Postmodernism and postcolonialism thus meet in Bhabha's new "geopolitical space, as a local or transnational reality" (Bhabha 1994: 6).

In fact, while most proponents of postcolonialism usually see it as offering an alternative road to a world literature that transcends the traditional limitations imposed upon it by Western thinking, my contention would be that what I will call its tangled relationship to postmodernism risks enclosing it yet again within those very same limitations. For Bhabha, postcoloniality is "a salutary reminder of the persistent 'neo-colonial' relations within the 'new' world order and the multinational division of labor," while at the same time bearing witness to what he calls cultures constituted "otherwise than modernity" (Bhabha 1994: 6). Such "cultures of postcolonial *contra-modernity*," he contends, "may be contingent to modernity, discontinuous or in connection with it, resistant to its oppressive, assimilationist technologies" (Bhabha 1994: 6). At the same time, he maintains, "they also deploy the cultural hybridity of their borderline conditions to 'translate', and therefore re-inscribe, the social imaginary of both metropolis and modernity" (Bhabha 1994: 6). Elsewhere (D'haen 1994), I have proposed the term "counter-postmodernism" to indicate the same relationship between metropolis, postcolonialism, and modernity, or, more precisely perhaps, to indicate how postmodernism and postcolonialism, the latter together with its twin multiculturalism, "shadow" postmodernism within the more general framework of modernity. Aijaz Ahmad I think intimated very much the same thing when in 1992, still using the earlier term "third-world literature," he proposed that: "There now appears to be, in the work of the metropolitan critical avant-garde, an increasing tie between postmodernism and the counter-canon of 'Third World Literature'" (Ahmad 1992: 125).

Hans Bertens (1991), contextualizing the debate on postmodernism around 1990, distinguishes an "avant-garde," a "poststructuralist" and an "aesthetic" postmodernism, and links these various postmodernisms both to different historical stages in the use of the term, roughly speaking the 1960s, 1970s and 1980s, and to different stances, inspired by opposing socio-political convictions, toward contemporary literature and culture in general. These stances, moreover, are perceptually defined. In other words, they depend upon how one *reads* a particular work rather than upon any "objective" quality of the work itself. An avant-garde reading, primarily associated with Ihab Hassan (1982 [1971], 1975, 1980, and 1987) and Douwe Fokkema (1984 and 1986), foregrounds the work's technical features distinguishing it from works in a previous mode, and specifically from modernism. It sees postmodernism as an artistic current, characterized in its literary manifestations, and particularly in fiction, by a common set of techniques, conventions and themes. A poststructuralist reading, associated with Brian McHale (1987 and 1992) and Linda Hutcheon (1984, 1985, 1988, and 1989), focuses on the de-centering of the (bourgeois) subject, the deferment of meaning, and the problematical status of the text. What Bertens calls an "aesthetic" reading fits the period approach of Jameson (1984 and 1991) and his neo-conservative humanist counterparts, and stresses the artificiality, the emptiness, the lack of depth, the purely formal interests of the postmodern work. This reading sees postmodern works as directly translating late capitalism's commodifying influence into an "aesthetic" experience, reduplicating as it were the very personality (or non-personality) make-up multinational late capitalism needs: functional man, broken up in disparate units, without any essence to him, man as malleable putty, what Gerhard Hoffmann (1982) has called "situational" man. In this sense, too, aesthetic postmodernism (both in its neo-Marxist and its [neo]-conservative reading) sees postmodern works, functionally speaking, as the continuation of earlier forms of mass-culture. Particularly in its neo-Marxist version, this reading blames postmodernism for having sold out to the culture-industry of late capitalist consumer society, thus also taking up Theodor Adorno's, and the Frankfurt School's, more general point with regard to mass culture after WWII (Adorno 1991a [1944] and 1991b [1967]). Since 1984, the date of publication of Jameson's article "Postmodernism, or, the Cultural Logic of Late Capitalism," and especially as of 1991, the date of appearance of the book with (almost) the same title, Jameson's view has largely monopolized discussions of postmodernism, at least in the United States. It is this view that we also see articulated in Jameson's 1986 article on third-world literatures.

What a counter-reading of postmodernism seizes upon is the latter's universalizing claim regardless of its being grafted upon an aesthetic avant-garde practice that was also highly specific in its conditions and circumstances, that is to say the United States (Huyssen 1986). After all, this is where late, multinational, consumer capitalism first flowered, and where the central categories of modernity leading to such late capitalism were worked out and applied most categorically. The United States, after all, is the most "true West". Kumkum Sangari (1990: 242–43) neatly summarizes the point:

> Postmodern skepticism is the complex product of a historical conjuncture as both symptom and critique of the contemporary economic and social formation of the West. But postmodernism does have a tendency to universalize its epistemological preoccupations – a tendency that appears even in the work of critics of radical political persuasion. ... the world contracts into the West; a Eurocentric perspective ... is brought to bear upon "Third World" cultural products; a "specialized" skepticism is carried everywhere as cultural paraphernalia and epistemological apparatus, as a way of seeing; and the postmodern problematic becomes *the* frame through which the cultural products of the rest of the world are seen. ... Such skepticism does not take into account either the fact that the postmodern preoccupation with the crisis of meaning is not everyone's crisis (even in the West) or that there are different modes of de-essentialization which are socially and politically grounded and mediated by separate perspectives, goals, and strategies for change in other countries.

The fact remains that some of the best-known postcolonial authors, Salman Rushdie probably being the prime example, on the basis of their literary techniques can be categorized just as easily as postmodern. Adam and Tiffin, for example, note that, "there is a good deal of formal and tropological overlap between "primary" texts variously categorised as "post-modern" or "post-colonial" (Adam and Tiffin 1991: vii). But, they also note, "If there is overlap between the two discourses in terms of 'primary' texts ... there is considerably less in the 'secondary' category. ... it is thus in the selection and reading of such 'primary' texts, and in the contexts of discussion in which they are placed, that significant divergences between post-colonialism and post-modernism are most often isolated" (Adam and Tiffin 1991: vii).

Stephen Slemon (1991: 4) makes the same point when he remarks that Hutcheon's (1988) analysis of intertextual parody as a constitutive principle of postmodernism resembles the post-colonial practice of "rewriting the canonical 'master texts' of Europe," but with the difference that "whereas a postmodernist criticism would want to argue that literary practices such as these expose the constructedness of *all* textuality, ... an *interested* post-colonial critical practice would want to allow for the positive production of oppositional truth-claims in these texts" (Slemon 1991: 5). Hutcheon herself concurs when she says that "the post-colonial, like the feminist, is a dismantling but also constructive political enterprise insofar as it implies a theory of agency and social change that the post-modern deconstructive impulse lacks ... while both 'posts' *use* irony, the post-colonial cannot *stop* at irony ... " (Hutcheon 1991: 183).

Counter-postmodernism can thus be seen as yet another reading of "postmodernism," complementary while at the same time oppositional to those enumerated before. Instead of submitting to the demise of the subject as posited by these other readings, and if we follow Simon Gikandi when he posits that "entry into the European terrain of the modern has often demanded that the colonized peoples be denied their subjectivity, language, and history" (Gikandi 1992; 2), a counter-postmodern reading such as here proposed "writes" the subjectivity, history, and language of those hitherto suppressed by the discourse of modernity as applied by Western bourgeois society. As such, it makes this discourse accessible to those traditionally excluded or repressed by Western modernity. Ironically, by thus marking the end of modernity as the exclusive instrument of hegemonic Western man, and the advent of modernity for the hitherto repressed, counter-postmodernism may well be the only truly "*post*-modern" reading of postmodernism in that it posits the transcendence of "orthodox" Western or metropolitan modernity, and the attainment of an-"Other" modernity. As such, counter-postmodernism also adds an emancipatory "counter-ethics" to those of poststructuralist and aesthetic postmodernism, breaking the free-play impasse of the one, and productively challenging the other. Counter-postmodernism thus posits a postmodernism practiced by subaltern, post-colonial or multicultural writers to recover the "history, language, and subjectivity" of the West's "Others." In the way counter-postmodernism seizes upon the Western hegemonic and colonial discourse of modernity, and of that discourse's reading of "postmodernism," it is not just the postmodernism of the West's "Others," but also the "Other" to postmodernism as we are accustomed to think of it. As the "Other" to Euro-American postmodernism, then, counter-postmodernism feeds "difference" back into the center. In fact, it is only in this return that postmodernism recognizes itself as not just Bhabha's "celebration of the fragmentation of the 'grand narratives' of postenlightenment rationalism" (Bhabha 1994: 4) but as an articulation of the particular condition of the West (or in first instance the United States) *in relation* to the rest of "the world." As Bhabha puts it in "The Postcolonial and the Postmodern": "We see how modernity and postmodernity are themselves constituted from the marginal perspective of cultural difference ... they encounter themselves contingently at the point at which the internal difference of their own society is reiterated in terms of the difference of the other, the alterity of the postcolonial site" (Bhabha 1994: 196).

Postcolonialism as Western projection

Bertens, although using a totally different vocabulary, predicates a similar return of a difference that already was, albeit only belatedly realized as such, when, drawing upon Ernesto Laclau and Chantal Mouffe's "radical democracy" from their *Hegemony and Socialist Strategy: Towards a Radical Democratic Politics* (1987), he sees postcolonialism and multiculturalism as part of "a new round in the realization of the potential of Enlightenment vision" (Bertens 1994: 244). In this "current round of democratization," he argues, "an older Enlightenment dispensation is giving way to a new one in a process in which the Enlightenment is – belatedly – forced by its own momentum to confront the problem of the Other" (Bertens 1994: 245). Contrary to Jameson's views Bertens argues that "one can see postmodernism, then, as Enlightenment principles finally coming home to roost, while, paradoxically, that home is simultaneously being subjected to a thorough deconstruction" (Bertens 1994: 245). Proponents of multiculturalism and postcolonialism will hardly feel like quarrelling with the emancipatory prospects sketched here for their respective constituencies. At the same time they may well fear this latest avatar of postmodern thinking to be yet another sly maneuver on the part of the West via theory to preserve its "imperious" (Sangari 1990: 243) grasp on an ever more refractory literary production worldwide. The room here made for multiculturalism and postcolonialism under the umbrella of "postmodernism" invites the risk of being construed as yet another attempt on the part of the West to appropriate to itself "some of the more forward-looking products" of "marginal" cultures (Tiffin 1991: viii), meaning not only some of the more highly regarded literary works from these cultures but likewise the very theory underlying multiculturalism and postcolonialism. Specifically, as the editors of *Past the Last Post* state it in their introduction, it may function as "a way of depriving the formerly colonised of 'voice', of, specifically, any theoretical authority, and [of] locking post-colonial texts which it does appropriate firmly within the European episteme" (Adam and Tiffin 1991: viii). Similar suspicions with regard to postcolonialism, along different lines of analysis, have been uttered almost from its very emergence, by Kwame Anthony Appiah (1991), Ella Shohat (1992), Vijay Mishra and Bob Hodge (1991), and Arif Dirlik (1994).

A world literature under the aegis of postmodernism and/or postcolonialism, then, at least in some interpretations projects a world that remains relentlessly "Western," whether in extending the postmodernism of the West, and perhaps even of only one nation of the West, to comprise all of the world, as happens for instance in Bertens and Fokkema's *International Postmodernism* (1997), or in countering such postmodernism with a post-colonialism that for its definition is finally dependent upon what it subverts. In fact, postcolonialism, even if only because of its "post"-status, but also for the reasons just adduced, might well be regarded as another instance of what the American-Chinese critic Rey Chow has called a "post-Europe and ... " construction, where whatever "new" theory or approach that defines itself through difference from European or American theory remains fatally beholden to the primacy of the latter (Chow 2004). Simon Gikandi goes so far as to consider postcolonial theory, the subject of which he sees as "global culture linked with postmodernism" (Gikandi 2001: 638), as the product of knowledge production about the nations newly independent from Britain by Third World intellectuals migrating themselves into the academic institutions of the First World, there to function as what Gikandi calls "émigré native informants" (Gikandi 2001: 646). What links them, according to Gikandi, is the submerged point of departure for their construction of a postcolonial literature in English as world literature in the attitude toward literature propagated (some would say preached) in England by F.R. Leavis from the 1930s through the 1960s, but disseminated throughout the British colonies and former colonies in secondary and university teaching, and which effectively posited Englishness and English literature as central to a particular worldview (Gikandi 2001: 649–50). The German literary historian Horst Steinmetz had, in 1988, already suggested that instead of interpreting world literature as either comprising all of the world's literatures in all their manifestations or as designating a canon of masterpieces, where both these interpretations basically applied to the past, we should heed Goethe's own hints that he saw world literature as a contemporary and future phenomenon. Specifically, Steinmetz says, we should see world literature as referring to the period stretching from Goethe's own lifetime to our own, and which he sees characterized by an ever-growing convergence between the lives led by people all over the world. The latter is caused by the same phenomena that Goethe too invoked when he saw a world literature coming into being: improved means of communication, faster circulation of cultural goods, mass media. The historical context of literature since Goethe's epoch, Steinmetz claims, is no longer national but global. Even what he sees as a return to the regional in these postmodern times is merely a locally differentiated manifestation of a global phenomenon. We might deduce that under these circumstances the postcolonial is merely one such form of "glocalization."

Even if one grants postcolonialism the power to truly represent the diversity of the peoples of the world beyond the West, there still remains the danger of reverse occlusion: "The political and disciplinary collisions between the Eurocentric premises of traditional comparative approaches to literary and cultural study and the inherently and necessarily anti-Eurocentric stance of postcolonial politics and theory appear to have colluded towards a subtle yet unmistakable reinforcement of a monolithic and monologic 'European' identity, in which the ideal notion of 'Europe as Subject' [Spivak 1988: 271], devoid of historical and geopolitical determinants of its own, is mirrored by the oppositional construct of Europe as Object, a staunchly self-identical metropolitan Other to the richly fragmented (post)colonial Self" (Klobucka 1997: 126). For "Europe," of course, we can here equally well read "the West."

It is precisely such dangers that Gayatri Spivak seems to warn of in the revised version of her famous 1988 article "Can the Subaltern Speak?" in the "History" chapter from *A Critique of Postcolonial Reason* (1999). In the original version of her article Spivak upbraids Michel Foucault and Gilles Deleuze in an interview these two French philosophers gave in 1977 when discussing the plight of the oppressed and agreeing that "reality" happens on the factory floor, in prison, at the police station, where "concrete experience happens," for not seeming to be "aware that the intellectual within socialized capital, brandishing concrete experience, can help consolidate the international division of labor" (Spivak 1988: 275). In the 1999 version she slightly elaborates on this by saying that Foucault and Deleuze, by exclusively concentrating on the experience of the Western "masses" help to "consolidate the international division of labor by making one model of 'concrete experience' *the* model" (Spivak 1999, 255–56) More importantly for our purposes, however, she then extrapolates this to literary studies when she continues that "we are witnessing this in our discipline daily as we see the postcolonial migrant become the norm, thus occluding the native once again" (Spivak 1999, 256). It is hard not to read this addition as a direct comment, critique even, of Bhabha's position in *The Location of Culture.*

Gayatri Chakravorty Spivak (1942–) is an Indian (Bengali)-born literary critic teaching at Columbia University in New York, where she was a colleague of Edward Said. Considered one of the most influential theoreticians of postcolonialism, Spivak combines insights taken from the French philosopher Jacques Derrida, whose *On Grammatology* she translated in the 1960s, Marxism, feminism, and the Indian historians' collective Subaltern Studies. She is an outspoken critic of the West, and especially of Western approaches to non-Western literatures.

Waïl S. Hassan makes the same point more directly and more topically when he remarks, in terms that I can only read as a direct and deliberate echo of Bhabha's, that "[the] emergent canon of postcolonial-literature-as-world-literature ... inscribes 'writing back,' diaspora, migrancy, border-crossings, in-betweenness, and hybridity as the defining features of the 'postcolonial condition'" (Hassan W. 2002: 60). While such issues are important, he continues, "they are extremely limited when we remember that the vast majority of African and Asian populations are not diasporic, migrants, or bilingual, and may, indeed, have never even traveled beyond the borders of their native countries" (Hassan W.2002: 60). And Neil Lazarus pointedly observes that, "Even if, in the contemporary world system the subjects whom Bhabha addresses under the labels of exile, migration, and diaspora, are vastly more numerous than at any time previously, they cannot reasonably be said to be paradigmatic or constitutive of 'postcoloniality' as such" (Lazarus 1999: 136–37).

World literature and "Anglophony"

One suspects that Spivak would judge the danger just signaled all the more acute as postcolonialism, in theory as well as in the primary literature it focuses upon, has mostly been confined to the Anglophone realm, thus even further prejudicing the world literature it potentially comprises in favor of an already hegemonic construct. Nicholas Brown, reflecting on "Anglophone literature" in the context of Goethe's commercial metaphors for speaking about *Weltliteratur* and on how Marx and Engels use similar metaphors in the *Communist Manifesto*, comments that "as plainly as we can see the legacy of the Goethean conception in contemporary multicultural discourse, it is just as clear that the Marxian narrative, where particular cultural forms colonize territory along with economic ones, represents the truth of Goethe's metaphor" (Brown 2001: 831). Waïl Hassan finds that, "One of the ironies of postcolonial studies is that colonial discourse analysis began with several theorists who studied colonialism in the Arab world: Albert Memmi (in Tunisia), Frantz Fanon (in Algeria), Edward Said (in the Levant)," but that "the sophisticated theoretical apparatus" built on their work rarely takes into account Arabic literature (Hassan W. 2002: 45). In fact, he notes, postcolonial studies seems to confine its attention to literatures written in former colonies or by authors emanating from former colonies and in the language of the ex-colonizer, in practice English and French (and even the latter only very recently, I would add). Therefore, he continues, "postcolonial studies profess to make the balance of global power relations central to its inquiry, yet seems [sic] to inscribe neocolonial hegemony by privileging the languages (and consequently the canons) of the major colonial powers, Britain and France … even the substantial colonial and postcolonial writing in other European languages such as Dutch, German, Italian, Portuguese, and Spanish, is no less excluded from post-colonial debates than texts written in the languages of the colonies: Arabic, Bengali, Hindi, and Urdu, not to mention the oral literatures of Africa, Native Americans, and Australia's Aborigines, which pose a serious challenge to postcolonial theories based on contemporary notions of textuality" (Hassan W. 2002: 46).

From the perspectives of Hassan and Gikandi someone like Salman Rushdie, who is often considered, at one and the same time, the quintessential postcolonial novelist and an exemplary postmodernist, might well be regarded as a prime example that, in Spivak's term, the subaltern cannot "speak," however linguistically inventive and eloquent his or her novels for the rest may be. "No novel that I know of articulates more powerfully the theme of postcolonial migrancy in a mutable postmodern world than Salman Rushdie's *The Satanic Verses*," according to Gilian Gane (2002: 18). Interpreting India, and Indian migrants in the world, to the West in the hegemonic language of the West, Rushdie can be seen as what Spivak in her *Critique of Postcolonial Reason* has called a "Native Informant" (Spivak 1999: ix). Rushdie would then be a member of that intermediate class that Spivak, in the language of Ranajit Guha, the founding editor of the "Subaltern Studies" Group, defines as the group that under colonialism would have stood between the "elite," that is to say "'dominant foreign groups,' and 'dominant indigenous groups at the all-India and at the regional and local levels' representing the elite" and "[t]he social groups and elements included in the terms 'people' and 'subaltern classes'" (Spivak 1999: 271, quoting Guha 1982). Such an intermediate group then represents "*the demographic difference between the total Indian population and all those whom we have described as the 'elite'*" (Spivak 1999: 271, quoting Guha 1982). "At the regional and local levels [these intermediate groups] ... if belonging to social strata hierarchically inferior to those of the dominant all-Indian groups acted in the interests of the latter and not in conformity to interests corresponding truly to their own social being" (Spivak 1999: 272, quoting Guha 1982). If we translate this as pertaining to postcolonial postmodern writers they can be seen as "subalterns" that cannot truly speak either but only ventriloquate in the language of "the master." In fact, Gikandi (2001) includes Rushdie in his group of "émigré native informants." In *Death of a Discipline* (2003) Spivak enlarged on her suspicions to the use of English as the necessary lingua franca for the study of world literature through anthologies. In the 1995 Bernheimer volume, though, Spivak had found a perhaps unexpected ally in the famous poetry scholar Marjorie Perloff, who lamented that, "because the United States is currently the only superpower in the world, it gets to call the shots when it comes to a lingua franca," and that "such essentializing of English ... perpetuates the old notion of centers and margins which the new comparative literature model is supposedly countering" (Perloff 1995: 178).

Subaltern Studies refers to an organized collective of Indian historians around the journal *Subaltern Studies*, and to the approach they have elaborated for dealing with the history of decolonized and postcolonial societies, and especially of India. Inspired by the theories of the Italian Marxist Antonio Gramsci, who coined the term "subaltern" to refer to groups or individuals that find themselves in a position of inferiority, they analyze history from the standpoint of those discriminated against because of race, cast, gender, language, or religion. The founder of the group is Ranajit Guha. Other historians and sociologists associated with subaltern studies are Gyan Prakash, Dipesh Chakrabarty, and Partha Chatterjee.

The "new" comparative literature that Perloff referred to was that of multiculturalism and postcolonialism. In 2003 Spivak also called for a "new" comparative literature, but hers is one of globalization and planetarity. Ritu Birla suggests that with *Death of a Discipline* Spivak has moved beyond "problems of historical representation," and hence of postcolonialism in its "historical" stage, we might add, to "the history and politics of globalization" and thereby from "the mechanics of othering to the possibilities of alterity" (Birla 2010: 97). Drawing upon ideas and a vocabulary inspired by the French philosopher Emmanuel Levinas (1906–95), *Death of a Discipline*, Birla posits, "has posed *the planet* as a name for an alterity that we inhabit, a way of being in the world that requires the imagination of what we cannot know, the universe, from a perspective that cannot produce mastery through mirroring" (Birla 2010: 97). Instead of "world," which as we have seen always implies someone's world, or "globe," which is tainted with the economic power imbalances of globalization, "planet" infers a view from outside, in which all is equal in its alterity, that is to say in that which we cannot, that we must not, fully apprehend of the other, but that we must nevertheless respect precisely in its difference. In order to respond to the other, though, we have to try and bridge the difference. This is where the imagination, and hence literature, is our only helpmate. World literature under this aegis, then, becomes not a way of "mastering" the world, but of respectfully experiencing it in, and as, difference. Wai Chee Dimock, in *Through Other Continents: American Literature Across Deep Time* (2006b) and in the volume she edited with Lawrence Buell, *Shades of the Planet: American Literature as World Literature* (2007), has taken up Spivak's call for a planetary approach, although it seems to me that she has not done so with an eye to the alterity that Spivak also calls for, but rather in the sense of "englobing" the world through, and in, American literature.

Littérature-monde

Earlier, in 1988, another comparative literature scholar, René Etiemble, had launched his *Ouverture(s) sur un comparatisme planétaire (Openings[s] towards a Planetary Comparatism)*. In this volume Etiemble republished the 1977 revised version of his 1963 *Comparaison n'est pas raison (The Crisis in Comparative Literature*, 1966), along with a number of texts in various ways reflecting upon that 1963 original. As in almost all his work, this volume too was a plea for a comparativism truly encompassing "the world," and not just a tiny Eurocentric part of it. For French comparative literature, let us recall, it was French literature that had always remained the yardstick of the discipline. So too had French literature remained the ideal against which were measured the "other" literatures in French, or of the so-called "francophonie," a term that always implied a second best next to the "real" thing – that is to say, French literature from France, the "hexagone," itself. This attitude was frontally attacked with the publication of "Pour une littérature-monde en français" (for a world literature in French) in the Parisian daily *Le Monde* of 16 March 2007. This manifesto bore the signature of forty-four authors, the best-known among them being the Moroccan Tahar Ben Jelloun, the Guadeloupeans Maryse Condé and Gisèle Pineau, Didier Daeninckx, the Martinican Edouard Glissant, the Canadians Jacques Godbout and Nancy Huston, the Haitian-Canadian Dany Laferrière, the future Nobel Prize winner (2008) J.M.G. Le Clézio, the Lebanese Amin Maalouf, Erik Orsenna, and Jean Rouaud.

> **Edouard Glissant** (1928–2011) was a Martinican writer and critic, who, next to a series of highly regarded novels, and various collections of poetry, all set in the Caribbean, also wrote a number of influential theoretical essays on the relationship of Caribbean, and particularly French-Caribbean or Antillean literature to French and European literature. Key works are *Caribbean Discourse* (*Discours antillais*, 1981) and *Traité du Tout-Monde* (1997). Glissant was the chief inspiration for the writers of *Créolité*, a group comprising Patrick Chamoiseau, Jean Bernabé, and Raphaël Confiant. In 1989 they published a pamphlet entitled *Eloge de la créolité/In Praise of Creoleness*, advocating the use of a hybrid language feeding upon the native creolised French of the Caribbean islands for their literature.

Noting that in autumn 2006 five of the seven major French literary prizes had gone to foreign-born authors, the manifesto proclaimed that this was a historical moment that signaled a Copernican revolution because it "reveal [ed] what the literary milieu already knew without admitting it: the center, from which supposedly radiated a franco-French literature, is no longer the center" (Toward 2009: 54). The result, the manifesto claims, is "the end of 'francophone' literature – and the birth of a world literature in French" (Toward 2009: 54). At the same time, it also means the return of "the world, the subject, meaning, history, the 'referent'" in French literature, and the overcoming of the stale pre-occupation with self-reflexivity that, for the longest time – in fact, ever since the *nouveau roman* – had plagued French literature (Toward 2009: 54). In Britain writers from the former Empire had been taking in the major literary prizes as of the 1980s, creating a new fiction from their plural identities. In France, meanwhile, foreign-born authors were still expected to "blend in" and become "French" to the core. Now, however, all was different: "the emergence of a consciously affirmed, transnational world-literature in the French language, open to the world, signs the death-certificate of so-called francophone literature ... no one speaks or writes 'francophone'" (Toward 2009: 56). In fact, the manifesto claims, "in a strict sense the 'francophone' concept presents itself as the last avatar of colonialism" (Toward 2009: 56). Instead, there will now be a "world-literature" or "littérature-monde" in French, and this in the sense of spanning the world because of the French language being spread around the world, and in the "worldly" sense of referring to the world, beyond "the age of suspicion" (a reference to Nathalie Sarraute's 1956 *L'ère du soupçon*, or *The Age of Suspicion*, the programmatic statement of the French *nouveau roman*) in a "vast polyphonic ensemble, without concern for any battle for or against the preeminence of one language over the other or any sort of 'cultural imperialism' whatsoever," and "with the center placed on an equal plane with other centers" and "language freed from its exclusive pact with the nation" (Toward 2009: 56).

The *Le Monde* manifesto immediately came under heavy critical fire, from the general secretary of the Organisation Internationale de la Francophonie (International Organisation of Francophone Countries) and former President of Senegal, Abdou Diouf, and from Nicolas Sarkozy, in the daily *Le Figaro*, almost on the eve of the presidential elections that he would go on to win, but also from Amadou Lamine Sall and Lylian Kesteloot (Forsdick 2010a: 125–26). Diouf obviously did battle for his own organization. Sarkozy lamented what he called the "Americanization" of "la francophonie," with a number of well-known writers in French, such as Condé and Glissant, living and teaching in the United States. Lamine Sall and Kesteloot, the latter an early anthologizer and critic of Francophone African and Caribbean literatures, pointed out that the celebration of the 2006 literary prize winners as signaling the sudden emergence of foreign-born authors writing in French blatantly disregarded earlier such generations active since the immediate post-WWII period. While this critique was certainly justified, and while there was undoubtedly, as Lamine Sall and Kesteloot implied, an element of self-marketing involved on the part of the signatories to the manifesto, it should also be said that there is a significant difference between the writers of the generation Lamine and Kesteloot referred to and those of the manifesto. The former were generally speaking anti-colonial and supportive of the newly independent nations they originated from. The latter rather fit the postcolonial mold of Anglophone transnational lineage. Forsdick notes that "Lamine Sall and Kesteloot concluded by critiquing the text's defence of a post-national, apolitical cultural utopianism that makes no attempt to grasp the consistently politicized postcolonial context of the Francosphere, a space in which the nation state, rightly or wrongly, may be seen as more important than ever" (Forsdick 2010a: 126).

Other critics took the Manifesto and its authors to task for imitating too closely English or Anglo-American models, particularly those of postcolonial and world literature studies, and for what Forsdick calls "the oxymoronic contradictions of a phenomenon that claims a global reach but persists with a monolingual definition" implied in the "en français" of the manifesto's title (Forsdick 2010a: 127). It is perhaps to forestall further such criticism that the 2007 volume collecting twenty-seven texts by signatories of the manifesto, *Pour une littérature-monde*, edited by Michel Le Bris, himself also a signatory of the *Le Monde* manifesto, and Jean Rouaud, quietly dropped the "en français." The volume's programmatic title article, to which Le Bris signed his name, remains a more elaborate version of the original manifesto though.

Nowhere does Le Bris use the term "postcolonial," but it is clear that the English-language writers he mentions – Kazuo Ishiguro, Salman Rushdie, Michael Ondaatje, Ben Okri, Hanif Kureishi, and Zadie Smith – fall under the rubric of what we would call the postcolonial or the multicultural. This leads Dominique Combe to venture that the Manifesto is "above all, based on an apparent inferiority complex with respect to the postcolonial anglophone novel" (Combe 2010: 231). Combe also links the Manifesto, in its title, but also in its views, such as for instance on the creolisation of the French language by "littérature-monde" authors, to the work of Glissant, especially to the latter's novel *Tout-Monde* (1993) and his *Traité du Tout-Monde* (1997), and to the French-Antillean "créolistes" Patrick Chamoiseau, Raphaél Confiant, and Jean Bernabé, even though Chamoiseau and Confant, "even though regularly featuring in Le Monde, keep ... surprisingly silent (Combe 2010: 239; pourtant habitués des colonnes du Monde, restent ... étonnamment silencieux).

In a companion piece to his article on the *littérature-monde* manifesto Forsdick elaborates on the role of Glissant within French-language literature and thought, defending the Martinican author from the barbed criticism of Chris Bongie (2008), itself to a large part based on Peter Hallward's 1998 reading of Glissant, that Glissant, as of the late 1990s, had shifted from his former oppositional stance, as instanced in *Le discours antillais* (1981; *Caribbean Discourse*), to an accomodationist one, with his signing of the *littérature-monde* manifesto being an instance of the latter. Instead, Forsdick maintains, "Glissant has continued to be instrumental in allowing the emergence, in the French-speaking world, of debates that we might recognize as *postcolonial*, but with which the French equivalent of that label has only been associated since 2005" (Forsdick 2010b: 128). In a changing world in which both France and its former colonies of the "francophonie" as well as its DOM-ROMs (*départements* and *régions d'outre-mer* – overseas departments and regions) need to rethink their relations, Forsdick argues, Glissant "has attempted to elaborate, as opposed to simply import, the conceptual and lexical apparatus by which such a situation may be analyzed" (Forsdick 2010b: 134). Mary Gallagher, in fact, suggests that one could go further and, instead of seeking the salvation of French-language literature in imitating Anglophone notions of postcolonialism, as does the manifesto, "ask whether the political and cultural orthodoxy of postcolonialism is not, in fact, a dominant global discourse against which francophone poetics sounds a singular or a refractory note, if not quite a dissident blow" (Gallagher 2010: 24). This in fact is what she sees Glissant's writings on poetics, on the relations between European and American literature, and on world literature, as doing. The manifesto, on the contrary, "shrinks the conceptual scale and content of the *world*, a term that comes to mean at worst 'anywhere but France' and at best 'anywhere else preferably with postcolonial cachet'" (Gallagher 2010: 32). The manifesto, she argues, "demonstrates none of that complex sense of the world that informs all of Edouard Glissant's writing on the Tout-monde ... for the complexity of Glissant's notion largely derives from his effort to conceive of the world as a nonreductive totality, as a(n imperfectly interconnected) whole, a whole that can no longer be thought about exclusively in terms of the postcolonial plot" (Gallagher 2010: 32). Of course, the fact remains that Glissant himself put his name to the manifesto …

If the manifesto, when compared to the subtlety of Glissant's ideas, can indeed only be called naïve, the same thing goes when one compares it to work on postcolonialism in English, while at the same time it avoids none of the pitfalls the latter also faces when fashioning itself as the pivot of a "world literature." Moreover, for all the admiration they express for English-language postcolonial developments, the drafters of the manifesto do not seem too much *au courant* with what had been going on there precisely with regard to French-language literature. Only a year before the publication of "pour une littérature-monde" Emily Apter had suggested that "francophonie might … no longer simply designate the transnational relations between metropolitan France and its former colonies, but linguistic contact zones all over the world in which French, or some kind of French, is one of many languages in play" (Apter 2006: 55). And even if one can understand that Le Bris and Rouaud may not have been aware of an article that had appeared only recently in a collective volume that did not immediately concern them, it is perhaps a little more strange that they also do not seem to have been aware of a book, in English it is true, that pretty much, though in far greater sophistication, outlined the kind of program they drew up in their manifesto: Charles Forsdick and David Murphy's 2003 *Francophone Postcolonialism*.

Forsdick (2010a) notes that the manifesto, apart from the early and mostly negative reactions just briefly sketched, drew little further attention in France itself. Outside France, however, it was taken up in academic circles and continues to be discussed. Perhaps we should add that the latter is particularly true in countries where debates with regard to "world literature" have been at the center of attention for some time now, particularly Anglo-America but also Denmark. An interesting twist is that one of the signatories to the 2007 manifesto since then has gained particular notoriety: Le Clézio won the 2008 Nobel prize for literature. It is well-known that the Swedish Academy keeps an ear to the ground for what is happening in literary Paris. "From the 1940s onwards, the Academy came to accept a set of literary ideals that have their roots in French modernism," the former Permanent Secretary of the Swedish Academy declared not so long ago (Engdahl 2008: 207). Perhaps Le Clézio's appearance in "pour une littérature-monde" has contributed at least some, then, to his canonization as a "world author"?

Conclusion

- Postcolonialism has been proposed as the new world literature.
- Postcolonialism and postmodernism, supposedly each other's opposites as expressions of, respectively, resistance and accommodation to the Western world, in fact have a tangled relationship.

- Postcolonialism can be seen as a projection of, rather than resistance to, Western thought.
- Postcolonial world literature has in practice largely meant English-language postcolonial literature.
- Recently, the debate on postcolonialism has also erupted in the French-language context, with heated debates around "la francophonie."

8 World literature and the literatures of the world

Overview

Earlier I cited Werner Friederich ironically referring to what in the late 1950s passed for "world literature" as NATO literature, and that this was already an overstatement as usually only about one fourth of the literatures in the then fifteen NATO languages received any actual sustained attention. The literatures in question were French, English, German, Spanish, and Italian, and discussion on world literature was almost exclusively restricted to German, French, and US comparative literature circles. This is not to say that there was no work being undertaken on world literature elsewhere, particularly in Europe, but this usually shadowed what was being done, primarily, in the major European French and German academic centers, filtered only rarely into the more general or "global" discussion, and the latter usually only when done straightaway in a "major" European language or translated therein. This situation has basically persisted to this day, with US academe, and the English language, increasingly supplanting German and French preponderance. Work on world literature done outside of Europe and the US usually has only been recognized as such retrospectively and as a result of the renewed interest in world literature in Europe, and particularly in the USA, as at the end of the twentieth century. In what follows I will concentrate, in particular, on examples from Europe's so-called "semi-periphery" and on China to gauge the impact of the renewal of interest in world literature beyond the core area of "comparative Literature talking about world literature." In most cases this will involve both a return to "native" precursors to claim an "alter-native" approach to world literature and an unspoken but I think nonetheless implied resistance to a world literature fashioned by Anglophone hegemony.

Europe's semi-periphery

In a 1997 special issue of *symploké* dedicated to "refiguring Europe," Anna Klobucka, drawing upon Immanuel Wallerstein's economics-based world-systems theory (although in his later writings Wallerstein has also pronounced on cultural matters), and invoking Goethe's frequent metaphorical use of the market to speak about the "value" of a particular literature, posits that "the almost uniform characterization of the biased perspective of traditional comparative literary studies as 'Eurocentric' generally fails to take into account the fact that literatures and cultures of the European periphery have only on token occasions been considered as rightful contributors to the common 'European' cultural identity" (Klobucka 1997: 128). The same thing is even more true for world literature, and recent theorizing about the latter offers little consolation to Europe's so-called "minor" literatures, in effect the literatures of Europe's semi-periphery. It should be noted that semi-periphery, at least in the cultural or literary context, not necessarily applies to geographically or economically ex-centric countries but may just as well pertain to the culture of countries that in all other respects would seem to be quite "central," such as for instance Holland or Belgium (Spoiden 1997).

The theories of both Casanova and Moretti, in their "irradiation" or "diffusionist" perspective centered upon Paris, or Paris and London, cast Europe's minor literatures as purely re-active in relation to the "centre" or "centres" of Europe. Moreover, as noted earlier, American academe has to a large extent replaced the earlier French and German dominance in comparative literature and literary theory, even though the latter often as a re-working of initially European, and again particularly French and German, ideas and theories. Under the twin pressures of multiculturalism and post-colonialism, arguably the reigning paradigms of literary study in the US in the more recent past, the renewed interest in world literature has led to an ever greater attention to non-European literatures, and hence to the progressive inclusion of ever more non-European texts in American anthologies of world literature, in practice the *only* such anthologies. If anything, this has led to an ever growing marginalization, or perhaps we should say "peripheralisation," of Europe's minor literatures. In fact, in such more recent re-castings of world literature it is the world's other "major" literatures – Chinese, Japanese, Arabic, Indian – that now seem to become semi-peripheral or even co-equal to the "old" European, or latterly perhaps rather Euro-American, "core." Europe's minor literatures then sink to the status of truly "peripheral" literatures. In what follows I will concentrate on three such semi-peripheral literatures: Scandinavian, especially Danish and Swedish, Spanish, and Portuguese.

Scandinavia

In Scandinavia, and particularly in Denmark, the renewed interest in world literature has led to a revival of the work of the Danish critic and literary historian Georg Brandes (1842–1927). Influenced by the positivism of the French historian Hippolyte Taine, under whom he studied in Paris in 1866–67, and also by the critical practice of the French critic Sainte-Beuve, and by German philosophy, especially that of Georg Wilhelm Friedrich Hegel

(1770–1831), Brandes between 1872 and 1890 wrote a ground-breaking six-volume series on European literature from 1800 to 1848 under the general title of *Hovedstrømninger*, translated as *Main Currents in Nineteenth-Century Literature*. Sainte-Beuve had shown the way towards a criticism that went beyond mere description and evaluation, situating works and authors in their various contexts, and comparing them with other works and authors. Brandes likewise advocated comparison as a fruitful entry into the world of European literature in the introduction to his first *Main Currents* volume. Comprised of *Emigrant Literature* [Emigrantlitteraturen] (1872), *The Romantic School in Germany* [Den romantiske Skole i Tyskland] (1873), *The Reaction in France* [Reaktionen i Frankrig] (1874), *Naturalism in England* [Den engelske Natur-alisme] (1875, where "naturalism" refers to nature poetry and not to the later literary movement that now goes by that same name), *The Romantic School in France* [Den romantiske Skole i Frankrig] (1882), and *Young Germany* [Det unge Tyskland] (1890), *Main Currents* switches from France to Germany to France to England, and then back to France and finally back to Germany, describing the literature of the period under investigation as a Hegelian process of action and reaction between revolution and restoration, progressivism and conservatism, the struggle for freedom and the wish for containment, in literature as in politics

In his entry on Georg Brandes in the *Routledge Companion to World Literature* Svend Erik Larsen highlights how the work of Brandes provoked diametrically opposed reactions in different parts of the world. In France, where his work has hardly been translated, at variance with Germany and the English-speaking countries where almost everything he ever wrote was diligently translated during his own lifetime, Brandes was vehemently opposed by Fernand Brunetière and later, in an obituary in 1927, derided by the equally eminent comparatist Ferdinand Baldensperger for "the superficiality of [his work's] knowledge and the lack of substance of its edifice" (Baldensperger 1927: 143, quoted in Larsen 2011: 24). In China, however, Brandes's cause was taken up by the famous novelist and critic Lu Xun (1881–1936), by many considered the most important Chinese writer of the first half of the twentieth century. Lu Xun, on the left of the political spectrum, praised Brandes for his progressivism. In his own country and in Germany, where he lived part of his life, Brandes's reputation fluctuated. In the middle of the twentieth century his work fell into oblivion, but more recently he, like Meltzl, has been reclaimed as an alternative "founding father" of comparative literature in a world perspective. The grounds for this are to be sought in his critical practice in *Main Currents*, but also in a brief essay on "World Literature" ("Verdens-litteratur" in Danish, but actually first published as "Weltliteratur" in the German journal *Das litterarische Echo*) that he wrote in 1899, and which is currently being reprinted in all kinds of collective volumes on world literature and on the "new" comparative literature, such as the 2009 *Princeton Source-book in Comparative Literature* and the 2011 *Routledge Reader in World Literature*.

Lu Xun or **Lu Hsün** was the penname of the Chinese novelist and essayist **Zhou Shuren** (1881–1936). He is considered the founder of modern Chinese literature. A liberal in politics, and a defender of a common humanity, he sympathized with the plight of the lower classes, and sided with what we would commonly call the Left. For this reason he was admired by Mao Zedong, the Communist leader who came to power in China after a decades-long struggle with the nationalists under Chang Kai-shek. Lu Xun's best-known story is *The True Story of Ah Q* (1921–22).

The reason for the revival of interest in Brandes is, according to Larsen (2011: 26–28), that Brandes, in four distinct ways, can be seen as anticipating what currently occupies the "new" comparatists. He is interested in the diffraction (perhaps we should say the "refraction") of local cultures: "World literature of the future will appear the more appealing, the stronger it represents the national particularity, and the more diversified it is, but only when it also has a general human dimension as art and science" (*Samlede Skrifter* 12: 28; quoted in Larsen 2011: 26). He is a proponent of a globalized cultural approach. He favored transnational themes in his dealings with literature: "Brandes would have been sympathetic to the resurfacing contemporary debate on cosmopolitanism and also to central global themes of literature: risk society, migration, trauma and forgiveness, international justice or genocide" (Larsen 2011: 28). Finally, he paid great attention to issues of translation, especially with regard to the imbalances of power involved. Brandes specifically took up the latter point in his 1899 essay on world literature. Though he starts off his essay by saying that, although he is aware that the term "Weltliteratur" has been coined by Goethe (erroneously, as we have seen in Chapter 1, but taken for granted at the time), he does not remember exactly what it refers to, and therefore he will start from his own assumptions on the matter. He notices that next to some writers who have become household names in world literature – Shakespeare for instance – there are others, such as Shakespeare's contemporary Christopher Marlowe, who although not necessarily less great have remained only nationally or locally famous. He then stresses the importance of translation in gaining an author or a work access to world literature, especially so in the modern period, that is to say since the rise of the vernaculars as literary languages, and he stipulates that "in no other language do translations play so great a role as in German" (Brandes 2009: 63), thus echoing, consciously or not, Goethe.

"It is incontestable," Brandes argues, "that writers of different countries and languages occupy enormously different positions where their chances of obtaining worldwide fame, or even a moderate degree of recognition, are concerned" (Brandes 2009: 63). French writers are luckiest when it comes to their chances of becoming known to the world, next come English and German writers, and then Italian and Spanish. Russians, even though few people know the language, are so many that they too have a fair chance of becoming world famous. "But whoever writes in Finnish, Hungarian, Swedish, Danish, Dutch, Greek or the like is obviously poorly placed in the universal struggle for fame ... in this competition he lacks the major weapon, a language – which is, for a writer, almost everything" (Brandes 2009: 63). With the clause that "when a writer has succeeded in France, he is known throughout the world" (Brandes 2009: 63), Brandes presciently seems to confirm, at least as far as the nineteenth-century situation is concerned, Pascale Casanova's (1999 and 2004) definition of Paris as the Greenwich Meridian of the literary world.

Translation, because of its "inescapable incompleteness" (Brandes 2009: 63), Brandes feels, cannot compensate for writing in a minor language, and this is why lesser writers writing in a world language easily gain far greater recognition than do far greater writers in lesser known languages. But sometimes it is also simply a matter of chance, he argues, taking as his example two Danish writers, namely Hans Christian Andersen and Søren Kiergegaard. The former, Brandes says, achieved world fame, the latter is "unknown in Europe" (Brandes 2009: 65). Yet, Brandes notes, "among us [Danes] Andersen is thought of as one among many, nothing more" while Kierkegaard is "the greatest religious thinker of the Scandinavian North" (Brandes 2009: 65). Nor does it help to write deliberately for fame and fortune, and with an eye to becoming a world author, in the process by-passing one's own roots and environment. Brandes concludes:

> When Goethe coined the term "world literature," humanism and cosmopolitanism were still ideas that everyone held in honour. In the last years of the nineteenth century, an ever stronger and more jealous national sentiment has caused these ideas to recede almost everywhere. Today literature is becoming more and more national. But I do not believe that nationality and cosmopolitanism are incompatible. The world literature of the future will be all the more interesting, the more strongly its national stamp is pronounced and the more distinctive it is, even if, as art, it also has its international side; for that which is written directly for the world will hardly appear as a work of art.
>
> (Brandes 2009: 66)

In 1872 Brandes, who had started teaching *Belles Lettres* at the University in Copenhagen in 1871, unsuccessfully applied for the professorship in Aesthetics at his university. This may seem to have been a strange move for somebody primarily interested in literature (actually, Brandes was interested in many things besides literature; he was for instance also involved in the founding of *Politiken*, still today one of Denmark's leading newspapers), but it was actually very logical in the Scandinavian situation. In Denmark, Sweden, and Norway, literature during the nineteenth century was taught as part of the wider discipline of "aesthetics," comprising all the arts, along the lines laid out by Kant in his *Critique of Judgment*. In Sweden, in 1906, a new discipline called "litteraturhistoria med poetik" (literary history and criticism) was created, and this in the 1970s was renamed "litteraturvetenskap" (literary "science" or scholarship). Swedish literature forms part, in fact the larger part, of this discipline, while foreign languages and literatures form subjects of their own. "World literature," then, is an integral part of the courses offered by "literaturvetenskap," along with Swedish literature and what elsewhere might well be called "theory of literature." As Anders Pettersson puts it: "There are no separate chairs in Swedish literature in Sweden, so all study of Swedish literature is incorporated into *litteraturvetenskap*, where it plays a very dominant role ... when presenting my academic subject in English-speaking contexts, I call it 'Swedish and Comparative Literature'" (Pettersson 2008: 464).

In Denmark and Norway foreign languages and literatures are subjects in their own right, as is "Nordisk litteraturhistorie" or "Scandinavian literature," comprising Danish, Norwegian, Swedish and Icelandic, with different emphases depending on the particular country. Next to this, Danish universities also have what is called an "Institut for Aestetiske Fag," at Aarhus translated as "Department of Aesthetic Studies," with various sections, one of which is the "Afdeling for Litteraturhistorie" (http://litteraturhistorie.au.dk/, accessed 28/11/10), which, on the English-language webpage, is not given a translation, but in the English-language course catalogue would correspond to "Comparative Literature" (http://mit.au.dk/coursecatalogue/index.cfm?elemid=37465&topid=37 465&elemid=40508&topid=40508&sem=F2011&udd=&art=&hom=, accessed 28/11/10). It is also as "Comparative Literature" scholars that members of the Faculty of Arts teaching "litteraturhistorie" announce themselves to their colleagues abroad. Under the heading "World Literature" the Aarhus University website states that "the degree programme in comparative literature focuses on European literature, but you also have the opportunity to discover Russian or South-East Asian literature, for example" (http://studieinfo.au.dk/bachelor_ introduction_en. cfm?fag=1231, accessed 28/11/10). The Department of Aesthetic Studies also has a research "Center for Verdenslitteraere Studier," or "Center for the Study of World Literature" (http://cvs.au.dk/, accessed 28/11/10). Rather ironically, given Brandes's own failure to win the Copenhagen chair, the Copenhagen PhD School in the Humanities is named The Georg Brandes School.

Although the way it is embedded in the academic structures is very different, the interest of the Scandinavians in world literature in some ways parallels that of the US Americans, in that it is very much pedagogically oriented. What predominates is a concern to expose beginning university students to a variety of works from different provenance. In fact, the Scandinavians take things even a stage further than the Americans in that over the last decade or so they have actively started to introduce world literature into high school teaching. In Sweden a mixed committee of academics and high school teachers is drawing up a list, a canon one could say, of world literature for use in high schools. The committee has not yet made its list public, but it seems fair to say already that the emphasis is on contemporary rather than historical works of literature, and on what can be deemed a fair geographical, and furthermore also gender, representation. The choice for contemporary works rather than works of historical importance is grounded in the (supposed) interest of the students and in the desire to make the chosen works relevant to the life-world of those students. It is also to a large extent governed by what is available in Swedish translation, thus once more showing up the intimate relationship, at least on the pedagogical level, between canonicity, or perhaps in this case better canonicability, and translation. The relative preponderance of works originally written in English, whether it be works of historical importance originating in Britain or the US, or contemporary so-called post-colonial works, is also to be explained from this conundrum: even though English is undoubtedly the foreign language most widely disseminated in Sweden, as in all Scandinavia (and the world, we might add), it also is the language from which most is translated into Swedish, thus offering a much wider range of choice of works than any other literature in any other language.

In Denmark there recently appeared a literary history for high school students called *litteraturDK* (2009). Written by the chairholder of comparative literature (*litteraturhistorie*) at Aarhus University, Svend Erik Larsen, in collaboration with three colleagues, academics and high school teachers, *litteraturDK* aims to study "local literature in a global perspective." *litteraturDK* starts from the premise that Denmark's being subject to an increasing process of globalization has implications for how literature is taught. Danish high school students live a "globalized reality as it is experienced in Denmark" and literature "belongs to a larger media landscape defined also by other languages than Danish and other media than verbal language"(Larsen 2010: 16). This reality "promotes an encounter between several cultures and it therefore inevitably contains a strong historical dimension, which more often than not is excluded from the close-reading strategies pursued in the teaching of literature or reduced to factual comments of varying relevance"(Larsen 2010: 16). Literature, then, needs to be re-conceptualized from a "world literature" perspective geared to local Danish conditions. Consequently, in *litteraturDK* "every chapter offers a different viewpoint on how literature during a thousand years has suggested answers to questions about what it means to face the conditions of human existence living in Denmark as a country within moving boundaries and with a changing but always crucial interaction with the larger world" (Larsen 2010: 24).

Moreover, *litteraturDK* "is not a literary history of *Danish* literature but a history of *literature in Denmark*, that is about the texts which have been read, used, imitated, remediated, arrived along labyrinthine routes, transformed completely once they arrived and thereby constituted examples of the permanent presence of the greater world inside the local confinement" (Larsen 2010: 25). Even if not a full-blown history of world literature, then, *litteraturDK* does bring into play insights and strategies gleaned from recent discussions on world literature as well as from older such reflections by Goethe and Brandes and translates them into a workable paradigm for a specific twenty-first century locale. At the same time, and even if only for its own local audience, teaching Danish literature in such a setting also lifts it from its otherwise restrictive national environment and recasts it as part of world literature, thus providing at least some solace for Brandes's lament about the relative invisibility of literatures from smaller nations and in less known languages. Of course, the real remedy to the imbalance of power that Brandes noted with regard to a writer's chances of gaining worldwide fame would lie in similar literary histories, for high school and/or university teaching, to also be created and published in major languages and countries, and preferably in English, and soon perhaps also in Chinese, or other emerging world languages. As we saw in a previous chapter, some of this is starting to happen at least in the USA, and at least on the university level.

The work Larsen and colleagues are undertaking on the level of high school anthologies and literary histories is paralleled on the research level by a study such as Mads Rosendahl Thomsen's *Mapping World Literature: International Canonization and Transnational Literature* (2008). While recognizing the merits of the works of Damrosch (2003), Casanova (1999 and 2004) and Moretti (2000 and 2005), Thomsen also offers some intriguing counter-proposals of his own, such as looking at world literature from what he calls "shifting focal points" (Thomsen 2008: 33–60), under which he subsumes "centers, temporary sub-centers, old and emerging world literatures, international canonization without the support of a major national literature, and temporal shifts in the historical horizon" (Thomsen 2008: 54). Examples he offers are, as far as centers are concerned, Athens, Alexandria, Rome, Paris, London, and New York, as temporary sub-centers Russia, with the Russian novel, in the period 1860–80, Scandinavia, with the theatre and the novel, in the decade 1890–1900, the US in the 1920s and the Latin America of the "boom" in 1960–80, the emergence of American literature in the 1920s versus the established major literatures of Europe in the 1920s, Borges as a "lonely canonical," and Modernism as moving from being "new" to being the "new antiquity" for post-post-modernism. Whatever one may think of some or all of these proposals, they show a definite desire to go beyond the old center-periphery constructions and to re-map the world of world literature along more, and more varied axes, than those hitherto prevailing and prejudicing a true evaluation of literatures beyond the pale of "traditional" world literature which Thomsen still sees as very much tied to the paradigm of comparative literature as it has been operative for the past one hundred-plus years, and as tied to national literatures as its constituent parts. Instead, when it comes to the present map of world literature, Thomsen proposes to start from what he calls "constellations of works," that is to say "very different texts [that] share features that make them stand out on the literary canopy" (Thomsen 2008, 4). Some such constellations he investigates in the second half of his book are migrant writers and holocaust writers. Again, one may differ in one's opinion as to the applicability of such criteria, and even as to the novelty of what Thomsen here proposes, as his "constellations," after all, sound very much like thematic groupings. For his metaphorical model Thomsen invokes stellar constellations as humanly imposed patterns upon heavenly bodies otherwise disparate in space. Although he nowhere mentions this, Thomsen presumably also has in mind Walter Benjamin's "constellations" yoking together past and present, thus lending even greater historical and theoretical weight to his construction (Benjamin 1982).

Spain and Portugal

Just a few paragraphs ago I referred to Chinese as a – perhaps even *the* – language of the future. In Europe too, though, and next to English and French as long-standing languages with global or near global reach (even though in changing relations of hegemony over the past few centuries), we find languages and cultures that, once powerful yet later considered "peripheral," have latterly re-surfaced as emergent world languages by dint of the former colonial empires in which they were disseminated. Along with Earl Fitz (2002) I am thinking here particularly of Spain and Portugal. Especially the latter, because of its smaller size, its geographically more ex-centric position, and its "eclipsed" history since at least the eighteenth century, would squarely seem to fit into Europe's "semi-periphery." In any of the going re-theorizations of world literature that I have just mentioned, the old home countries of Spanish and Portuguese – that is to say, Spain and Portugal themselves, and their literatures – would seem destined to play only a minor role. Pride of place would go to literatures in Spanish and Portuguese produced in the former colonies, that is to say Spanish America and Brazil, and in the longer run also Lusophone Angola and Mozambique. In this respect the situation of Spain and Portugal is significantly different from that of, for instance, England, and particularly France.

England, because of its relatively small number of English speakers as compared to many of its former colonies, partially in the singular but certainly in the aggregate, risks being eclipsed, and is already partially at least eclipsed, by literature in English produced outside of the British Isles, first in the United States, later in the so-called "settler colonies" (Canada, Australia, and partially South Africa), and latterly also in India and perhaps in the future likewise sub-Saharan Africa. For the time being, though, and also because of the status of English, in whatever variant, as the undisputed world language of commerce and diplomacy, England continues to be an important linguistic, cultural, and literary center. France, meanwhile, easily remains the largest French-speaking country in the world, at least for the moment, although of course in the longer run it might well be equaled by some "Francophone" African countries. Perhaps most importantly, though, both France and England are indisputably part of the European cultural "core." Indeed, for Moretti, and at least as far as the period since 1800 is concerned, they are "the" core. For Casanova, of course, the matter is even simpler: Paris is the core.

Spain, and even less so Portugal, cannot lay claim to the same centrality in Europe. Moreover, as compared to their former colonies, both Spain and Portugal these days are almost tiny in terms of numbers of speakers. At the same time, while London and Paris continue to function as major clearing-houses and publishing centers for English and French language literature, in Spanish and Portuguese rival centers have arisen with Mexico City, Buenos Aires, and São Paulo, even though Barcelona still plays a major role in Spanish-language literature publishing and the same thing goes for Lisbon at least with regard to Lusophone Africa. There is a tension, then, between the role Spanish and Portuguese literature risk being reduced to under the logic of the "new" world literature thinking, and their networked position because of historical conditions. The acute awareness of these tensions is leading to initiatives aimed at raising the visibility of Spanish and Portuguese literature in world literature terms. I will here concentrate on two such initiatives: one, more modest, from Spain; the other, quite ambitious, from Portugal. In both cases, these initiatives also build on longer-standing native traditions of comparative literature and literary history writing and anthologizing.

In Spain, an ancestor to be recovered is the Spanish and, after his flight from Spain because of the Civil War in 1936, Argentinian writer and critic Guillermo de Torre (1900–71). Not long after the conclusion of WWII, in 1949, de Torre pondered on "Goethe y la literatura universal" (Goethe and world literature). Goethe, while unleashing a most important idea on the world, had not been very precise in its definition, de Torre found. When having to choose between two definitions offered in Shipley's then well-known and widely used *Dictionary of World Literature*, namely that of all literature in the world and the totality of those works that have gained recognition beyond their national borders, de Torre opts for the second possibility, or for what he denominates, using quotation marks, as "literatura mundial" (De Torre 1956: 282). However, he immediately objects – and here he starts sounding like Brandes in his 1899 article on world literature – if we then take translation, a necessary instrument for cross-border dissemination, as our yardstick, we notice that many coincidental factors intervene, such as a given country's socio-economic importance driving its cultural irradiation, the popularity of certain genres, or other aleatory facts. Some works are even written especially for a world market, he claims. Any such works he labels, denigratingly, "cosmopolitan" rather than "world" literature. Still, we should also not fall over into only applauding what is rooted in local or national conditions. The proper instance to really stake out world literature, then, de Torre asserts, is comparative literature. As an example he invokes *A Short History of Comparative Literature from the Earliest Times to the Present Day* (1906, 1904 in French, 1905 in Spanish) of Frédéric Loliée. Loliée in his conclusion sees all literatures "blend in harmonious unity" (Loliée 1906: 314) and "united in an all-embracing unity" (Loliée 1906: 358); in fact, he con-fidently propounds, "we are approaching unity" (Loliée 1906: 374). De Torre finds such a trust in the coming of a *Weltliteratur* not overly utopian in the early years of the twentieth century, before the World Wars. Since then however, he contends, things of course have changed dramatically. Still, he also thinks, it is inevitable that from the recent disasters a federal Europe will emerge, a "Superestado" (superstate) which alone can guarantee a lasting peace. Why, he asks, should we not then conceive in such a world "the effective realization of a world literature, on a par with the national literatures, and in which would figure representative entries from the latter, but more equitably so, and chosen less capriciously, than at present?" (De Torre 1956: 289; la realización efectiva de una *literatura universal*, coexistente con las demás literaturas nacionales, y en cuyo dominio entrarían representaciones de estas últimas, pera más equitativas y menos caprichosamente elegidas que las actuales?).

One attempt at such a more equitable representation is at present going on at the University of Santiago de Compostela, in Spain, where César Domínguez offers a course on "literatura y arte en el mundo antiguo y medieval" (literature and art in the classical and medieval world) in which he discusses, along with the usual suspects from Greek and Latin antiquity as well as the usual medieval romances, knights' tales, and lyrical poetry from Romance, Germanic and Celtic languages, also the Mesopotamian *Epic of Gilgamesh* (in an English translation), a "selección de poemas, hispanoárabes, trovadorescos provenzales y chinos" (a selection of Spanish-Arab, troubadour, and Chinese poetry), a selection from the Japanese Murasaki Shikibu's *Genji Monogatari* (*The Tale of Genji*), and a selection from *The Travels of Ibn Battuta* in a translation from the Arabic. As general anthology and background, he uses the first volume of Martín de Riquer and José María Valverde's *Historia de la literatura universal* (*History of World Literature*) mentioned in Chapter 1, and Jordi Llovet's *Lecciones de literatura universal: siglos XII a XX* (*Readings in World Literature: Twelfth to Twentieth Centuries*). With the Spanish-Arab poems and the *Travels of Ibn Battuta*, Domínguez includes a number of items that at least potentially stress the relationship of Spain to the world of Islam, and especially to the Arab world, in line with recent Spanish ambitions, also in the diplomatic and economic spheres, to bank on its medieval "three cultures" (Christian, Islamic, Jewish) past in order to claim the role of mediator between Europe and the Arab world. At the same time Domínguez is at least partially also applying the "regionalist" principles of Dionýsz Ďurišin, particularly as they apply to the Mediterranean space of which Spain has been so integral a part for most of its history.

More importantly, in reading *The Tale of Genji* next to European medieval romances, and Chinese poems next to medieval Spanish-Arab and Provençal poetry, Domínguez is also picking up on what another Spanish comparative literature ancestor, namely Claudio Guillén (1924–2007), has dubbed the B and C models of supranationality. The B model applies "when phenomena or processes that are *genetically independent*, or belong to different civilizations, are collected and brought together for study" on the grounds of "*common sociohistorical conditions*" (Guillén 1993: 70). The C model applies when "some *genetically independent* phenomena make up supranational entities in accordance with principles and purposes derived from the *theory of literature*" (Guillén 1993: 70). The A model implies direct contact or chronological line-arity, and it is clear that in the particular cases Domínguez here treats this is out of the question. For models B and C Guillén specifically refers to East/ West examples, thus showing Domínguez the lead. For model B, though, he also specifically points to work in comparative literature then going on in East and Central Europe by V.M. Zhirmunsky (1881–1971) and Dionýsz Ďurišin (Guillén 1993: 82). Here too we can see how diffusionist models of literary history – in this case when it comes to theory rather than creative literature – can easily miss what is really going on "on the ground," so to speak, because of their superior level of aggregation. Ďurišin, while hardly acknowledged in the Euro-American "core" of comparative literature, has been extensively translated, and his theories taken up, in Spain, and especially at the Department of Comparative Literature at Santiago de Compostela, by Dario Villanueva, Fernando Cabo, and César Domínguez himself (Domínguez 2011). In Italy too the work of Ďurišin has had indubitable impact, even if only because of the 2000 book he co-edited with the Italian comparatist Armando Gnisci on the literary Mediterranean.

In Portugal, as in many other European countries, there have long existed book series especially designed to disseminate what we would now call "world literature," whether in the form of single translated volumes or anthologies. Portugália Editora, in Lisbon, for instance, from 1942 until the 1970s, ran a series called "Antologías Universais." But there is also a series of five volumes published between 1966 and 1997 by the poet Herberto Helder of what he called "Poemas mudados para Português por Herberto Helder." Helena Buescu and João Ferreira Duarte (2007: 175) describe these five volumes as follows:

> The 1966 volume (*O Bebedor nocturno* [The Night Drinkard]) collects materials from Ancient Egypt, the Old Testament, Maya and Nahuatl lore, Ireland, Scotland, Finland, Japan, Indochina, Indonesia, Greece and Madagascar, together with Zen poems, Arab and Al-Andaluz poems, "Eskimo" and Tartar poems, Haikus and "Red-Skin poems". *As Magías* (1987), in turn, offers poems from the Belgian poet Henri Michaux, D.H. Lawrence, Robert Duncan, Blaise Cendrars and Stephen Crane, among others, lined up with native materials from Central Asia, Equatorial Africa, Sudan, Gabon, British Columbia, India, Panama, Australia, Colombia, Ancient Greece, Mexico and Mongolia. As to the 1997 tril-ogy, *Ouolof* collects texts from Mayan and Amazonian sources, as well as poetry by Zbignew Herbert, Jean Cocteau, Emilio Villa, Marina Tsvetaieva and Malcom Lowry. *Poemas ameríndios* starts out with a long poem by Ernesto Cardenal [he himself working with several sources of 16th Cen-tury Nahuatl texts, as well as the Florentine Codex] and goes on to gather texts culled from Aztec and Quichua cultures, as well as texts from

an array of native North and South American sources. Finally, *Doze nós numa corda* seems to shift away from the logic governing the previous volumes by privileging Western sources: Antonin Artaud, Carlos Edmundo de Ory, Henri Michaux (whose poetry takes up almost two-thirds of the book) and a short poem by Hermann Hesse which closes the collection.

While this is perhaps the most salient example of a series of volumes covering a, in this case highly personal, selection of "world poetry," there are also other, more systematic Portuguese anthologies, edited, by, amongst others, Jorge de Sena, Vasco Graça-Moura, Diogo Pires Aurélio, Nina e Filipe Guerra, and Pedro Tamen.

The examples just mentioned predate the re-emergence of thinking about world literature at the turn of the twenty-first century. In 2002, though, Earl Fitz, clearly influenced by the renewed interest in world literature, suggested that, "While English departments may regard globalization as a threat to their long-standing hegemony within the Academy, for Luso-Africanists and Luso-Brazilianists it represents an *abertura* (opening) of tremendous poten-tial, an opportunity to bring our literature to the attention of the rest of the world" (Fitz 2002: 442). A major effort in this vein is presently under way at the University of Lisbon's Centro de Estudos Comparatistas, where Helena Buescu is putting together a worldwide team of collaborators to assemble a two-volume anthology of what, taking her cue from the 2007 French pub-lication on "littérature-monde," she calls "literatura-mundo" in Portuguese. She starts from the premise that this "literatura-mundo" comprises both lit-erature written in Portuguese and translated into Portuguese, and that it should lead to an integrated vision of the relationships obtaining between both of these (2010 working document of the CEC). Invoking the original ideas of Goethe, as expressed by himself and as taken up by later proponents of world literature, particularly Guérard, Etiemble and Damrosch, Buescu posits that "this anthology is, then a way of upholding a 'conversational' vision of literature, a legitimate complement to other visions, equally legit-imate in terms of their own specializations, but incapable of covering the entire field of what literature can do (and always does): a concept of literary conversation that not only points to the transnational and trans-historical nature of the phenomena it comprises, but that also projects an awareness of literature that is potentially planetary and, to speak the truth, humanist" (2010 working document of CEC; esta antología é pois uma forma de defen-der uma visão conversacional da literatura, legítima forma de complementar outras visões, igualmente legítimas em termos de especialização, mas não capazes de cobrir todo o campo do que a literatura pode fazer (e sempre fez): uma concepção de conversa literária que não só indica o carácter transna-cional e trans-histórico dos fenómenos que abriga, mas ainda projecta uma consciência potencialmente planetária e, em boa verdade, humanista da literatura). The first volume of the projected anthology would contain,

[a] closely reasoned collection of texts from the various literatures in Portuguese, opening up the possibility of reading each of these literatures starting from various intersections, thus to contribute to their mutual (re) cognition ... such a perspective would undoubtedly enrich each of the individual national literatures concerned ... but it would contribute, above all, to their mutual illumination through a comparativist perspective that allows for the recognition of the global dimension shared by the literatures written in Portuguese.

Um conjunto muito significativo de textos escritos nas várias literaturas de língua portuguesa, oferecendo a possibilidade de ler cada uma das literaturas a partir de cruzamentos vários, bem como de construir o seu (re)conhecimento mútuo, ... uma tal perspectiva contribui sem dúvida para o enriquecimento de cada uma das literaturas nacionais individualmente consideradas. ... mas contribui, sobretudo, para a sua iluminação mútua, através de uma perspectiva comparatista que permita reconhecer a dimensão mundial para que apontam as literaturas escritas em português.

(2010 working document of CEC)

[The second volume] would gather a closely reasoned collection of world literature texts, holding out the possibility of reading them on the basis of translations made, with few exceptions, especially for this volume. Its publication will therefore permit and promote cross-cultural reading and understanding. Such a perspective would contribute to elaborating a comparativist approach that would allow for the recognition of a global dimension to which the translations into Portuguese of texts from an enormous diversity of genres, ages, languages and historical-cultural periods would contribute.

Pretende reunir ... um conjunto muito significativo de textos escritos nas várias literaturas de âmbito mundial, oferecendo a possibilidade de os ler a partir de traduções feitas, com poucas excepções, especialmente para este volume. A sua publicação permitirá assim construir cruzamentos vários, bem como abrir a uma leitura e o conhecimento mútuos. Uma tal perspectiva contribui para a complexificação de uma perspectiva comparatista que permita reconhecer a dimensão mundial para que apontam as traduções para português de textos pertencentes a uma enorme diversidade de géneros, épocas, línguas e períodos histórico-culturais.

(2010 working document of CEC)

A double-barreled anthology such as envisaged here would implicitly reaffirm the centrality of Portugal, and of Portuguese literature, for literatures in Portuguese, for world literature in Portuguese, and for literature in Portuguese as world literature. Such an anthology would relocate the country and its literature parallel to what the Portuguese writer and Nobel Prize winner

José Saramago does with the Iberian peninsula in his novel *The Stone Raft*. As Klobucka puts it: "The island that used to be the Iberian Peninsula does not, after all, go on floating aimlessly around the Atlantic: it becomes (perhaps provisionally) anchored and reterritorialized in a sort of de-centered central position, 'in the middle of the Atlantic, between Africa and South America,' reflecting contemporary Iberia's, and particularly Portugal's, desire to capitalize on its historically irreversible colonial experience by assuming a major (sic) mediating function in the global community of nations" (Klobucka 1997: 132). Paradoxically, such an anthology would also emphasize the peripherality of Portugal vis-à-vis Europe by converting its ex-centricity into a new centrality, not with regard to Europe but to the world, a world of "its own," so to speak. As my discussion of Domínguez's course relative to Spain's positioning vis-à-vis the Arab world has intimated, and as the colonial heritage of Spain warrants also with regard to Latin America, and in fact increasingly also to North America with its rapidly growing Hispanic population, a similar claim could easily be made for Spain and Spanish literature.

I hasten to add, though, that Lisbon's Centro de Estudos Comparatistas also collaborates on a one-volume anthology of European literature, inclusive of Portuguese literature, as part of a European project coordinated by the University La Sapienza in Rome, and aiming at constituting a canon of European literature leading to an anthology to be disseminated throughout Europe, in all European languages. The latter project should eventually yield teaching materials for high schools around Europe, thus echoing the Danish case described earlier. In Italy itself, Armando Gnisci and Franca Sinopoli for a long time now have been pleading for opening up the study of literature beyond narrow national boundaries, and for re-situating Italian literature within the wider contexts of European literature, of the Mediterranean (Ďurišin and Gnisci 2000), and of the wider world.

What transpires from these cases, then, is that also at the beginning of the third millennium, the "world" of world literature looks different from different locations. As we saw in previous chapters, this was already the case with earlier histories and anthologies of world literature, usually depending upon the national point of departure of the author or authors. It was certainly also the case with the research carried out in the former Soviet Institutes of World Literature in Moscow, and in Ďurišin's Institute for World Literature in Brno. In the Yugoslavia of Josip Broz Tito, from the 1960s to the 1980s, the creation of the Non-Aligned Movement (of which Tito was one of the leaders) led to yet a wholly different "alignment" of the world's literatures as researched and taught in Yugoslavia's Institute of World Literature (Bahun 2011). At present, however, we see wholly new alignments appearing.

Global South and Chinese world literature

Fitz, in the article I mentioned a little while ago, feels that especially Brazilian literature might fruitfully be studied in the increasingly important field of inter-American, or hemispheric American, Studies. "Freighted with the kind of suspicion and rancor, however, that stem from centuries of economic exploitation, political intervention, and both cultural hegemony and cultural disdain, [this] remains an issue that has long divided many Brazilian (and Spanish American) intellectuals," Fitz says, and he points to the "anthropologist, novelist, and intellectual Darcy Ribeiro" arguing "that the proper destiny of Latin Americans is to join together in 'common opposition to the same antagonist, which is Anglo-Saxon America, in order to bring together, as is happening in the European Community, the Latin American Nation dreamed of by Bolivar' (Ribeiro 2000: 321–22)" (Fitz 2002: 443). Joshua Lund explicitly posits that "in Ribeiro's view from the margin, Europe's centrality is relativized (decentered) within a global context" and Lund sees Ribeiro, along with for instance the Cuban historian Fernando Ortíz and the Brazilian critic Antonio Candido, putting a peripheral position and vision to "the sometimes polemical task of carving out their own centers from which to enunciate" (Lund 2001: 72). Ribeiro, Ortíz, and Candido are carrying out this task by turning the theories and instruments of hegemonic Eurocentrism against themselves, Lund argues, quoting Walter Mignolo to the effect that "Ribeiro – as much as Ortíz or Candido – is identifiable as 'someone who was trained as [a Western academic]' … and at the same time was part of the 'other'" (Mignolo 1988: 50). (Lund 2001: 73). Finally, Efraín Kristal, in an essay I mentioned earlier, is doing something similar when he opposes Franco Moretti's diffusionist and Eurocentrist view of World Literature and instead casts Spanish America as center. What we see emerging here is a "world literature" emphasizing what has increasingly come to be called "the global South," and that is rooted in resistance to Northern hegemonies – political, economic, linguistic, and literary.

Fernando Ortíz (1881–1969) was a Cuban writer and ethnomusicologist. Trying to understand the culture of his native Cuba he coined the term "transculturation" as indicating the convergence of various cultures into a new hybridized culture. His most famous work is *Cuban Counterpoint: Tobacco and Sugar* (*Contrapunteo cubano del tabaco y el azúcar*, 1940).

This is a message that recently also has been taken up by the Chinese Institute for World Literature at Peking University. Writing in the mid-1980s, A. Owen Aldridge in *The Reemergence of World Literature: A Study of Asia and the West* reminded his readers at the outset that "in the mind of many Third World critics, the concentration [in comparative literature studies] on European values and texts represents a survival or reflection of a colonialist mentality" (Aldridge 1986: 10). "Even when Eastern masterpieces have been recognized as such," he continues, "they have often been treated as precursors of later European works, not as models or cultural achievements in their own right … it is now time for the classics of the East to be viewed as the foundations of independent traditions and made available to Western students" (Aldridge 1986: 10). However, Aldridge also admits that no satisfactory methodology for the study of literature East-West has yet been devised. Practice in the West is usually to simply add a couple of Eastern masterpieces to the traditionally Western canon of world literature. The custom in the East has been to unleash Western theory upon Eastern literatures. And yet, he notes, there is the promising beginning of the emergence of comparative literature departments especially in Japan, and along what he terms the "Taiwan-Hong Kong Axis," and in the participation of scholars from these departments in international conferences such as those of the International Comparative Literature Association, as well as increasing attention from Western scholars for Asian literatures. Aldridge dedicated his book to René Etiemble, the French scholar who already in 1963 had called for a widening of comparative literature practice, and for discussions on world literature, to take in all of the world, and particularly such major literary traditions as the Arabic, the Indian, the Japanese and the Chinese. In fact, he had even suggested that the future of comparative literature and world literature might well lie with Chinese (Etiemble 1966, 27–30).

Antonio Candido do Mello e Souza (1918) is a Brazilian writer, critic, and academic. His most famous work available in English is *On Literature and Society* (*Literatura e sociedade*, 1965). Candido was trained as a sociologist, and in his critical work he always relates literature to society. He wrote on European as well as Brazilian literature.

Deeney (1981 and 1990) and Aldridge (1986) maintained that comparative literature, and the interest in world literature, emerged only late in the Chinese context, basically as of the 1970s and 1980s, and they mostly refer to examples from Taiwan and Hong Kong. Since Deeney's and Aldridge's days, things have changed. In their overview of the history of comparative literature in China in the twentieth century Zhou Xiaoyi and Q.S. Tong (2000) chronicle a thriving academic practice of comparative literature before the 1940s and again as of the 1970s, even crediting the discipline, after its re-introduction into mainland China in the late 1970s, with having been one of the most liberal areas of study in contemporary China. At the same time, though, they also point out that the enthusiastic responses to the call for a "Chinese School of Comparative literature" launched by John Deeney in 1986, a school which he saw destined to take the lead in a "Third World" comparative literature context, have fed into "a politics of recognition that aims to establish Chinese comparative literature as an equal partner on the international stage of comparative literature" (Zhou and Tong 2009: 352). As such, Zhou and Tong argue, "Chinese comparative literature as a critical practice may thus be considered a product of China's pursuit of modernity in the twentieth century" (Zhou and Tong 2009: 353). Such a pursuit also implies the tacit primacy, if not the superiority, of the West, as it comprises, according to Zhou and Tong, the "total acceptance of Enlightenment values and practices" (Zhou and Tong 2009: 353). The deconstruction of Eurocentrism as of the 1990s, they further argue, has discredited these values, and hence also the binary premises upon which comparative literature rests. Therefore, they suggest, instead of "comparative literature," with its ingrained imbalance between the West and the Rest, the term "cross-cultural studies," implying equality between all cultures concerned, might be more appropriate all around, in the East as well as the West (Zhou and Tong 2009: 354). For much the same reasons Anders Pettersson proposes the term "transcultural literary history" (Pettersson 2008).

As elsewhere, the more recent renewal of interest in world literature has also in China, that is to say mainland China, led to the reclamation of "forgotten" or "submerged" precursors. Indeed, whereas the revival of comparative literature in mainland China, after the caesura in Chinese intellectual life occasioned by Maoism and the Cultural Revolution, and after the liberalization of the late 1970s, mainly under the guidance of Peking University's Yue Daiyun, took its bearings primarily from American academe, more recent research insists on "native" ancestors pre-dating 1949. Longxi Zhang (2011) makes a case for Qian Zhongshu (1910–98) and particularly the latter's 1948 book of criticism in classical Chinese *Tan yi lu* or *Discourses on the Art of Literature*. The book refers to, and quotes, not only Chinese but also Western writers, often in the original. For Zhang, Qian Zongshu "effectively lays down the foundation of East-West comparative studies buttressed by a traditional philosophical argument ... demonstrating that in assimilating ideas from the West, Chinese scholars follow an intellectual genealogy of their own, rather than just act upon a desire to emulate the West" (Zhang 2011: 82).

Jing Tsu recovers even earlier ancestors. Tsu (Tsu 2010 and 2011) points out that the term "world literature" (*shijie de wenxue*) was introduced in China as early as 1898, when Chen Jitong, a mandarin and Chinese military attaché in Europe, used it in a conversation – appropriately so given Goethean antecedents! – with another Chinese writer, Zeng Pu. Chen Jitong, according to Tsu, was "motivated by a felt indignation, rather than humility, over the lack of proper recognition of Chinese literature by western readers" (Tsu 2011: 165) Given Europe's centrality in matters cultural and literary, however, "entry into its literary platform was key to forging a more even nexus of cultural exchange" (Tsu 2011: 165). When Chen Jitong first used "world literature" in Chinese the Chinese Empire was still a reality, albeit very much weakened under the onslaught of Western and Japanese economic, political, and military pressure. In the early years of the twentieth century it became increasingly apparent that the days of the Chinese Empire were numbered. It was against this background that Lu Xun (1881–1936), who would subsequently become the greatest Chinese writer of the first half of the century, and his brother Zhou Zuoren (1885–1967), in 1909 put together *A Collection of*

Fiction from Abroad (*Yuwai xiaoshuo ji*). Tsu labels this collection "a formally expressed literary concern with the experiences of the perishing nations and ethnicities ... devoted to the struggles of oppressed races and nations" (Tsu 2011: 166). Instead of Chen's "nostalgic, if genuine, wish to regain the cultural grandeur befitting erstwhile empires" (Tsu 2011: 165), with Lu Xun we find a socially progressive vision that links those excluded by both the traditional centers of power in China itself and the hegemonic powers of Western colonialism. As Tsu puts it, the Lu Xun/Zhou Zuoren collection "helped to shift the literary focus of cultural hegemony to the interstices of emergent, minor, oppressed, injured, and subglobal narratives" (Tsu 2011: 166) As such, she contends, "a new conceptual grammar for world literature gained ground, differentiating the national and world literary space along lines of conflict rather focusing on a common literary humanity ... if Goethe had imagined *Weltliteratur* to emerge from a world community with little in common, Lu Xun responded with a borderless literature of oppression without global triumph" (Tsu 2011: 166).

Zheng Zhenduo between 1914 and 1927 wrote *Wenxue dagang* (*The Outline of Literature*) which Tsu characterizes as "the first important, systematic attempt at a world literary history in China" (Tsu 2010: 299). However, to say that Zheng Zhenduo "wrote" his *Outline of Literature* is misstating the case. In fact, as Tsu demonstrates, Zheng Zhenduo compiled his work largely on the basis of John Drinkwater's *The Outline of Literature* (1923), with additional material taken from John Albert Macy's *The Story of the World's Literature* (1925), mostly simply translating the originals. To this Zheng added a number of chapters on Chinese literature. The principle of the universality of humanity upon which he inspired himself he had gleaned from Caleb Thomas Winchester's *Some Principles of Literary Criticism* (1899), and Richard Green Moulton's *World Literature and Its Place in General Culture* (1911) and *The Modern Study of Literature* (1915). To frame anthologies or studies of world literature along overall human categories rather than along historical, national or generic lines was not unusual in the first half of the twentieth century: Arthur E. Christy and Henry H. Wells emphatically titled their 1947 volume *World Literature: An Anthology of Human Experience*. Tsu also points out that Macy's book was translated no less than five times between 1935 and 1992, and that at least 4 other histories of world literature appeared in Chinese between 1932 and 1937. Specifically with regard to Zheng Zhenduo's *Outline of Literature*, however, she comments that the "idea of world literature allows for national interests to overlap and cross bounds but keeps the fundamental concern with power intact ... world literature ... is neither an exception to nor innocent of the modality of power that is created in any context of prestige" (Tsu 2010: 309). In fact, she claims, while it was "convenient for Zheng to make a passionate case for relinquishing national interests ... it was precisely his preoccupation with such a nation-bound identity that motivated him to turn to the world as the desired forum for China's literary participation" (Tsu 2010: 309).

Pre-occupations similar to those of Zheng Zhenduo also seem to undergird at least some of the more recent Chinese forays into world literature. China's increasing profilation as a major, perhaps in future *the,* world power, leads to a re-thinking of world literature in line with China's commercial and political ambitions. In first instance this makes for a desire for a greater participation of Chinese literature in world literature. Second, it makes for a recasting of what in the wake of Lu Xun and Zhou Zuoren's 1909 collection of translated fiction became all the rage in the 1920s and 1930s in China, that is to say the championing of the "weak and small races/nations" (Tsu 2010: 299), into the present Chinese enthusiasm for the "global South" that I mentioned not so long ago.

The implications of some of these views clearly appear from the more recent essays of Wang Ning, who as of the early 1990s has been one of the most prolific, and I would say almost "seismographic," interpreters of the relation of Chinese literary scholarship to Western theory and practice. In a 2010 article he reflects on the size of the Chinese population, its wide and increasing spread to all corners of the earth, China's rising economic might, how the Chinese language is therefore bound to gain a greater purchase on the world, and what the implications are for Chinese literary historiography. Unabashedly he compares Chinese to English in its wide diffusion, but also in how this implies a certain measure of hybridization. "Quite a few scholars are greatly worried about this phenomenon," he notes, but to him, "if it really achieved the effect of being inclusive and hybridized like English, Chinese would become the second major world language next to English, for it could play the unique role that English cannot play, and in more aspects, it could function as a major world language in an interactive and complementary way to English" (Ning 2010a: 167). He points out the growing role of government efforts and institutionalization, and compares the hundreds of "Kongzi xueyuan" (Confucius Institutes) the Chinese government has been setting up worldwide over the last decade or so to the British Council institutes that until a short while ago spread Britain's language, culture, and influence abroad. With the "rise of 'Chinese fever' in the world," he asks, "what shall [Chinese] literary scholars ... do to remap world literature?" (Ning 2010a: 170). Just as English literature has been transformed from "a national literature to a sort of world literature since English literature is more and more 'postnational'," so too "Chinese literature: also from a national literature to a sort of transnational and postnational literature" (Ning 2010a: 172).

Invoking "the pioneering Neo-Confucianist ... Tu Wei-ming's concept of 'Cultural China'," Ning maintains that "we can for the time being define Chinese literature in two senses: one is the literature produced in greater China: mainland China, Hong Kong, Macao and Taiwan in Chinese which is the people's national language or mother tongue; and the other is the litera-ture produced overseas in Chinese which is the writers' mother tongue although not necessarily their national language" (Ning 2010a: 173). Such international Chinese literature studies will become, Ning says, "like its counterpart of international English literature, a sub-discipline in the broader context of comparative literature and world literature. ... since to Spivak, a new Comparative Literature must be encountered within area studies, international Chinese literature studies will have both characteristics and, therefore, will undoubtedly have a bright prospect along with the popularization of Chinese worldwide" (Ning 2010a: 173–74). Literature in Chinese, then, as a world literature, similar to literatures in English or Anglophone, in French or Francophone, in Portuguese or Lusophone literatures. Only bigger. Although Ning is careful to invoke the fate of English and literature(s) in English as an example, it is clear that he is seeing the new Chinese literary historiography also, and perhaps in first instance, as rival to this example.

In another 2010 article Ning posits "that the globalization of material, cultural, and intellectual production, accompanied by the dissolution of Eurocentrism and "West-centrism" and by the rise of Eastern culture and literature, has assisted at world literature's birth from the ashes of comparative literature" (Ning 2010b: 2). World literature, Ning argues, implies translation, and translation in Chinese literary history has mostly served foreign literatures to colonize Chinese literature and culture. However, Ning opines, "the recent trend of cultural globalization in the Chinese context by no means augurs the further colonization of Chinese culture; instead, it will help promote Chinese culture and literature worldwide" (Ning 2010b: 13). Such promotion also seems to be very much part of the mission of the Peking University Institute of World Literature: "The institute aims at breaking the national boundaries in literary studies and serving as a bridge between the East and the West ... The institute is mainly engaged in training scholars at teaching, researching and editing comparative literature and world literature. Meanwhile, it also nurtures talents in the fields of foreign cultures, cultural management, international communication and Sino-overseas media. (http://english.pku.edu.cn/Schools_Departments/542_6.htm, accessed 3/12/10). In 2011 the Peking University Institute of World Literature hosts the first session of the Institute for World Literature which has its permanent and administrative home in Harvard, with David Damrosch as its director, and which will run yearly one-month institute sessions somewhat modeled on those of the long-established School of Criticism and Theory, but obviously with a specific orientation toward world literature. The 2011 Peking session pays particular attention to the Global South.

As Ning (2006: 163) reminds us elsewhere, the Chinese Ministry of Education in 1998 integrated comparative literature and world literature into one discipline for graduate study. Consistently, there is a Chinese journal, published in Beijing, called *Comparative and World Literature*. Perhaps the most recent Chinese vision of world literature here sketched is the realization of what Rey Chow in 2004 envisaged as a "new" form of East/West comparison, in which Asian literatures would be freed from what she calls the "post-European and ... " complex in which the implicit awareness of "the European" as the original term of comparison always haunts the term after the "and," thus allowing in its stead for "other possibilities of supplementarity, other semiotic conjunctions mediated by different temporal dynamics, … as yet unrealized comparative perspectives, the potential range and contents of which we have only just begun to imagine" (Chow 2004: 307). One wonders though whether this particular new perspective is necessarily more equal than that which she so eloquently criticizes.

Conclusion

- For most of its history world literature has been not only an almost exclusively European, or by extension Western, concern – the discussion on world litera-ture has also almost exclusively been conducted in just a few major European languages
- This has led to the semi-peripherilization of most "minor" European literatures
- With the shift of attention in the United States to other parts of the world than Europe, and hence also to other "major" literatures, the semi-peripherality of those minor European literatures has turned into full peripherality
- In a number of European reactions to this state of affairs we can recognize attempts to re-contextualize some of these minor literatures within the newly emerging world literature paradigm – quite often this involves the recovery of native precursors
- Beyond Europe, we see similar developments taking place in for instance Latin America but also China.

Guide to further reading

Below is a further explanation of some of the books that are listed in the bibliography along with other titles that might be useful for those wishing to dig deeper ...

Chapter 1

Damrosch, David (2003) *What is World Literature?* Princeton and Oxford: Princeton University Press.

Wide-ranging discussion of the idea of world literature, concentrating on issues of circulation, translation and production, each of them illustrated with a number of case studies. This book serves as consolidation and validation of the explosively growing interest in world literature in American academe.

D'haen, Theo, Damrosch, David, and Djelal Kadir (eds) (2011) *The Routledge Companion to World Literature.* London: Routledge.

Collection of 50 comprehensive articles on all aspects of world literature.

D'haen, Theo, Domínguez, César, and Mads Rosendahl Thomsen (eds) (2011) *The Routledge Reader in World Literature.* London: Routledge.

Collection of 30 seminal publications on world literature, from Goethe to Damrosch.

Pradeau, Christophe and Samoyault, Tiaphine (eds) (2005) *Où est la littérature mondiale?* Vincennes: Presses Universitaires de Vincennes – 150pp.

Collection of articles on world literature by French scholars, a.o. Pascale Casanova and the editors of the volume.

Schmeling, Manfred (ed.) (1995) *Weltliteratur Heute.* Würzburg: Königshausen und Neumann – 213pp.

Useful collection, in German, providing a snapshot of thinking about world literature in the mid-1980s, thus before the renewed interest in the subject as of the new millennium.

Schmeling, Manfred, Schmitz-Emans, Monika, and Walstra, Kerst (eds) (2000) *Literatur im Zeitalter der Globalisierung.* Würzburg: Königshausen und Neumann – 318pp.

Rich collection on globalization as affecting the study of literature. Contributions from around the world, a.o. by Paul Cornea, Joel Black, Jean Bessière, Wladimir Krysinski, Horst Steinmetz, and Hans-Jürgen Lüsebrink.

Strich, Fritz (1949) *Goethe and World Literature.* Transl. C.A.M. Sym. New York: Hafner Publishing Company – 362pp.

Continues to be indispensable for anyone interested in Goethe and world literature.

Chapter 2

Treml, Martin and Barck, Karlheinz (eds.) (2007) *Erich Auerbach: Geschichte und Aktualität eines europäischen Philologen.* Berlin: Kadmos – 512pp.

Useful collection, in German, of articles highlighting all aspects of Auerbach's work and career. Contributions by a.o. Carlo Ginzburg, Geoffrey Hartmann, Luiz Costa Lima and Herbert Lindenberger. Also contains a CD with a recording of a talk on Dante Auerbach gave at Pennsylvania State College in 1948.

Chapter 3

Bassnett, Susan (1993) *Comparative Literature: A Critical Introduction.* Oxford: Blackwell – 183pp.

Brisk, comprehensive, useful, and accessible introduction to comparative literature.

Damrosch, David, Melas, Natalie, and Buthelezi, Mbongiseni (eds) (2009) *The Princeton Sourcebook in Comparative Literature.* Princeton: Princeton University Press – 442pp.

Comprehensive collection of seminal articles on comparative literature from Johnn Gottfried Herder in the eighteenth century to Gayatri Spivak, Franco Moretti, and Emily Apter in the twenty-first.

Guillén, Claudio (1993) *The Challenge of Comparative Literature.* Transl. Cola Franzen. Cambridge, Mass: Harvard University Press – 450pp.

Still one of the most stimulating, if idiosyncratic, introductions to comparative literature.

Jost, François (1974) *Introduction to Comparative Literature.* Indianapolis: Pegasus.

Probably still the most even-handed introduction to comparative literature.

Saussy, Haun (ed.) (2006) *Comparative Literature in an Age of Globalization.* Baltimore: The Johns Hopkins University Press – 261pp.

Collection of essays issuing from the American Comparative Literature Association gauging the state of the discipline during a certain decade; world literature is the focus of almost all contributions.

Schulz, Joachim and Rhein, Philip (eds) (1973) *Comparative Literature: The Early Years*. Chapell Hill: The University of North Carolina Press – 241pp.

Seminal collection of texts from the early history of comparative literature from Goethe to Benedetto Croce.

Chapter 4

Damrosch, David (2009) *Teaching World Literature*. New York: The Modern Language Association of America – 432pp.

Collective volume on ways and means of teaching world literature including discussions of issues and definitions, program strategies, teaching strategies, actual courses, and resources.

Lawall, Sarah (ed) (1994) *Reading World Literature: Theory, History, Practice*. Austin, TX: Texas University Press.

Especially useful for the very thorough introduction by the volume's editor giving an overview of world literature practice in the United States.

Pizer, John (2006) *The Idea of World Literature: History and Pedagogical Practice*. Baton Rouge, Louisiana: Louisiana State University Press – 190pp.

Comprehensive overview of especially the German discussion on "Weltliteratur" as related to the American practice of "world literature."

Chapter 5

Casanova, Pascale (2004) *The World Republic of Letters*. Cambridge, MA: Harvard University Press; English translation of *La république mondiale des lettres* (1999) Paris: Seuil.

A systemic discussion, mostly inspired on Pierre Bourdieu, of the idea of a world system of literature emerging in and from Europe as of the seventeenth century and anchored in Paris.

Moretti, Franco (2005) *Graphs, Maps, Trees*. London: Verso – 119pp.

Best brief yet comprehensive exposition of Moretti's highly original and stimulating ideas on world literature; enjoyable also for its brisk style.

Prendergast, Christopher (2004) *Debating World Literature*. London and New York: Verso – 353pp.

A useful collection of articles, many of them published earlier elsewhere, and by various authors, on the subject. Not an overview, but rather active contributions to the discussion.

Chapter 6

Bassnett, Susan (2002) *Translation Studies*. London and New York: Routledge – 176pp.

The classical brief introduction to translation studies, here updated from the original 1980 version.

Bermann, Sandra and Wood, Michael (eds) (2005) *Nation, Language, and the Ethics of Translation*. Princeton: Princeton University Press – 411pp.

Important collection of essays by a.o. Emily Apter, David Damrosch, Edward Said, Gayatri Spivak. and Lawrence Venuti.

Delabastita, Dirk D'hulst, Lieven, and Meylaerts, Reine (eds) (2006) *Functional Approaches to Culture and Translation: Selected Papers by José Lambert*. Amsterdam and Philadelphia: John Benjamins – 225pp.

Selection of essays by one of the pioneers of translation studies using a polysystem approach.

Schulte, Rainer and Biguenet, John (eds) (1992) *Theories of Translation: An Anthology of Essays from Dryden to Derrida*. Chicago and London: The University of Chicago Press – 254pp.

Collection of important essays by both practitioners and theoreticians of translation.

Tymocko, Maria (2007) *Enlarging Translation, Empowering Translators*. Manchester: St. Jerome Publishing – 353pp.

Provides a history of translation studies and calls for greater attention to matters of translation and to the role of the translator.

Venuti, Lawrence (ed.) (2000) *The Translation Studies Reader*. London and New York: Routledge – 524pp.

Comprehensive collection of seminal twentieth-century articles on translation from Walter Benjamin to Lawrence Venuti himself.

Chapter 7

Ashcroft, Bill, Griffiths, Gareth, and Tiffin, Helen (eds) (1995) *The Postcolonial Studies Reader*. London and New York: Routledge – 526pp.

Important essays by a.o. George Lamming, Abdul JanMohamed, Gayatri Spivak, Homi Bhabha, Chinua Achebe, Edward Said, Jamaica Kincaid, Kwame Anthony

Appiah, Kumkum Sangari, Partha Chatterjee, Timothy Brennan, Trin T. Minh-ha, Wilson Harris, Dipesh Chakrabarty, Robert Kroetsch, and Graham Huggan.

Bertens, Hans. (1995) *The Idea of the Postmodern: A History.* London and New York: Routledge – 284pp.

Docherty, Thomas (ed.) (1993) *Postmodernism: A Reader.* London and New York: Harveste/Wheatsheaf – 528pp.

Collection of seminal essays on postmodernism by a.o. Jean-François Lyotard, Jürgen Habermas, Fredric Jameson, Gianni Vattimo, Zygmunt Bauman, Ihab Hassan, Jean Baudrillard, Umberto Eco, Andreas Huyyssen, Christopher Jencks, Simon During, and Rey Chow.

Ezli, Özkan, Kimmich, Dorothee, and Werberger, Annette (eds) (2009) *Wider den Kulturenzwang: Migration, Kulturalisierung und Weltliteratur.* Bielefeld: Transcript – 407pp.

Essays on "minor" literatures and works by minority authors.

Guttman, Anna, Hockx, Michel, and Paizis, George (eds) (2006) *The Global Literary Field.* Newcastle: Cambridge Scholars Press – 251pp.

Gathers essays by (predominantly) younger scholars on "minor" literatures undei the following headings: national literatures in global contexts, reading across cultures, practices of circulation and communities of consumption, politics of translation.

Loomba, Ania, Kaul, Suvir, Bunzl, Matti, Burton, Antoinette, and Esty, Jed (eds) (2005) *Postcolonial Studies and Beyond.* Durham and London: Duke University Press – 499pp.

Important collection of essays, many of them by prominent practitioners of postcolonialism, evaluating the achievements and the future of postcolonial studies.

Natoli, Joseph and Hutcheon, Linda (eds) (1993) *A Postmodern Reader.* Albany: State University Press of New York – 584pp.

Collection of seminal essays on postmodernism, with many of the same contributors as the collection edited by Docherty earlier, along with contributions by Hans Bertens, Jacques Derrida, Linda Hutcheon, bell hooks, and Houston A. Baker Jr.

Mongia, Padmini (ed.) (1996) *Contemporary Postcolonial Theory.* London: Arnold – 407pp.

Collection of essays containing much of the same material as Ashcroft et al. above and Williams and Chrisman below, but next to this also interesting and important essays by Arif Dirlik and Ella Shohat.

Sturm-Trigonakis, Elke (2007) *Global Playing in der Literatur,* Würzburg: Königshausen und Neumann – 275pp.

Theorizes migrant literatures as world literature.

Schwartz, Henry and Sangeeta Ray, Eds. (2000) *A Companion to Postcolonial Studies*, London: Blackwell – 608pp.

In-depth essays on all aspects of postcolonial studies by leading academics.

Williams, Patrick and Chrisman, Laura (eds) (1993) *Colonial Discourse and Post-Colonial Theory*. London and New York: Harvester/Wheatsheaf – 570pp.

Collection of basic essays by a.o. Léopold Sédar Senghor, Frantz Fanon, Gayatri Spivak, Homi Bhabha, Edward Said, Aimé Césaire, Sara Suleri, Anne McClintock, Ania Loomba, Arjan Appadurai, Stuart Hall, Paul Gilroy, Ngugi wa Thiong'o, and many others.

Chapter 8

Simonsen, Karen-Margrethe and Stougaard-Nielsen, Jakob (eds) (2008) *World Literature, World Culture: History, Theory, Analysis*. Aarhus: Aarhus University Press – 283.

Interesting collection of articles on world literature also from the perspective of "minor" literatures – mostly by younger scholars.

Thomsen, Mads Rosendahl (2008) *Mapping World Literature: International Canonization and Transnational Literatures*. London and New York: Continuum – 176pp.

Not a history of the term, concept and usage of "world literature," but rather an active contribution to the ongoing discussion on the subject.

Bibliography

Adam, Ian and Helen Tiffin (eds) (1991) *Past the Last Post: Theorizing Post-Colonialism and Post-Modernism*. London: Harvester/ Wheatsheaf.

Adorno, Theodor W. and Max Horkheimer (1988) [1944] *Dialektik der Aufklärung*. Frankfurt: Fischer.

Adorno, Theodor W (1969) [1951] *Minima Moralia*. Frankfurt: Suhrkamp.

——(2003) [1966] *Negative Dialektik*. Frankfurt: Suhrkamp.

——(1974) "Ist die Kunst heiter?" In *Noten zur Literatur IV.* Frankfurt a.m.: Surhrkamp, 147–57.

Adorno, Theodor (1991a) "The Schema of Mass Culture." In *The Culture Industry: Selected Essays on Mass Culture.* London: Routledge, 61–97 (originally "Das Schema der Massenkultur," in Theodor Adornmo and Max Horkheimer, 1944, *Dialektik de Aufklärung* [*Dialectic of Enlightenment*]).

——(1991b) "Culture Industry Reconsidered." In *The Culture Industry: Selected Essays on Mass Culture.* London: Routledge, 98–106 (originally transl. by Anson G. Rabinbach in *New German Critique* 6 [Fall 1975]: 12–19, from Theodor W. Adorno, *Ohne Leitbild*, Frankfurt am Main: Suhrkamp, 1967).

Ahmad, Aijaz (1992) *In Theory: Classes, Nations, Literatures.* London: Verso.

Aldrige, Owen A. (1986) *The Reemergence of World Literature.* Cranbury, NJ: Associated University Presses.

Andreasen, B., M. Jørgensen, S.E. Larsen and D. Ringgard (2009) *litteraturDK.* Copenhagen: Lindhardt & Ringhof.

Appiah, Kwame Anthony (1991) "Is the Post- in Postmodernism the Post- in Post-colonial?" *Critical Inquiry* 17.2 (Winter 1991): 336–57.

Apter, Emily (1995) "Comparative Exile: Competing Margins in the History of Comparative Literature." In Charles Bernheimer (ed.) *Comparative Literature in the Age of Multiculturalism.* Baltimore and London: The Johns Hopkins University Press, 86–96.

——(2003) "Global *Translation*: The 'Invention' of Comparative Literature, Istanbul, 1933." In *Critical Inquiry*, 29: 253–81.

——(2006a) "'Je ne crois pas beaucoup a la littérature comparée'." In Haun Saussy (ed.) *Comparative Literature in an Age of Globalization.* Baltimore: Johns Hopkins University Press, 54–62.

——(2006b) *The Translation Zone: A New Comparative Literature.* Princeton and Oxford: Princeton University Press.

——(2008) "Untranslatables: A World System." In *New Literary History* 39, 3 (Summer 2008): 581–98.

Arac, Jonathan (2002) "Anglo-Globalism?" In *New Left Review* 16 (July–August 2002): 35–45.

——(2004) "Global and Babel: Two Perspectives on Language in American Literature." In *ESQ* 50, nos. 1–3 (2004): 94–119.

——(2007) "Babel and Vernacular in an Empire of Immigrants: Howells and the Languages of American Fiction." In *boundary 2* 34,2 (2007); 1–20.

——(2008) "Commentary: Literary History in a Global Age." In *New Literary History* 39, 3: 747–60.

Arnold, Matthew (1978) [1869] *Culture and Anarchy.* Cambridge: Cambridge University Press.

Assmann, Aleida (2010) "Re-framing memory: between individual and collective forms of constructing the past." In Karin Tilmans, Frank van Vree and Jay Winter (eds) *Performing the Past: Memory, History, and Identity in Modern Europe.* Amsterdam: Amsterdam University Press, 35–50.

Auerbach, Erich (1953) *Mimesis: The Representation of Reality in Western Literature.* Transl. Willard Trask. Princeton: Princeton University Press.

——(1969) [1952] "Philology and *Weltliteratur.*" transl. Maire and Edward Said. In *The Centennial Review* 13, 1 (Winter 1969), 1–17.

——(2009) [1952] "Philology and *Weltliteratur.*" In *The Princeton Sourcebook in Comparative Literature* (eds) David Damrosch, Natalie Melas and Mbongiseni Buthelezi. Princeton: Princeton University Press, 125–38.

Bahun, Sanja (2011) "The Politics of World Literature." In *The Routledge Companion to World Literature* (eds) Theo D'haen, David Damrosch and Djelal Kadir. London: Routledge, 373–82.

Baldensperger, Fernand (1927) "Georg Brandes (1842–1927)." In *Revue de littérature comparée* 7 (1927): 368–71.

Bassnett-McGuire, Susan (1980) *Translation Studies.* London and New York: Methuen.

Bassnett, Susan (1993) *Comparative Literature: A Critical Introduction.* Oxford: Blackwell.

Bassnett, Susan and André Lefevere (1992) *Translation, History and Culture.* London: Pinter.

Bassnett, Susan, and Harish Trivedi (eds) (1999) *Post-Colonial Translation: Theory and Practice.* London: Routledge, *Questia.* Web. 7 Dec. 2010.

Bassel, Naftoli and Ilana Gomel (1991) "National Literature and Interliterary System." In *Poetics Today* 12, 4 (Winter 1991): 773–79.

Batts, Michael S. (1993) *A History of Histories of German Literature, 1835–1914.* Montreal: McGill-Queen's University Press.

Beecroft, Alexander (2008) "World Literature Without a Hyphen: Towards a Typology of Literary Systems." In *New Left Review* 54 (November-December 2008): 87–100.

Benjamin, Walter (1982) "Theses on the Philosophy of History." In *Illuminations,* edited and with an introduction by Hannah Arendt, translated by Harry Zohn. London: Fontana/Collins.

——(2000) [1968, 1923] "The Task of the Translator." Transl. Harry Zohn. In Lawrence Venuti (ed.) *The Translation Studies Reader.* London and New York: Routledge, 15–25.

Berczik, Árpád (1963) "Eine ungarische Konzeption der Weltliteratur. (Hugo v. Meltzls vergleichende Literaturtheorie.)" In *La Littérature comparée en Europe orientale* (ed) István Sötér, et al. Budapest: Akadémiai, 287–94.

——(1972) "Die ersten ungarischen Verkünder der Weltliteratur und der vergleichenden Literaturwissenschaft." In *Zagadnienia rodzajw literackich* 10.112: 156–73.

Berman, Antoine (1984) *L'Epreuve de l'étranger: culture et traduction dans l'Allemagne romantique.* Paris: Gallimard. Engl. Transl. S. Heyvaert. *The Experience of the Foreign: Culture and Translation in Romantic Germany.* Albany, NY: State University of New York Press, 1992.

Bernheimer, Charles (ed.) (1995) *Comparative Literature in the Age of Multiculturalism.* Baltimore and London: The Johns Hopkins University Press.

Bertens, Hans (1986) "The Postmodern Weltanschauung and its Relation with Modernism: An Introductory Survey." In Douwe Fokkema and Hans Bertens (eds) *Approaching Postmodernism.* Amsterdam and Philadelphia: John Benjamins, 9–51.

——(1991) "Postmodern Cultures." In Edmund J. Smyth, ed. *Postmodernism and Contemporary Fiction.* London: Batsford, 123–37.

——(1994) *The Idea of the Postmodern: A History.* London and New York: Routledge.

Bertens, Hans and Douwe Fokkema (eds) (1997) *International Postmodernism: Theory and Practice.* A Comparative History of Literatures in European Languages Sponsored by the International Comparative Literature Association, Vol. XI, Amsterdam and Philadelphia: John Benjamins.

Bhabha, Homi K. (1994) *The Location of Culture.* London and New York: Routledge.

Birla, Ritu (2010) "Postcolonial Studies: Now That's History." In *Can the Subaltern Speak? Reflections on the History of an Idea.* New York: Columbia University Press, 87–99.

Birus, Hendrik (2000) "The Goethean Concept of World Literature and Comparative Literature." In *CLCWeb* Volume 2, 4 (December 2000) Article 7. http://docs.lib.purdue.edu/clcweb/vol2/iss4/7 (accessed 3 January 2011).

Boldrini, Lucia (2006) "Comparative Literature in the Twenty-First Century: A View from Europe and the UK." In *Comparative Critical Studies* 3, 1–2: 13–23.

Bongie, Chris (2008) *Friends and Enemies: The Scribal Politics of Post/Colonial Literature.* Liverpool: Liverpool University Press.

Boyle, Nicholas (1991–2000) *Goethe.* 2 vols. Oxford: Oxford University Press.

Brandes, Georg. (1899–1910) *Samlede Skrifter.* Copenhagen: Gyldendal.

——(1902) [1899] "Verdenslitteratur." *Samlede Skrifter* 12. København: Gyldendal, 23–28. Engl. trans. http://global.wisc.edu/worldlit/readings/brandes-worldliterature Pdf (Accessed 18 August 2010).

——(2009) [1899] "World Literature." In David Damrosch, Natalie Melas and Mbongiseni Buthelezi (eds) *The Princeton Sourcebook in Comparative Literature.* Princeton: Princeton University Press, 61–66.

Brown, Calvin S. (1953) "Debased Standards in World Literature." In *Yearbook of Comparative and General Literature* 2: 10–14.

Brown, Nicholas (2001) "The Eidaesthetic Itinerary: Notes on the Geopolitical Movement of the Literary Absolute." In *The South Atlantic Quarterly* 100, 3 (Summer 2001): 829–51.

Brunetière, Ferdinand (1973) [1900] "European Literature." In Hans-Joachim Schulz and Philip H. Rhein (eds) *Comparative Literature: The Early Years.* Chapel Hill, NC: The University of North Carolina Press, 157–82.

Buescu, Helena C. and João Ferreira Duarte (2007) "Communicating Voices: Herberto Helder's Experiments in Cross-cultural Poetry." In *Forum for Modern Language Studies* 4.3: 173–86.

Buescu, Helena (2011) "The Republic of Letters and the World Republic of Letters." In *The Routledge Companion to World Literature* (eds) Theo D'haen, David Damrosch and Djelal Kadir. London: Routledge, 126–35.

Buck, Philo M., Jr (ed) (1934) *An Anthology of World Literature.* New York: Macmillan.

Carré, Jean-Marie (2009) [1951] "Preface to *La littérature comparée.*" In David Damrosch, Natalie Melas, Mbongiseni Buthelezi (eds) *The Princeton Sourcebook in Comparative Literature.* Princeton: Princeton University Press, 158–60.

Carrière, Moritz (1884) *Die Poesie. Ihr Wesen und ihre Formen mit Grundzügen der vergleichenden Literaturgeschichte.* Leipzig, 1884 (second revised edition of *Das Wesen und die Formen der Poesie,* 1854).

Casanova, Pascale (1999) *La République mondiale des lettres.* Paris: Seuil.

——(2004) *The World Republic of Letters.* Transl. M. DeBevoise. Cambridge, MA: Harvard University Press.

Catford, J.C. (1965) *A Linguistic Theory of Translation: An Essay in Applied Linguistics.* London: Oxford University Press.

Chakrabarty, Dipesh (2000) *Provincializing Europe: Postcolonial Thought and Historical Difference.* Princeton and Oxford: Princeton University Press.

Chasles, Philarète (1973) [1835] "Foreign Literature Compared." In Hans-Joachim Schulz and Philip H. Rhein (eds) *Comparative Literature: The Early Years.* Chapel Hill, NC: The University of North Carolina Press, 16–37.

Chow, Rey (2004) "The Old/New Question of Comparison in Literary Studies: A Post-European Perspective." In *ELH,* 71, 2 (Summer 2004): 289–311.

Christy, Arthur E. and Henry H. Wells (eds) (1947) *World Literature: An Anthology of Human Experience.* New York: American Book Company.

Clark, Kenneth (1972) [1953] *The Nude: A Study in Ideal Form.* Princeton: Princeton University Press.

Combe, Dominique (2010) "Littératures francophones, littérature-monde en français." In *Modern & Contemporary France* 18, 2: 231–49.

Cooppan, Vilashini (2004) "Ghosts in The Disciplinary Machine: The Uncanny Life of World Literature." In *Comparative Literature Studies* 41, 1: 10–36.

Corstius, J.C. Brandt (1963) "Writing Histories of World Literature." In *Yearbook of Comparative and General Literature* 12: 5–14.

Culler, Jonathan (2006) "Whither Comparative Literature?" In *Comparative Critical Studies* 3, 1–2: 85–97.

Curtius, Ernst Robert (1953) *European Literature and the Latin Middle Ages.* Transl. Willard Trask. Princeton: Princeton University Press.

——(1973) *Essays on European Literature.* Transl. Michael Kowal. Princeton: Princeton University Press.

Damrosch, David (2003) *What Is World Literature?* Princeton and Oxford: Princeton University Press.

——(2004) "From the Old World to the Whole World." In Jeffery R. DiLeo (ed.) *On Anthologies: Politics and Pedagogy.* Lincoln and London: University of Nebraska Press, 31–46.

——(2006) "Rebirth of a Discipline: The Global Origins of Comparative Studies." In *Comparative Critical Studies* 3, 1–2: 99–112.

——(2011) "Hugo Meltzl and 'the principle of polyglottism'." In Theo D'haen, David Damrosch and Djelal Kadir (eds) *The Routledge Companion to World Literature.* London and New York: Routledge, 12–20.

Damrosch, David; David L. Pike, et al (eds) (2004) *Longman Anthology of World Literature*. New York: Longman.

Davis, Paul; Gary Harrison et al (eds) (2003) *The Bedford Anthology of World Literature*. New York: Bedford/St. Martins.

Deeney, John J. (1981) "Chinese Literature from Comparative Perspectives." In *Chinese Literature: Essays, Articles, Reviews* (CLEAR) 3, 1 (Jan. 1981): 130–36.

——(1990) *Comparative Literature from Chinese Perspectives*. Shenyang: Liaoning University Press.

D'haen, Theo (1990) "The Dutch Byron: Byron in Dutch Translation."In *Centennial Hauntings: Pope, Byron and Eliot in the Year 88* (eds) C.C. Barfoot and Theo D'haen, Amsterdam/Atlanta: Rodopi, 232–51.

——(1991) "W. B. Yeats and A. Roland Holst: (S)Elective Affinities." In *Yeats: An Annual of Critical and Textual Studies* 8 (1990). Ann Arbor: The University of Michigan Press, 49–70.

——(1994) "Countering Postmodernism." In *REAL* (Yearbook of Research in English and American Literature)10. Tübingen: Gunter Narr Verlag, 49–64.

——(2005) "'A Splenetic Englishman': The Dutch Byron." In Richard A. Cardwell, ed., *The Reception of Byron in Europe, Volume II: Northern, Central and Eastern Europe*, London and New York: Thoemmes Continuum, 269–82.

——(2006) "Yeats in the Dutch-language Low Countries." In *The Reception of W.B. Yeats in Europe*, ed. Klaus Peter Jochum., London and New York: Continuum, 12–24.

——(2009) "Mapping Modernism: Gaining in Translation – Martinus Nijhoff and T.S. Eliot." In *Comparative Critical Studies* 6, 1: 21–41.

Dimock, Wai Chee (2006a) "Genre as World System: Epic and Novel on Four Continents."In *Narrative* 14, 1 (Jan., 2006): 85–101.

——(2006b) *Through Other Continents: American Literature Across Deep Time*. Princeton: Princeton University Press.

Dirlik, Arif (1994) "The Postcolonial Aura: Third World Criticism in the Age of Global Capitalism." In *Critical Inquiry* 20, 2 (Winter 1994), 328–356.

Domínguez, César (2011) "Dionýz Ďurišin and a Systemic Theory of World Literature." In Theo D'haen, David Damrosch and Djelal Kadir (eds) *The Routledge Companion to World Literature*. London: Routledge, 99–107.

Drinkwater, John (1923–24) *The Outline of Literature*. New York, London: G.P. Putnam's Sons.

During, Simon (2004) "Comparative Literature." In *ELH* 71 (2004): 313–22.

Ďurišin, Dionýsz. (1992) *Čo je svetová literatúra?* (What Is World Literature?), Bratislava: Vydavateľstvo Obzor.

Ďurišin, Dionýsz and Armando Gnisci (eds) (2000) *Il Mediterranea: una rete interletteraria*. Roma: Bulzoni.

Eisler, Rudolf (1930) *Kant-Lexicon*. http://www.textlog.de/32413.html, accessed 23 July 2010.

Engdahl, Horace (2008) "Canonization and World Literature: The Nobel Experience." In Karen-Margrethe Simonsen and Jakob Stougaard-Nielsen (eds) *World Literature, World Culture: History, Theory, Analysis*. Aarhus: Aarhus University Press, 195–214.

English, James (2005) *The Economy of Prestige*. Cambridge, Mass.: Harvard University Press.

Etiemble, René (1966) *The Crisis in Comparative Literature*. Transl. and with a Foreword by Herbert Weisinger and Georges Joyaux. East Lansing, MI: Michigan State University Press. (Translation of *Comparaison n'est pas raison*, 1963)

——(1975) [1964, 1966] "Faut-il réviser la notion de *Weltliteratur?*" In *Essais de littérature (vraiment) générale*. Paris: Gallimard.

——(1977) [1963] *Comparaison n'est pas raison*. Paris: Gallimard.

——(1988) *Ouverture(s) sur un comparatisme planétaire*. Paris: Christian Bourgois.

Even-Zohar (2000) [1978/1990] "The Position of Translated literature Within the Literary Polysystem." In Lawrence Venuti (ed.) *The Translation Studies Reader*. London and New York: Routledge, 193–97.

Ferguson, Frances (2008) "Planetary Literary History: The Place of the Text." In *New Literary History*, 39: 657–84.

Fitz, Earl (2002) "Internationalizing the Literature of the Portuguese-Speaking World." In *Hispania* 85, 3 (Special Portuguese Issue, Sept. 2002): 439–48.

Fokkema, Douwe 1984. *Literary History, Modernism, and Postmodernism*, Amsterdam and Philadelphia: John Benjamins.

——(1986) "The Semantic and Syntactic Organization of Postmodernist Texts," in Fokkema and Bertens 1986: 81–98.

Fokkema, Douwe and Hans Bertens (eds) (1986) *Approaching Postmodernism*. Amsterdam and Philadelphia: John Benjamins.

Forsdick, Charles (2010a) "World Literature, *Littérature-Monde*: Which Literature? Whose World?" In *Paragraph* 33,1: 125–43

——(2010b) "Late Glissant: History, 'World Literature,' and the Persistence of the Political." In *Small Axe* 33, 14 (November 2010): 121–34.

Forsdick, Charles and David Murphy (eds) (2003) *Francophone Postcolonialism: A Critical Introduction*. London: Arnold.

Friederich, Werner, with the collaboration of David Henry Malone (1954) *Outline of Comparative Literature; from Dante Alighieri to Eugene O'Neill*. Chapel Hill: University of North Carolina Press.

Friederich, Werner P. (1960) "On the Integrity of Our Planning." In *The Teaching of World Literature*, Ed. Haskell M. Block. UNC Studies in Comparative Literature 28. Chapel Hill, N.C.: The University of North Carolina Press, 9–22.

——(1970) "Great Books Versus 'World Literature'." In *The Challenge of Comparative Literature and Other Addresses*. Chapel Hill, N.C.: The University of North Carolina Press, 25–35.

Fuller, Margaret (1839) *Conversations with Goethe in the Last Years of his Life, Translated from the German of Eckermann*. Specimens of Foreign Standard Literature Vol. IV. Edited by George Ripley. Boston: Hilliard, Gray, and Company.

Gallagher, Mary (2010) "Connection Failures: Discourse on Contemporary European and Caribbean Writing in French." In *Small Axe* 33, 14 (November 2010): 21–32.

Gane, Gillian (2002) "Migrancy, The Cosmopolitan Intellectual, and The Global City in *The Satanic Verses*." In *MFS Modern Fiction Studies* 48, 1 (Spring 2002): 18–49.

Gasché, Rodolphe (2009) *Europe, or the Infinite Task: A Study of a Philosophical Concept*. Stanford: Stanford University Press.

Gayley, Charles Mills (1973) [1903] "What is Comparative Literature?" In Hans-Joachim Schulz and Philip H. Rhein (eds) *Comparative Literature: The Early Years*. Chapel Hill, NC: The University of North Carolina Press, 85–103.

Gikandi, Simon (1992) *Writing in Limbo: Modernism and Caribbean Literature*. Ithaca: Cornell University Press.

——(2001) "Globalization and the Claims of Postcoloniality." In *The South Atlantic Quarterly* 100, 3 (Summer 2001): 627–58.

Glissant, Edouard (1981) *Le discours antillais*. Paris: Seuil. Transl. J. Michael Dash 1989. *Caribbean Discourse*. CARAF Books. Charlottesville, NC and London: University Press of Virginia.

——(1993) *Tout-monde*. Paris: Gallimard.

——(1997) *Traité du Tout-monde*. Paris: Gallimard.

Goethe, Johann Wolfgang von (1819) *West-Östlicher Diwan*. Stuttgard: in der Cottaischen Buchhandlung. http://www.deutschestextarchiv.de/goethe/divan/1819/viewer/image/9; accessed 20 December 2010.

——(1970) *Italian Journey*. Transl. By W.H. Auden and Elizabeth Mayer. London: Penguin.

——(1986) *Essays on Art and Literature* (ed.) John Gearey. Goethe's Collected Works, Vol. 3. New York: Suhrkamp.

——(2007) *Italienische Reise*. Jubilaeumsausgabe. Munich: C.H. Beck.

Gorky, Maxim (1969) [1919] "Weltliteratur." In *Maxim Gorki. Über Weltliteratur*. Leipzig: Philipp Reclam, 31–40.

Gossens, Peter (In press) "Weltliteratur: eine historische Perspektive." (preprint)

Guérard, Albert (1940) *Preface to World Literature*. New York: Henry Holt and Company.

Guha, Ranajit (1982) *Subaltern Studies*. Delhi: Oxford University Press.

Gumbrecht, Hans Ulrich (2002) *Vom Leben und Sterben der grossen Romanisten*. Munich: Carl Hanser Verlag.

Guillen, Claudio (1993) [1985] *The Challenge of Comparative Literature*. Transl. Cola Franzen. Cambridge, Mass: Harvard University Press.

Graff, Gerald (1987) *Professing Literature: An Institutional History*. Chicago: University of Chicago Press.

Gutzkow, Karl (1836) *Über Goethe. Im Wendepunkt zweier Jahrhunderte*. Berlin: Verlag der Plan'schen Buchhandlung (L. Nitse). http://books.google.be/books?id=unsuAAAAYAAJ&printsec=frontcover&dq=Karl+Gutzkow+Ueber+Goethe&source=bl&ots=nrsHycGrSr&sig=mwzFajj7jtjS6mJJHtW5hni20W0&hl=en&ei=y0h5Td7PGIaWhQe0hoj4Bg&sa=X&oi=book_result&ct=result&resnum=4&ved=0CCwQ6AEwAw#v=onepage&q&f=false accessed 9 March 2011.

Habermas, Jürgen (1992) [1980] "Modernity – An Incomplete Project." In Peter Brooker (ed.) *Modernism/Postmodernism*. London: Longman, 125–38.

Hallward, Peter (1998) "Edouard Glissant between the Singular and the Specific." In *The Yale Journal of Criticism* 11.2: 441–64.

Hassan, Ihab (1975) *Paracriticisms: Seven Speculations of the Times*. Urbana: University of Illinois Press.

——(1980) *The Right Promethean Fire: Imagination, Science, and Cultural Change*. Urbana: University of Illinois Press.

——(1982) [1971] *The Dismemberment of Orpheus: Toward a Postmodern Literature*. New York: Oxford University Press.

——(1987) *The Postmodern Turn: Essays in Postmodern Theory and Culture*. Ohio State University Press.

Hassan, Waïl S. (2000) "World Literature in the Age of Globalization: Reflections on an Anthology." In *College English* 63, 1 (Sep., 2000): 38–47.

——(2002) "Postcolonial Theory and Modern Arabic Literature: Horizons of Application." In *Journal of Arabic Literature* 33, 1 (2002): 45–64.

Henrion, Matthieu-Richard-Auguste (1827) *Histoire littéraire de la France*. Paris: J.J. Blaise. (http://books.google.be/books?id=pj_Is1MkThoC&printsec=frontcover&dq=Matthieu

+Richard+Auguste+Henrion&source=bl&ots=30gsYMBqOg&sig=Sb4C76gK6T1f
P3aGmN_ZNpXCQFs&hl=en&ei=E80pTZzsJYOAhAe838nlAQ&sa=X&oi=book_
result&ct=result&resnum=1&ved=0CBkQ6AEwADgK#v=onepage&q&f=false,
accessed 9 January 2011).

Hensbroek, P.A.M. Boele van (1911) *Der Wereld Letterkunde voor Nederlanders bewerkt.* Leiden and Antwerp: A. W. Sijthoff's Uitgeversmaatschappij and De Nederlandsche Boekhandel.

Hermans, Theo (1985) *The Manipulation of Literature: Studies in Literary Translation.* London: Croom Helm.

Hertel, Hans. (ed.) (1985–94) *Gyldendals Verdens litteraturhistorie.* 7 vols. Copenhagen: Gyldendal.

Hesse, Herman (2008) [1929, 1953, 1978] *Eine Bibliothek der Weltliteratur.* Stuttgart: Reclam.

Hightower, James Robert (1953) "Chinese Literature in the Context of World Literature." In *Comparative Literature* 5, 2 (Spring, 1953): 117–24.

Hoesel-Uhlig, Stefan (2004) "Changing Fields: The Directions of Goethe's *Weltliteratur.*" In Christopher Prendergast (ed.) *Debating World Literature,* London: Verso, 26–53.

Hoffmann, Gerhard (1982) "The Fantastic in Fiction: Its 'Reality' Status, Its Historical Development and Its Transformation in Postmodern Narrative," in *REAL* (Yearbook of Research in English and American Literature) 1: 267–364.

Holmes, James S. (2000) [1972] "The Name and Nature of Translation Studies." In Lawrence Venuti (ed.) *The Translation Studies Reader.* London and New York: Routledge, 172–85.

Hutcheon, Linda (1984) *Narcissistic Narrative: The Metafictional Paradox.* New York and London: Methuen.

——(1985) *A Theory of Parody: The Teachings of Twentieth-Century Art Forms.* New York and London: Methuen.

——(1988) *A Poetics of Postmodernism: History, Theory, Fiction.* New York and London: Routledge.

——(1989) *The Politics of Postmodernism.* London and New York: Routledge.

——(1991) " 'Circling the Downspout of Empire'." In Adam and Tiffin 1991, 167–89.

Huyssen, Andreas (1986) *After the Great Divide: Modernism, Mass Culture, Postmodernism.* Bloomington and Indianapolis: Indiana University Press.

Jameson, Fredric (1984) "Postmodernism, Or the Cultural Logic of Late Capitalism." In *New Left Review* 146 (July-August 1984): 59–92.

——(1991) *Postmodernism, or, The Cultural Logic of Late Capitalism.* Durham, NC: Duke University Press.

——(2000) *The Jameson Reader.* Edited by Michael Hardt and Kathi Weeks. Oxford: Blackwell.

Jost, François (1974) *Introduction to Comparative Literature.* Indianapolis: Pegasus.

Kadir, Djelal (2004) "To World, to Globalize – Comparative Literature's Crossroads." In *Comparative Literature Studies* 41.1 (2004): 1–9.

——(2006) "Comparative Literature in a World Become Tlön." In *Comparative Critical Studies* 3, 1–2: 125–38.

——(2011) *Memos from the Besieged City: Lifelines for Cultural Sustainability.* Stanford: Stanford University Press.

Kliger, Ilya (2010) "World Literature Beyond Hegemony in Yuri M. Lotman's Cultural Semiotics." In *Comparative Critical Studies* 7.2–3 (2010): 257–74.

Klobucka, Anna (1997) "Theorizing the European Periphery." In *symploke* 5.1 (1997): 119–35.

Koch, Max (1973) [1877] "Introduction." In Hans-Joachim Schulz and Philip H. Rhein (eds) *Comparative Literature: The Early Years.* Chapel Hill, NC: The University of North Carolina Press, 67–77. ("Zur Einführung," in *Zeitschrift für vergleichende Litteraturgeschichte* 1: 1–12)

Kristal, Efraín (2002) "Considering Coldly ... A Response to Franco Moretti."In *New Left Review* 15 (May-June): 61–74.

Kumar, Amitava (ed.) (2003) *World Bank literature.* Foreword by John Berger; afterword by Bruce Robbins. Minneapolis: University of Minnesota Press.

Laclau, Ernesto and Mouffe, Chantal (1987) *Hegemony and Socialist Strategy: Towards a Radical Democratic Politics.* London: Verso.

Larsen, Svend Erik (2010) "Local Literatures, Global Perspectives: On Writing a Literary History for Secondary Schools." In *Otherness: Essays and Studies* 1.1 (October): 1–30. (http://www.otherness.dk/journal/vol 1, accessed 29 November 2010).

——(2011) "Georg Brandes: The Telescope of Comparative Literature." In *The Routledge Companion to World Literature.* Theo D'haen, David Damrosch and Djelal Kadir, (eds) London: Routledge, 21–31.

Lawall, Sarah (1988.) "The Alternate World of World Literature."In *ADE Bulletin* 90: 53–58.

——(1996) "Richard Moulton and the Idea of World Literature." In *No Small World: Visions and Revisions of World Literature (ed.)* Michael Thomas Carroll Urbana, Illinois: National Council of Teachers of English, 3–19.

——(2004) "Anthologizing 'World Literature'." In *On Anthologies: Politics and Pedagogy.* Edited and with an introduction by Jeffery R. Di Leo. Lincoln and London: University of Nebraska Press, 47–89.

Lawall, Sarah (ed.) (1994) *Reading World Literature: Theory, History, Practice.* Austin, TX: Texas University Press.Lazarus, Neil (1999) *Nationalism and Cultural Practice in the Postcolonial World.* Cambridge: Cambridge University Press.

Le Bris, Michel and Jean Rouaud (eds) (2007) *Pour une littérature-monde.* Paris: Gallimard.

Lefevere, André (ed.) (1992) *Translation/History/Culture: A Sourcebook.* London: Routledge.

Lefevere, André (2000) [1982] "Mother Courage's Cucumbers: Text, system and refraction in a theory of literature." In Lawrence Venuti, ed. *The Translation Studies Reader.* London and New York: Routledge, 233–49.

Lernout, Geert (2006) "Comparative Literature in the Low Countries." In *Comparative Critical Studies* 3, 1–2: 37–46.

Lindenberger, Herbert (1990) "On the Sacrality of Reading Lists: The Western Culture Debate at Stanford University." In Herbert Lindenberger. *The History in Literature: On Value, Genre, Institutions.* New York: Columbia University Press. (http://www.pbs.org/shattering/lindenberger.html accessed 29 October 2010)

Lionnet, Françoise (2011) "World Literature, *Francophonie*, and Creole Cosmopolitics." In Theo D'haen, David Damrosch and Djelal Kadir (eds) *The Routledge Companion to World Literature.* London: Routledge, 325–35.

Llovet, Jordi (ed.) (2003) *Lecciones de literatura universal: siglos XII a XX.* Madrid: Cátedra.

Loliée, Frédéric (1906) [1903] *A Short History of Comparative Literature from the Earliest Times to the Present Day*, translated by M. Douglas Power. London: Hodder and Stoughton.

Luhmann, Niklas (1989) *Ecological Communication*. Cambridge: Polity Press.

Lukács, Geörgy (1974) [1916] *The Theory of the Novel*. Cambridge, Mass.: MIT Press.

——(1983) [1937] *The Historical Novel*. Omaha: University of Nebraska Press.

——(2001) [1938] "Realism in the Balance." In Vincent B. Leitch (ed.) *The Norton Anthology of Theory and Criticism*. New York: Norton, 1033–58.

Lund, Joshua (2001) "Barbarian Theorizing and the Limits of Latin American Exceptionalism." In *Cultural Critique* 47 (Winter 2001): 54–90.

Macaulay, Thomas Babington (2011) [1835] *Minute on Indian Education*. http://www.columbia.edu/itc/mealac/pritchett/00generallinks/macaulay/txt_minute_education_1835.html accessed 8 February 2011.

Macy, John Albert (1925) *The Story of the World's Literature*. Garden City, NY: Garden City Publishing Co.

Marno, David (2008) "The Monstrosity of Literature: Hugo Meltzl's World Literature and its Legacies." In Karen-Margrethe Simonsen and Jakob Stougaard-Nielsen (eds) *World Literature, World Culture: History, Theory, Analysis*. Aarhus: Aarhus University Press, 37–50.

Marx, Karl and Friedrich Engels (2010) [1848] *Communist Manifesto*. http://www.marxists.org/archive/marx/works/download/pdf/Manifesto.pdf, accessed 14 December 2010.

McGann, Jerome (2008) "Pseudodoxia Academica." In *New Literary History* 39.3 (Summer 2008): 645–56.

McHale, Brian (1987) *Postmodernist Fiction*. New York and London: Methuen.

——(1992) *Constructing Postmodernism*. New York, London: Routledge.

Meltzl de Lomnitz, Hugo (1973) [1877] "Present Tasks of Comparative Literature, Parts I and II." In Hans-Joachim Schulz and Philip H. Rhein (eds) *Comparative Literature: The Early Years*. Chapel Hill, NC: The University of North Carolina Press, 56–62. ("Vorläufige Aufgaben der vergleichenden Literatur", *Acta comparationis litterarum universarum* 1 [January 1877]: 179–82 and 2 [October 1877]: 307–15).

Menand, Louis (2005) "All That Glitters: Literature's Global Economy." In *The New Yorker*. December 26, 2005.

Mignolo, Walter (1988) "Globalization, Civilization Processes, and the Relocation of Languages and Cultures." In *The Cultures of Globalization*, ed. Fredric Jameson and Masao Miyoshi. Durham and London: Duke University Press, 32–53.

Mishra, Vijay and Bob Hodge (1991) "What is Post(-)Colonialism?" In *Textual Practice* 5.3 (1991): 399–414.

Møller, Peter Ulf (1989) "Writing the History of World Literature in the USSR." In *Culture and History* 5: 19–37.

Moretti, Franco (1998) *Atlas of the European Novel, 1800–1900*. London: Verso.

——(2000) "The Slaughterhouse of Literature." In *Modern Language Quarterly* March 2000: 207–27.

——(2003) "More Conjectures." In *New Left Review 20* (March-April 2003): 73–81.

——(2004) [2000] "Conjectures on World Literature." In *Debating World Literature* (ed.) Christopher Prendergast. London: Verso, 148–62; originally in *New Left Review* 1 (January-February 2000): 54–68.

——(2005) *Graphs, Maps, Trees: Abstract Models for Literary Study*. London: Verso.
——(2009a) [2006] "Evolution, World-System, *Weltliteratur*." In *The Princeton Sourcebook in Comparative Literature* (eds) David Damrosch, Natalie Melas, Mbongiseni Butheluzi. Princeton, NJ: Princeton University Press, 399–408. Originally in *Studying Transcultural Literary History*, ed. Gunilla Lindberg-Wada, Berlin: De Gruyter, 113–21.
——(2009b) "Style, Inc. Reflections on Seven Thousand Titles (British Novels, 1740–1850)." In *Critical Inquiry* 36 (Autumn 2009): 134–58.
——(2010) "History of the Novel, Theory of the Novel." In *Novel* 43, 1 (Spring 2010): 1–10.
Moulton, Richard Green (1915) *The Modern Study of Literature: An Introduction to Literary Theory and Interpretation*. Chicago: University of Chicago Press.
——(1921) [1911] *World Literature and Its Place in General Culture*. New York: The Macmillan Company.
Ning, Wang (2006) " 'Death of a Discipline?' Toward a Global/Local Orientation of Comparative Literature in China." In *Neohelicon* 23, 1 (2006): 149–63.
——(2010a) "Global English(es) and Global Chinese(s): toward rewriting a new literary history in Chinese." In *Journal of Contemporary China* 19, 63: 159 – 174.
——(2010b) "World Literature and the Dynamic Function of Translation." In *Modern Language Quarterly* 71,1 (March 2010): 2–14.
Orsini, Francesca (2002) "Maps of Indian Writing." In *New Left Review* 13 (January-February 2002): 75 88.
Perloff, Marjori (1995) "'Literature' in the expanded Field." In Charles Bernheimer (ed.) *Comparative Literature in the Age of Multiculturalism*. Baltimore and London: The Johns Hopkins University Press, 175–86.
Pettersson, Anders (2005) "The Possibility of Global Literary History." In Suthira Duangsamosorn, et al (eds) *Re-Imagining Language and Literature for the 21st Century*. Amsterdam and New York: Rodopi, 55–66.
——(2008) "Transcultural Literary History: Beyond Constricting Notions of World Literature." In *New Literary History* 39: 463–79.
Pichois, Claude and A.M. Rousseau (1967) *La littérature comparée*. Paris: Armand Colin.
Pizer, John (2006) *The Idea of World Literature: History and Pedagogical Practice*. Baton Rouge, LA: Louisiana State University Press.
Pollock, Sheldon (1996) "The Sanskrit Cosmopolis, 300–1300: Transculturation, Vernacularization and the Question of Ideology." In Jan Houben, ed., *Ideology and Status of Sanskrit: Contributions to the History of the Sanskrit Language*, Leiden: Brill, 197–249.
"Pour une 'littérature-monde' en français," *Le Monde* 16 mars 2007.
Posnett, Hutcheson Macaulay (1886) *Comparative Literature*. London: Kegan Paul, Trench & Co.
——(1973) [1901] "The Science of Comparative Literature." In Hans-Joachim Schulz and Philip H. Rhein (eds) *Comparative Literature: The Early Years*. Chapel Hill, NC: The University of North Carolina Press, 186–206.
——(2009) [1886] "The Comparative Method and Literature." In David Damrosch, Natalie Melas, Mbongiseni Buthelezi (eds) *The Princeton Sourcebook in Comparative Literature*. Princeton: Princeton University Press, 50–60.
The Editors "Preface" (2009) In *SubStance* 119, Vol. 38, 2: 3–7.
Prendergast, Christopher (ed.) (2004) *Debating World Literature*. London and New York: Verso.

Prendergast, Christopher (2004) [2001] "The World Republic of Letters." In Christopher Prendergast (ed.) *Debating World Literature.* London: Verso, 1–25. Originally as "Negotiating World Literature," in *New Left Review,* second series, 8 (March/April 2001).

Querrien, Anne (1986) "The Metropolis and the Capital." In *Zone* 1–2: 219–21.

Remak, H.H. (1961) "Comparative Literature: Its Definition and Function." In Newton P. Stallknecht and Horst Frenz (eds) *Comparative Literature: Methods and Perspective.* Carbondale and Edwardsville. London: Southern Illinois University Press, 1961, 1–57.

Ribeiro, Darcy (2000) *The Brazilian People: Formation and Meaning of Brazil.* Trans. by Gregory Rabassa. Gainesville: UP of Florida.

Riquer, Martín de and José María Valverde (2010) *Historia de la literatura universal.* 2 Vols. Madrid: Gredos.

Said, Edward (1979) [1978] *Orientalism.* New York: Random House.

——(1983) *The World, the Text, and the Critic.* Cambridge: Harvard University Press.

——(1993) *Culture and Imperialism.* London: Chatto and Windus.

——(2003) "*Orientalism* 25 Years Later: Worldly Humanism v. the Empire-builders." In *CounterPunch,* August 4, http://www.counterpunch.org/said08052003.html, Accessed 1 March 2011.

——(2004) *Humanism and Democratic Criticism.* New York: Columbia University Press.

Sangari, Kumkum (1990) "The Politics of the Possible." In JanMohamed, Abdul R. and David Lloyd (eds) *The Nature and Context of Minority Discourse.* New York and Oxford: Oxford University Press, 216–45.

Saussy, Haun (ed.) (2006a) *Comparative Literature in an Age of Globalization.* Baltimore: The Johns Hopkins University Press.

Saussy, Haun (2006b) "Exquisite Cadavers Stitched from Fresh Nightmares: Of Memes, Hives, and Selfish Genes." In Haun Saussy (ed.) 2006. *Comparative Literature in an Age of Globalization.* Baltimore: The Johns Hopkins University Press, 3–42.

Schamoni, Wolfgang (2008) " 'Weltliteratur' zuerst 1773 bei August Ludwig Sclözer." In *Arcadia* 43: 288–98.

Scherr, Johannes (1848) *Bildersaal der Weltliteratur.* Stuttgart: Ad. Becher.

——(1851) *Allgemeine Geschichte der Literatur von den ältesten Zeiten bis auf die Gegenwart. Ein handbuch für alle Gebildeten.* Stuttgart: Franck'sche Buchhandlung.

——(1895) *Illustrierte Geschichte der Weltliteratur. Ein Handbuch in zwei Bänden.* Neunte Auflage. Durchgesehen und bis auf die neueste Zeit ergänzt von Otto Haggenmeister. Stuttgart: Franck'sche Verlagsbuchhandlung.

Schlözer, August Ludwig von (1792–1801) *Weltgeschichte nach ihren Haupttheilen im Auszug und Zusammenhange (Main elements of world history in excerpts and context),* 2 vols. Göttingen.

Schneider, Jost (2004) "Psychische Globalisierung? Vom projekt einer weltliteratur zur Realität des Weltunterhaltungskultur." In *TRANS: Internet-Zeitschrift für Kulturwissenschaften* 15 (April 2004).

Schulz, Hans-Joachim and Philip H. Rhein. (eds) (1973) *Comparative Literature: The Early Years.* Chapel Hill: The University of North Carolina Press.

Seeba, Hinrich C. (2003) "Ernst Robert Curtius: Zur Kulturkritik eines Klassikers in der Wisschenschaftsgeschichte." In *Monatshefte* 95, 4: 532–40.

Shackford, Charles Chauncey (1973) (1871) "Comparative literature." In Hans-Joachim Schulz and Philip H. Rhein (eds) *Comparative Literature: The Early Years.* Chapel Hill: The University of North Carolina Press, 42–51.

Shohat, Ella (1992) "Notes on the Post-Colonial." In *Social Text* 31–32 (1992): 93–11.

Shurtleff, Oliver (1947) "World Literature." In *The Clearing House* 21, 9 (May, 1947): 575.

Simonsen, Karen-Margrethe and Jakob Stougaard-Nielsen. (eds) (2008) *World Literature, World Culture: History, Theory, Analysis.* Aarhus: Aarhus University Press

Slemon, Stephen (1991) "Modernism's Last Post" In Ian Adam and Helen Tiffin (eds) *Past the Last Post: Theorizing Post-Colonialism and Post-Modernism.* London: Harvester/Wheatsheaf, 1–11.

Spivak, Gayatri (1988) "Can the Subaltern Speak." In Cary Nelson and Lawrence Grossberg (eds) *Marxism and the Interpretation of Culture.* Basingstoke: Macmillan, 271–313.

——(1999) *A Critique of Postcolonial Reason: Toward a History of the Vanishing Present.* Cambridge, Mass.: Harvard University Press.

——(2000) [1992] "The Politics of Translation." In Lawrence Venuti (ed.) *The Translation Studies Reader.* London and New York: Routledge, 397–416.

——(2003) *Death of a Discipline.* New York: Columbia University Press.

——(2010) "Can the Subaltern Speak?" revised edition, from the "History" chapter of "Critique of Postcolonial Reason." In Rosalind C. Morris, ed. *Can the Subaltern Speak? Reflections on the History of an Idea.* New York: Columbia University Press, 21–78.

Spólden, Stéphane (1997) "The Treachery Of Art: This Is Not Belgium." In *symplokē* 5, 1–2 (Special Issue: Refiguring Europe): 137–52.

Steiner, Ann (2011) "World Literature and the Market." In *The Routledge Companion to World Literature.* Theo D'haen, David Damrosch and Djelal Kadir (eds). London: Routledge, 316–24.

Steinmetz, Horst (1988) "Weltliteratur: Umriss eines literaturgeschichtlichen Konzepts." In Horst Steinmetz. *Literatur und Geschichte.* Munich: Iudicium Verlag, 103–26.

Stern, Adolf (1888) *Geschichte der Weltliteratur in übersichtlicher Darstellung.* Stuttgart: Rieger'sche Verlagsbuchhandlung.

Strich, Fritz (1957) [1946] *Goethe und die Weltliteratur.* Bern: Francke Verlag.

Strich, Fritz (1949) *Goethe and World Literature.* Transl. C.A.M. Sym. New York: Hafner Publishing Company.

Swiggers, Pierre (1982) "A New Paradigm for Comparative Literature." In *Poetics Today* 3, 1 (Winter 1982): 181–84.

Tagore, Rabindranath (2001) "World Literature." In *Rabindranath Tagore: Selected Writings on Literature and Language* (ed.) Sukanta Chaudhuri. New Delhi: Oxford University Press, 138–50.

Tanoukhi, Nirvana (2008) "The Scale of World Literature." In *New Literary History* 39: 599–617.

Texte, Joseph (1898) "L'histoire comparée des littératures." In *Etudes de littérature européenne.* Paris: Colin, 1–24.

Thomsen, Mads Rosendahl (2008) *Mapping World Literature: International Canonization and Transnational Literatures.* London and New York: Continuum.

Tiffin, Helen (1991) "Introduction," In Ian Adam and Helen Tiffin (eds) *Past the Last Post: Theorizing Post-Colonialism and Post-Modernism.* London: Harvester/Wheatsheaf, vii-xvi.

Torre, Guillermo de (1956) "Goethe y la literatura universal." In *Las Metamórfosis de Proteo.* Buenos Aires: Losada, 278–89.

Toury, Gideon (1995) *Descriptive Translation Studies – and Beyond.* Amsterdam: John Benjamins.

"Toward a 'World-Literature' in French." Transl. Daniel Simon. 2009. In *World Literature Today* 8, 2 (March–April 2009): 54–56 ("Pour une 'littérature-monde' en français," *Le Monde* 16 mars 2007)

Tsu, Jing (2010) "Getting Ideas about World Literature in China." In *Comparative Literature Studies* 47, 3 (2010): 290–317.

Tsu, Jing (2011) "World Literature and National Literature(s)." In *The Routledge Companion to World Literature* (ed.) Theo D'haen, David Damrosch and Djelal Kadir. London: Routledge, 158–68.

Valéry, Paul (1960) [1939] "La liberté de l'esprit." In *Oeuvres*, Vol. II. Bibliothèque de la Pléiade. Paris: Gallimard.

Van Tieghem, Paul (1931) *La littérature comparée.* Paris: Colin.

Venuti, Lawrence (ed.) (2000) *The Translation Studies Reader.* London: Routledge.

Venuti, Lawrence (2011) "Translation Studies and World Literature." In Theo D'haen, David Damrosch and Djelal Kadir (eds) *The Routledge Companion to World Literature.* London: Routledge, 180–93.

Viswanathan, Gauri (1989) *The Masks of Conquest: Literary Study and British Rule in India.* New York: Columbia University Press.

Weitz, Hans J. (1987) "Weltliteratur zuerst bei Wieland." In *Arcadia* 22: 206–8.

Wellek, René (2009) [1959] "The Crisis of Comparative Literature." In David Damrosch, Natalie Melas, Mbongiseni Buthelezi (eds) *The Princeton Sourcebook in Comparative Literature.* Princeton: Princeton University Press, 162–72.

Wienbarg, Ludolf (1982) [1835] "Goethe und die Weltliteratur." In *Literaturkritik des Jungen Deustchlands: Entwicklungen – Tendenzen – Texte.* Ed. Hartmut Steinecke. Berlin: Erich Schmidt, 155–64.

Woodberry, George (1973) [1903] "Editorial." In Hans-Joachim Schulz and Philip H. Rhein (eds) *Comparative Literature: The Early Years.* Chapel Hill, NC: The University of North Carolina Press, 211–14.

Young, Robert J.C. (1995) *Colonial Desire: Hybridity in Theory, Culture and Race.* London and New York: Routledge.

——(2010) "The Legacies of Edward W. Said in Comparative Literature." In *Comparative Critical Studies* 7,2–3: 357–66.

Zabus, Chantal (2002) *Tempests after Shakespeare.* London: Palgrave/Macmillan.

Zhang, Longxi (1999) *Mighty Opposites: From Dichotomies to Differences in the Comparative Study of China.* Stanford, Cal.: Stanford University Press

——(2003) *The Tao and the Logos : Literary Hermeneutics, East and West.* Durham: Duke University Press.

——(2005) *Allegoresis: Reading Canonical Literature East and West.* Ithaca, NY: Cornell University Press.

——(2011) "Qian Zhongshu as Comparatist." In *The Routledge Companion to World Literature.* Theo D'haen, David Damrosch and Djelal Kadir, (eds). London: Routledge, 81–88

Zhou, Xiaoyi and Q.S. Tong. (2009) [2000]. "Comparative Literature in China." In *The Princeton Sourcebook in Comparative Literature* (eds) David Damrosch, Natalie Melas and Mbongiseni Buthelezi. Princeton: Princeton University Press, 341–57.

Index

Mundt, Theodor, *Geschichte der
Literatur der Gegenwart* 13
Murphy, David 150

Nair, K.K. *see* Chaitanya, Krisha
naming world literature 5–26
national context 115
nationalism 9, 13, 34
national literature 9–12, 81
NATO literature 85–86, 152
Neuhumanismus 29–30
"New Criticism" 84–85
Ngal, Mwbil, *Giambatista Viko* 107
Niethammer, Friedrich Immanuel 29
Nijhoff, Martinus 127–28
Ning, Wang 171–72
Noël, Jean-François-Michel, *Cours de
littérature comparée* 51

Orsini, Francesca 112
Ortíz, Fernando 167
Ouspensky, Boris 67

Palladio, Andrea 31–32, 33
panchoric system 49, 115
Pannwitz, Rudof 121, 122
Parisian Athénée lectures 51
Patocka, Jan 34
Pavič, Milorad 107
Penguin Classics 118–19
Perloff, Marjori 145–46
Petöfi, Sándor 57, 67
Petrarch, Francesco 86, 103
Pettersson, Anders 16, 17, 157, 169
philology 34–37, 40–41, 45, 51, 56
Pichois, Claude 19, 51, 52; *La
Littérature comparée* 66
Pizer, John 5, 13, 78, 83, 95; *The Idea of
World Literature* 2, 12
Plantin, Christoffel 29
Pléiade, *Histoire de des littératures* 21
Poirier, Richard 42
Pollock, Sheldon 49
polyglottism 55, 57, 69
polysystem theory 101, 109, 126
Pope, Alexander 118
popular literature 8
positivism 58, 59, 62, 153
Posnett, Hutcheson Macaulay 118;
Comparative Literature 61–63, 75
postcolonialism 24–25, 42, 46, 68, 71,
123, 125–26, 133–51
postmodernism 25, 133–51
postnationalism 130

Poulet, Georges 87
Pound, Ezra 121
Prampolino, G., *Storia universale della
leteratura* 21
Prendergast, Christopher 1, 90, 105,
107, 108; *Debating World Literature* 1
provincializing 46

Qian Zhongshu 169
Quadrio, Francesco Saverio, *Della storia
e della ragione d'ogni poesia* 48
Queneau, Raymond, *Histoire des
littératures* 21
Querrien, Anne 107

reader reception theories 66–67
Reclam Verlag 119
Remak, H.H. 65–66
Renaissance 27, 29, 31, 38, 45
"Republic of Letters" 7–8, 50, 105
Rhein, Philip H. 15, 57, 58, 59, 61, 63
Ribeiro, Darcy 167
Riquer, Martín de, *Historia de la
literatura universal* 21, 162
Robinet, Jean-Baptiste-René,
*Considérations sur l'état présent de la
littérature en Europe* 48
Robinson, Edwin Arlington 82
Romanticism 9, 11, 30, 49
Rosenkranz, Karl 16
Rouaud, Jean 148, 150
Rousseau, André-M. 19, 51, 52; *La
Littérature comparée* 66
Rushdie, Salman 139, 144–45
"Russian" school 67

Said, Edward 24, 27, 35–36, 41–44, 112,
135, 144; Apter's work 44–45; *Culture
and Imperialism* 42; *Humanism and
Democratic Criticism* 36, 38, 39, 42,
44, 68; *Orientalism* 35, 36, 43; *The
World, The Text, and the Critic* 41,
92–93
Said, Maire 35, 44, 45–46
Sainte-Beuve, Charles-Augustin 52,
153–54
Saint Maur monks 10
Saint-Simonism 53
Samarin, R.M. 24
Sangari, Kumkum 139
Saramago, José 166
Sarkozy, Nicolas 148
Saussy, Haun 2, 55–56, 74–75
Schamoni, Wolfgang 5

www.routledge.com/literature

Also available...

Routledge Critical Thinkers Series

Series Editor: **Robert Eaglestone**, Royal Holloway, University of London, UK

Routledge Critical Thinkers is designed for students who need an accessible introduction to the key figures in contemporary critical thought. The books provide crucial orientation for further study and equip readers to engage with theorists' original texts.

The volumes in the Routledge Critical Thinkers series place each key theorist in his or her historical and intellectual context and explain:

- why he or she is important
- what motivated his or her work
- what his or her key ideas are
- who and what influenced the thinker
- who and what the thinker has influenced
- what to read next and why.

Featuring extensively annotated guides to further reading, *Routledge Critical Thinkers* is the first point of reference for any student wishing to investigate the work of a specific theorist.

Titles include:

Martin Heidegger
Gilles Deleuze
Giorgio Agamben
Jean-Paul Sartre
Sigmund Freud
Edward Said
Emmanuel Levinas

For more information and to order a copy visit
www.routledge.com/literature

Available from all good bookshops

US Popular Print Culture (Oxford UP)